BLOODING AT GREAT MEADOWS

Young George Washington and the Battle that Shaped the Man

BY ALAN AXELROD

RUNNING PRESS

PHILADELPHIA · LONDON

For Anita and Ian

9   8   7   6   5   4   3   2   1

Digit on the right indicates the number of this printing
Library of Congress Control Number: 2006940108

ISBN-13: 978-0-7624-2769-7
ISBN-10: 0-7624-2769-8

Cover and interior design by Matthew Goodman
Cover art: George Washington as Colonel of the Virginia Regiment, 1772,
by Charles Willson Peale. Washington-Custis-Lee Collection,
Washington and Lee University, Lexington, Virginia.
Back cover: *A Charming Field for an Encounter,* special thanks to Artist Robert Griffing
and his publisher, Paramount Press Inc.
Edited by Jennifer Kasius
Typography: Garamond, and Trajan

This book may be ordered by mail from the publisher.
Please include $2.50 for postage and handling.
But try your bookstore first!

Running Press Book Publishers
2300 Chestnut Street
Philadelphia, PA 19103-1371

Visit us on the web!
www.runningpress.com

CONTENTS

"The volley fired by a young Virginian in the backwoods of America set the world on fire."

—Horace Walpole,
Memoirs of the Reign of King George II (1822)

THE FLESH BENEATH
THE MARBLE

Horatio Greenough, born in Boston on September 6, 1805, was from earliest childhood unmistakably a sculptor. He dazzled the adults around him with his uncanny ability to mold from clay exact miniatures of "objects that impressed themselves on his mind." He was just fifteen when a Boston-based French sculptor known to history only as J. B. Binon took him as a student. Later, the precocious Greenough enrolled in Harvard College, was befriended by the celebrated American painter Washington Allston, and, while still in his teens, drew up the design for the Bunker Hill monument. On the advice of Allston and with encouragement and funding from a wealthy Boston family, Greenough, after graduating from Harvard in 1825, went to Florence and Rome for advanced study. There he was steeped in the glories of classical art, executed a number of Greco-Roman-looking busts of prominent men, and, in 1832, received the first artistic commission ever made by the United States Congress. It was for a heroic statue of George Washington, intended to commemorate the centennial of his birth.

Greenough followed the example of the statue of Zeus at Olympia by the ancient Greek sculptor Phidias, seating his monumentally scaled Washington on a Grecian throne, right arm upraised, the left holding a sheathed sword, handle toward the viewer, his lap, legs, and right bicep draped in a toga, his feet shod in sandals, and his upper torso quite naked.

Therein lay the problem. In 1841, the completed work was installed in the place for which Congress had commissioned it, the Rotunda of the Capitol, where it immediately drew objections from Representatives and Senators as well as visitors. The classical attitude and accoutrements of the figure certainly presented no difficulty. After all, the great American governmental and other public buildings were all being designed on Greek or Roman models, the national mottoes—*E pluribus unum, Annuit coeptus,* and *Novus ordo seculorum*—were written in classical Latin, and George Washington himself had been depicted, even before his death in 1799, as the very embodiment of Roman virtue. In May 1783, officer veterans of the American Revolution founded the Society of the Cincinnati with membership open to Revolutionary officers and their eldest male descendants. The founders took the name of their organization from Lucius Quinctius Cincinnatus, who (according to semilegendary history) left his farm in 458 B.C. when the Roman Senate called on him to rescue a consular army surrounded on Mount Algidus by the Aequi, tribesmen of central Italy. Given all the powers of an absolute dictator, Cincinnatus defeated the invaders in a single day; then, his duty done, he promptly resigned the dictatorship and returned to his farm. The Revolutionary officers saw Cincinnatus as the quintessential citizen soldier and themselves as *Cincinnati*—his spiritual descendants. In electing George Washington their first president, these charter members demonstrated their view of him as what the poet Byron would call him years later in his 1815 "Ode to Napoleon Buonaparte": the "Cincinnatus of the West." Like the noble Roman, Washington had left his farm—Mount Vernon— to rescue his country and, having rescued it, duly renounced the tyrant's power that could have been his, quietly returning instead to his plantation. This same early American habit of framing the new republic in the

Roman past moved contemporaries to honor Washington with the title "Pater Patriae." Later generations have translated this into the familiar "Father of His Country," but the original intent of the Latin, "Father of the Fatherland," was intended explicitly to mirror an official honor conferred by the Roman Senate on the likes of Marcus Tullius Cicero, Julius Caesar, and Caesar Augustus for great and fundamental service to the nation. Thus Washington, as Pater Patriae, was the exact equivalent of the most virtuous leaders of Rome.

No question, depicting Washington in twelve tons of classical marble was hardly controversial. However, evoking the image of the Greek Zeus rather than, say, the Roman Augustus or even Cincinnatus himself was profoundly disquieting.

The trouble with incorporeal gods is their remoteness from the human beings who worship them. The Greeks never tolerated such. Their gods dwelled on Mount Olympus, not so very high above the rest of humanity, and, though immortal, were of flesh and blood. But the half nudity that suited Zeus and delighted the Greeks would not do for Washington and the Americans who worshipped him.

Many found the spectacle of a half-naked founding father offensive, and even more thought it hilarious. In 1843, the statue was exiled from the Rotunda to the east lawn of the Capitol, where passersby jeered that it depicted a discomfited Washington desperately grasping for his clothes—which were, at the time, on exhibit at the Patent Office several blocks to the north. The statue was moved indoors to the Smithsonian Institution in 1908, remaining in the old Castle until 1964, when it was moved to the second floor of the just-completed Museum of History and Technology (now the National Museum of American History).

It would be easy to write off mid-nineteenth-century objections to the Greenough sculpture as so much Victorian prudery were it not for the fact that the work remains for us today at the very least incongruous. The Father of His Country, sandal-shod, bedsheet wrapped, and bare of chest and shoulders? Something is *still* wrong with this picture.

George Washington is at once the most familiar and most remote of the founding fathers. He remains today what he was in 1841, an icon more marble than flesh—and when the flesh is permitted to show through the marble, we are made uneasy. Unlike the ancient Greeks, we *want* our gods to be aloof.

But there is more to this god's remoteness than our desire to have him so. Washington's early life lacks the rich anecdotal surface of the lives of, say, Benjamin Franklin or Thomas Jefferson. Doubtless it is for this reason that the best-known "Young George" anecdote is wholly fictitious. The tale of how the Virginia lad decided to test his brand-new hatchet on one of his father's prized cherry trees then admitted the crime to him— "Father, I cannot tell a lie"—made Parson Weems's 1800 *Life and Memorable Actions of George Washington* a bestseller for generations. Here was a parable that managed to combine a humanizing flaw with what in a child was the precocious, if not superhuman, virtue of honesty. It was a brilliant piece of fantasy in that it satisfied a craving for homely humanity in Washington, yet did so while further burnishing instead of tarnishing the gleaming marble surface of his popular image.

Perhaps it is high time to go beneath the surface and, without fabrication, search the character of George Washington the boy, the youth, and the young man for some clues to what made him what he was to become—in every sense, truly, the father of his country.

❧

Easier said than done. For Washington's first years present themselves as neither more nor less remarkable than those of any number of young men of the Southern planter class. Yet that class was itself remarkable. Euro-American civilization began abortively, in August 1585, in the place Sir

Walter Raleigh named Virginia for his sovereign, the Virgin Queen, Elizabeth I. After depositing a few colonists on Roanoke Island in what are today North Carolina's Outer Banks, the colony was quickly abandoned, but in July 1587 another 150 colonists showed up to try again. Their leader, John White, sailed back to England the following month to fetch supplies. His return was delayed by war with Spain, and by the time he got back to Roanoke Island on August 17, 1590, he was stunned to find no trace of the settlers other than the single, cryptic word "Croatoan" carved into a tree trunk. It was May 14, 1607, before a new party founded Jamestown, the first permanent English colony in what would, 169 years later, become the United States.

Jamestown, too, had a most precarious start—half the colonists died in the "Starving Time" of winter 1609-1610—but, unlike Roanoke Island, the new colony reaped the benefit of a benevolent dictatorship under Royal Governor Thomas West de la Warr, who arrived on June 10, 1610, and dragged the colony not only through survival but toward its first faint glimmer of prosperity.

What could possibly move anyone to abandon the familiar Old World for the New, where the only certainty was that of infinite hazard? For some, doubtless, it was the very promise of newness. For the religious, it seemed a new Eden, a fresh start in the most profound spiritual sense. Many others saw it as a fresh start in a more personal way. For the fact was that, by the beginning of the seventeenth century, Europe was pretty well used up. England, like most other Old World places, labored under the yoke of primogeniture, the legally enforced tradition dictating that the first son in a family inherited all titles and at least most property upon the death of the father. This left younger offspring to await whatever scraps the firstborn might give them, which could well be nothing at all. Beyond this, England had no more really important titles to confer, no more land to distribute, no way, really, for a man born to a shoemaker, say, ever to become anything other than a shoemaker—which meant that, as bad as things were for the more-or-less disinherited younger sons of the gentry, they were far worse for the poor and even those of the middling sort.

The middling sort. Beginning in the 1640s, a handful of "gentle-men"—as the scions of the upper crust were called—began settling Virginia's Northern Neck, the area between the Potomac and Rappahannock Rivers. Far more numerous than the gentlemen, however, were the petty farmers, tradesmen, clerks, and artisans: the middling people. Among these was John Washington, about twenty-five years old when he arrived early in 1657 aboard the *Sea Horse of London,* a modest ketch of which he was both mate and voyage partner. As the son of a clergyman, he was better educated than many of his class, but he had no future in the Church of England, his father having been kicked out of his parish by the Puritans in 1643.

John arrived in Virginia with no intention of staying. After picking up a cargo of tobacco, the *Sea Horse* set out on the return voyage to England, only to be driven aground by a winter storm. She sank, tobacco and all, and it was only while he labored to raise her that John decided his prospects in Virginia were probably more promising than what either England or the sea had to offer. *Sea Horse* skipper Edward Prescott released him from his obligations as mate, settled up on his partnership, and wished him well. In fact, John Washington had already made a fateful connection in the New World. He had been befriended by a prosperous Maryland planter named Nathaniel Pope, to whose daughter Anne he now became attracted. Shortly after the *Sea Horse* left without him, John Washington married Anne, and her father gave them the wedding present of 700 hundred Virginia acres and a loan of some £80.

Events moved with surprising speed in seventeenth-century Virginia. Less than a half-century before John Washington arrived, survival there had been a very long shot indeed. But now there was something more than the rudiments of a stratified, sophisticated society. At the top were those who had already acquired great estates, with acreages well into the thousands. Below them were the smaller, but still self-dependent, farmers, who worked perhaps 250 acres of cleared land. Many in this group may have owned far more than their cleared acreage, but, as forest and swamp, that land was worth little. Some of the small farmers were destined to make their way more or less comfortably, a few might advance into the class above them, but many would descend to the next lower stratum—that of the struggling farmer or even the farm laborer, who did fieldwork for other.s.

By the time of John Washington's arrival, another class was rapidly developing—that of the merchants and factors, who dealt in the export of what the plantations and farms produced. With skill and luck, members of this class could ascend to the highest planter class; in the absence of one or both, however, they could just as easily plummet to the depths of the lowest laboring class.

On the rung beneath the merchants and factors were the sailors. As a voyage partner, John Washington arrived in Virginia somewhat above this class, the members of which rarely had John's good fortune to marry above their station. Such marriages would become something of a Washington tradition. George Washington's beloved half-brother Lawrence would marry into wealth, as would George himself.

Below the sailors were the frontiersmen, who settled on small subsistence farms beyond the established Tidewater civilization and who owned no more than a hovel, a few animals, and whatever patches of cultivated ground they could hack out of the woods. Most hung on by the skin of their teeth, but a few, who aggressively acquired large land patents, retailed small tracts to the next wave of settlers and thereby grew wealthy.

Below even the people of the frontier were the indentured servants, who bound themselves to a period of years of service in exchange for passage to Virginia and subsistence during the term of their servitude. Indentured servitude was slavery, albeit for a limited period. As if cheap labor were not sufficient inducement for planters and others to import indentured servants, they also came with "headrights," a government grant of fifty acres per immigrant (of whatever station in life, convicts and slaves excepted), which the importer of the servant could in turn acquire for himself. At its best, indentured servitude offered economic opportunity and was no more oppressive than an apprenticeship back in England. At its worst, it was a cruel bondage, however limited in time. Nevertheless, in Virginia society, an indentured servant who had learned a good trade during his term of obligation was generally respected as a tradesman or artisan once he was released.

At the very bottom of the New World's New Eden were the convicts and, below even them, the slaves. Political prisoners—including Scotch and Irish troops of the English civil wars—as well as common criminals were often sentenced to "transportation," that is, deportation to the colonies, where they were offered by the shipload mainly to planters in need of cheap labor. So many were dumped in Virginia's Northern Neck that the colonial assembly, the House of Burgesses, passed laws to segregate them from the rest of the population or to ensure that they were summarily conscripted into the Royal Army.

Even transported convicts were eventually freed—though they rarely had the means to return to England. Slaves, however, were slaves for life, unless their masters freed them. Slavery came very early to Virginia, the first shipment of twenty arriving at Jamestown aboard a Dutch vessel in 1619. By the time John Washington was settling in the colony, Virginia was importing about 1,000 African slaves annually. By the time George Washington neared his majority, in the early 1750s, that number had risen to more than 4,000. And, of course, slaves were a form of self-renewing property. The master owned the imported slave as well as any of his or her children and grandchildren, throughout the generations and without limit. Predictably, it was this, the lowest class of Virginians, which was increasing most rapidly.

Ensconced on their 700 acres, John and Anne Washington had their first son, Lawrence, in the fall of 1659, and early the next year Nathaniel Pope died, specifying in his will the cancellation of John's debt. Thus endowed and freed up, John aggressively added to his 700-acre gift by importing indentured servants and claiming their headrights, by buying more land, and by assuming the grants of lands declared to have been deserted. The result was that, by 1668, John Washington owned in excess of 5,000 acres. Although land alone did not elevate one in Virginia society, it was essential to that rise, and John's growing prominence enabled him to capture profitable and prestigious public offices and appointments. In this year of 1668, having borne a total of five children, Anne Pope Washington died, whereupon John married another Anne, Anne Gerrard, already twice widowed.

John Washington died in 1677, leaving to his firstborn, Lawrence, a substantial share of his property. But even before he had inherited his father's lands, Lawrence, thanks to his father's successes, embarked on life already considerably elevated in Virginia society. As befitted a gentleman, he had been sent to England for his education, and before he reached the age of twenty-one, he was appointed a justice of the peace. By twenty-five, he was a Burgess (a representative in the Virginia assembly), and then was appointed a sheriff. As well established as he quickly became, even Lawrence married somewhat above his station, forming a union with the daughter of the speaker of the House of Burgesses who was also a member of the all-powerful Virginia Council. Unfortunately, he did not long enjoy his prosperity and position. He died in 1698, at age thirty-eight, leaving three children, seven-year-old John, three-year-old Augustine, and Mildred, an infant who was named for her mother. That woman, now a widow, married one George Gale in 1700 and, with him and her children, sailed to England. There Mildred Gale died shortly after childbirth, and George Gale sent his stepsons to Appleby School in Westmoreland, where they would be raised as proper English gentlemen.

Here, so far as American history is concerned, the story might have ended or, rather, might never have begun, had not members of the Washington family in Virginia disputed Mildred Gale's will, insisting that, based on the terms of Lawrence Washington's will, she had had no right to bequeath any part of the Washington estate, income, or custody of the children to her second husband, George Gale. As a result of legal proceedings, the three children, having lived two years in England, were returned to Virginia and put under the care of their cousin, another John Washington, known to his contemporaries as John of Chotank.

Augustine—Gus—Washington turned twenty-one in 1715. He was remarkably tall for the era, about six feet, handsome, and strong. In 1715 or 1716, he married Jane Butler, the daughter of a prominent Westmoreland, Virginia, landowner. Combined, his lands and hers amounted to 1,740 acres, a modestly impressive holding. Like both his father and grandfather, Gus became a justice of the peace. Like them, too, he set about aggressively augmenting his property. We do not know the full extent of his dreams and ambitions. Did he aspire to become a second Robert Carter—known as "King" Carter—who, at his death in 1732, owned more than 300,000 acres and 1,000 slaves, plus some £10,000 in cash? Certainly Augustine strained his cash resources to buy up property, but he did not push his holdings nearly as far west as the greatest of the Virginia planters, and his "empire" did not begin to approach that of King Carter and his ilk. Although reasonably prosperous, Augustine Washington was well back in the second rank of planters—more than a simple farmer, to be sure, but hardly a land baron. His acquisition of land on Little Hunting Creek in 1726 put him twenty-four miles east of the Great Falls of the Potomac, which was the beginning of the frontier—that is, the dividing line between the older and the newer settlements.

Augustine Washington also ventured in one other direction. He acquired land on Accokeek Creek about eight miles northeast of Fredericksburg, which was known to be rich in iron ore, and he built a refining furnace there. The very first colonial iron furnace had been started just a few years earlier, in 1718, when a British dispute with Sweden cut off iron imports from that country. Augustine began to realize profits from his iron venture early on, but he was uneasy with his British-based partners, and in 1729 took ship for London to meet with them personally. He did not return to his house on Pope's Creek until May 26, 1730—and discovered, when he did, that he had become a widower, his wife, Jane, having died on November 24, 1729.

With three children on his hands—Lawrence, Augustine (called Austin), and Jane—he set about finding a new wife as aggressively as he acquired land, and on March 6, 1731, married twenty-three-year-old Mary Ball. She was no woman of wealth and connections, but a mere orphan, plump, pleasing of voice, and pregnant by June. Her firstborn, delivered on February 22, 1732, was George Washington.

❦

The common denominator of childhood in early America was death. Infants and children died routinely and in large numbers. The twentieth-century American poet and essayist William Carlos Williams once wrote that colonial mothers "shot babies against the wilderness like cannon-balls." Perhaps for this reason, early American parents did not dote on their offspring in the way moderns do. They dutifully recorded the birth and the baptism, but very little else before the child, if he or she survived, approached manhood or womanhood. The early childhood of George Washington was no exception. Frustratingly little is known about it. His first years were spent in a growing family. Sister Betty was born on June 30, 1733, and brother Samuel on November 16, 1734. The house on Pope's Creek was simple, although well appointed, with fine wood paneling in the best of its rooms. Outside was a realm of farm animals and horses. And we may assume, too, that there was at least some tension in this household. Augustine had a fair amount of land, and he certainly provided well for his family, yet the land never seemed to produce as much as he anticipated that it would, and the iron furnace, though it turned a profit, turned it grudgingly. Moreover, it required constant attention, which meant a very long ride from Pope's Creek.

Did young George sense any of his father's discontent? Perhaps—but more probably not. Between the furnace, the farmlands, and the restless probing for promising real estate at bargain prices, Augustine Washington was rarely home for long. Did George wonder what his father saw and did when he was away? The toddler must have heard the adults around him discussing what they called "McCarty's sugar lands," a place forested with trees whose rich sap was sweet and delicious. Did his father go to the sugar lands? Did George's mouth—and imagination—water to go there, too? Of course, we do not know. But something, from an early age, excited in George Washington a hunger for new places, sweet places, untrodden lands beyond Pope's Creek and even beyond the mountains the people of Virginia called the "Bleu Ridge."

In 1735, George's world changed in two ways. His half-sister Jane, nearly three years old, died on January 17, 1735, and later that year, Augustine decided to move his family up the Potomac to the 2,500 acres he had purchased on Little Hunting Creek at a place called Epsewasson. This would bring Augustine closer to his labor-intensive iron furnace, and—incidentally—it also meant that little George would grow up closer to the frontier. The house at Epsewasson was smaller than that at Pope's Creek, to be sure, but the family was small as well. With Lawrence and Austin away at school in England, there were only Father, Mother, Mary, George, Betty, and Samuel to shelter—at least until January 24, 1736, when John Augustine was born.

The year 1735 saw another change for the Washingtons as well. Augustine's local partner in the iron furnace, John England, died, and with him died the expertise he possessed. Augustine needed another iron-master, but these were not easy to find in Virginia. Besides, the furnace, while profitable, was only marginally so. Augustine was concerned that the iron ore would run out sooner rather than later, and he was unsure of the continuing demand for the product in any case. Moreover, the kind of British trade regulations that would, in less than forty years, drive the colonies to fight for independence from the mother country had begun to

weigh heavily on the fledgling colonial iron industry. British law forbade
the export of colonial bar iron as well as the local manufacture of many
kinds of castings, including pots, firebacks, andirons, and the like. Having
settled into his new residence at Epsewasson in part to live closer to the
furnace, he decided to sail yet again for England at the end of 1736 or
beginning of 1737 to discuss with his English partners the future of the
furnace. Once in England, however, he ended up simply negotiating a
larger share of the business, which also entailed his assuming greater
responsibility for its operation. Although Epsewasson was closer to the
furnace than Pope's Creek had been, it was still about thirty miles distant.
Augustine returned to Virginia, resolved to find land for a home even
closer to Accokeek Creek.

Augustine found what he was looking for early in the spring of 1738,
when George got another new brother, Charles, born on May 2, and
about the time that his twenty-year-old half-brother, Lawrence, returned
from school in England. George immediately attached himself to
Lawrence, who largely assumed the role of father to him. Like Augustine,
Lawrence was tall and strong. In some contrast to Augustine, however, he
was also highly polished, his English education having produced in him
English manners. George idolized Lawrence, and from an early age, deliberately modeled himself on him. This apparently pleased Augustine, who
relied on Lawrence to give George the kind of fatherly instruction he
himself lacked the time to provide.

Augustine purchased 260 acres on the left bank of the Rappahannock
River, two miles below the falls and a very easy ride to Accokeek. He
closed the deal, leased some additional adjacent acreage, and on
December 1, 1738, moved himself and his family into the house that was
part of the property, a place dubbed Ferry Farm. Although Ferry Farm
was close to the frontier, it was also just across the narrow Rappahannock
from something entirely new in seven-year-old George's world: a town.
Among other things, Fredericksburg offered schooling. Although no
authentic record of the boy's education survives, it is likely that George

began learning reading and "ciphering" (as arithmetic was called) in the town—although he may have been tutored at home.

George found arithmetic especially appealing, but he had probably also progressed far enough in reading to take in for himself the exciting news in the *Virginia Gazette* concerning Britain's developing war with Spain and Admiral Edward Vernon's thrilling victory at Porto Bello on the Panamanian isthmus. Closer to home there was also excitement as, on June 21, 1739, a new sister, Mildred, was born.

Lawrence was stirred by the war news and thrilled by the announcement that three thousand of the troops to be recruited for the overland campaign against the Spanish in the Caribbean were to come from the colonies, with Virginia contributing four hundred. Governor William Gooch was authorized to commission the officers to lead the Virginia contingent, and Lawrence, hungry for martial glory and the opportunity for advancement it offered, lobbied vigorously for one of the positions. Gooch chose him as one of four company leaders.

Surely, George viewed his half-brother's commission with some mixture of emotions. On the one hand, the prospect of his sailing away must have filled him with sadness and trepidation, yet it must also have excited him. Here was his hero, about to embark on truly heroic deeds of military glory. Whatever he felt, George was obliged to hold his boyish emotions in long suspense, since bureaucratic and logistical delays kept the Virginians at home until October 1740, five months after the selection of the officers. After Lawrence finally set sail, little Mildred died, George attended to his studies, Augustine labored (often in frustration) at the furnace, and the whole family waited impatiently for Lawrence's letters, news, and even rumors from Jamaica and Cartagena.

It was not a cheerful time. For one thing, a fire destroyed a building or buildings (perhaps the Washingtons' former house, which Augustine still owned) at Little Hunting Creek. For another, the news from the front at Cartagena was not good. Delays in mounting the land attack against that city gave the Spanish ample time to reinforce their defenses, and the first

British assault was repulsed with heavy losses. As the British troops regrouped for another attack, their ranks rapidly withered in the rainy season of a most unhealthy climate, with scores succumbing to yellow fever. So many sickened and died that the attack had to be called off, the surviving troops evacuated, and Cartagena left in the hands of the Spanish.

As George saw it, what was worse? The prospect of Lawrence wounded, sick, or dead? Or that of Lawrence involved in a shameful and humiliating failure of British arms?

Fortunately, the choice turned out not to be among any of those grim alternatives. A letter dated May 30, 1741 arrived in which Lawrence explained that he was perfectly safe and had his honor intact, too, having been denied a role in the catastrophic land operations. British general Thomas Wentworth, commander of land forces, had such a low opinion of the "provincials"—as the American officers and troops were called—that he refused to use them in combat. Lawrence and his company, along with most of the other colonials, were ordered to remain on Admiral Vernon's flagship, Lawrence acting as captain of marines. Nevertheless, Lawrence had learned a thing or two about war, writing to his family that "the enemy killed of ours some 600 and some wounded and the climate killed us in greater number." Did young George pay close attention to this recitation of the battle's "butcher's bill," or did he focus more sharply on what his brother wrote next? "War is horrid in fact but much more so in imagination. We there have learned to live on ordinary diet; to watch much and disregard noise or shot of cannon." One is tempted to say that this is the very lesson young Colonel Washington would learn at the Battle of Great Meadows thirteen years later, except that he seems to have entered that battle already aware of the difference between fact and imagination in war and already able to "disregard noise or shot of cannon." As he awaited the inevitable French assault on his makeshift "Fort Necessity" at Great Meadows, he would write to his brother John Augustine on May 31, 1754, of the victory he had achieved in the fight three days earlier: "I can with truth assure you, I heard Bulletts whistle and believe me there was something charming in the sound." Thirteen years earlier almost to the day, Lawrence had written very nearly the same thing.[1]

By the time Lawrence Washington returned to Ferry Farm, Austin Washington was there as well, having completed his schooling in England. George grew fond of Austin, but his attachment to him was nothing like what he felt for Lawrence, the valiant veteran who had learned to "disregard" the roar and reality of cannon fire.

❧

And Lawrence was about to mean even more to George Washington. In the spring of 1743, George was packed off to Chotank on the Potomac to spend some time with his cousins on their farm. His play was interrupted by the arrival of a messenger who summoned him back to Ferry Farm. His father was gravely ill.

George Washington left no record of how this news affected him, nor of the impact of the sight of his father—the strapping figure who often rode out to the iron furnace, dismounted, rolled up his sleeves, and pitched in with his laborers to do the heavy work of refining ore and casting metal—now supine and pallid on his deathbed. Doubtless, George was anxious and sad, but after all, he had barely known his father and, recalling him in later years could say nothing more than that he had been tall, fair, well proportioned, and, oh yes, fond of children.[2] Augustine Washington died on April 12, 1743, and his will, probated the following month, divided an estate of seven or more tracts totaling more than 10,000 acres and worked by some forty-nine slaves.

To Lawrence, the eldest, went Little Hunting Creek, land on Mattox Creek, and his father's interest in the iron furnace. To Austin went various lands in Westmoreland County. To George went Ferry Farm and some smaller tracts, including three lots in the town of Fredericksburg and ten slaves. Samuel, John Augustine, and Charles Washington each received farms and slaves. Mary Washington divided Augustine's personal property with her sons, and she was also entrusted with the care of her children's estates until they should reach their majority. In addition, she inherited some slaves and the right to the crops and proceeds of certain properties. It was, as these things go, a straightforward will, befitting a man who had bequeathed to his heirs what in the eighteenth century was called a "competence," a living, albeit hardly in baronial high style. It was the legacy of a second-tier planter, enough to put George Washington in the position of making a momentous life decision: either follow his father and remain a second-tier planter, or risk all that he had in order to achieve something more.

The decision—at any rate, action on the decision—would necessarily be postponed until George reached his majority; however, Lawrence, now more than just a surrogate father to George, pointed the way almost immediately. Ensconced at Little Hunting Creek, Lawrence courted Anne Fairfax, daughter of Colonel William Fairfax, who was both cousin and agent of Thomas, Lord Fairfax, the proprietor of much of northern Virginia. Little more than two months after his father was buried, Lawrence married Anne, on July 19, 1743, forming a socially splendid union with a young woman who owned thousands of acres (with patents on even more) and whose family was among the most powerful in the colony. Clearly, the second tier was too narrow for Lawrence Washington—and George was learning to see it the same way.

Lawrence ushered his half-brother, fourteen years his junior, into the stratospheric realm of the Fairfaxes. Their houses were bigger and grander than anything George had known, and their interests and conversation were commensurately larger as well. George was proud of and delighted by the ease with which Lawrence talked and moved among them, and he was all the more resolved to watch, to learn, and to emulate his hero-model half-brother. If Lawrence was George's entrée into the top tier of

Virginia planter society, he also set the pattern for George's behavior within that society. His manners were polished, his mind was sharp—albeit rather more literary than mathematical, whereas George had more of a head for numbers than words—his business sense was savvy and sound, if not brilliant. If Lawrence had a passion, it was, in a gentlemanly sort of way, arms. All of these qualities, in combination, appealed mightily to the Fairfaxes and their circle. And all of it rubbed off on young George, to whom Colonel Fairfax in particular took a great liking and became for the youth a model supplementary to Lawrence.

Lawrence translated his newfound stature into wood and stone. It is not known whether he tore down the small house at Little Hunting Creek in which George had lived during 1735–1738 or if the fire of 1740 had destroyed it, but, in either case, he built over the cellar and foundation of the original house a larger structure. He christened the new house Mount Vernon, after the admiral in whose expedition he had served. Named for a celebrated military commander, the house became the frequent scene of stirring martial conversation, in which George, during extended visits from Ferry Farm, reveled.

Mount Vernon was on the frontier of the frontier. Travel eastward, and you reached the centers of sophisticated Tidewater civilization, the American ports that regularly communicated with Europe. Turn to the west, and you ventured through the frontier and into the wilderness. In addition to tales of battle in and about far-off Cartagena, talk at Mount Vernon was much more local. Lawrence and his circle spoke constantly of land, especially of the two great pending land issues of the day. By treaty with the Indians—the great Five Nations—the Blue Ridge was set as the western boundary of white settlement. The excited talk now was about renegotiating that line to push it westward to the Alleghenies. That would open up vast tracts to speculation and settlement.

Potentially, at least. Lord Fairfax, the great proprietor of most of Virginia's Northern Neck, laid claim to the lands between the Blue Ridge and the Alleghenies that were under negotiation with the Indians. This claim—to some 5.3 million acres—conflicted with royal claims to these same lands. If Fairfax prevailed, he would surely retail his lands to speculators. If the Crown won the day, it was likely that those lands would remain out of reach, as they would be awarded to others at the pleasure of the king or royal colonial officials.

Yet even as George listened to this westward-looking conversation, he also heard much talk in the other direction. To the west lay a great figurative ocean of land, but to the east—a real ocean. In the New World, land was the opportunity denied most men in the Old. Get enough of it, work it wisely, sell it productively, and any man might be a king—or, at least, a "King" Carter. Still, it was a very long shot. Lawrence knew that Augustine Washington had been as fine and strong a man as any in the Northern Neck, yet he never acquired more than ten thousand acres, sufficient to make him and his family reasonably comfortable, yes, but hardly rich and certainly not kings. What, Lawrence must have thought, were George's most realistic prospects for advancement? He looked upon him as a son, and he wanted the best for him. After serious thought, Lawrence sought to turn the thirteen-year-old's eyes from the west to the east. A whole class of competing, clamoring young land speculators was growing up around the Washingtons, and Lawrence decided that the more promising course for George was the sea. The British army may have been disgraced at Cartagena, but, under the great Vernon, the Royal Navy had triumphed gloriously. Perhaps the very best career for a young man pulled, as it were, between the New World and the Old was to be found on the ocean.

There was growing within George Washington an appetite for adventure, and at this point, it apparently did not matter to him whether his adventure would be had in the Shenandoah Valley or on the Atlantic and the planet's other seas. He would follow whatever course his half-brother prescribed for him.

The final decision, however, was neither Lawrence's nor George's to make. Lawrence may have thought of George as a son, but it was Mary

Ball Washington who was in fact his mother and, therefore, his legal guardian. We know that on September 8, 1746, young George took the ferry from Ferry Farm across the Rappahannock to Fredericksburg. There Colonel Fairfax gave him a pair of letters from Lawrence. One was for George—doubtless discussing the prospects of a seagoing career—and the other was for him to deliver to his mother. Presumably this letter pleaded the cause of the sea to her. Mary Washington, however, was inclined against it. She did not put her foot down, but she did withhold her approval, and so George Washington remained suspended between land and sea.

In the meantime, he completed his formal schooling. Unlike Lawrence, Austin, and his father, he was not sent to England for the education of a gentleman, but, either at home or in Fredericksburg, he learned mathematics—at which he excelled—and he learned how to write, developing a clear and strong hand and fine vocabulary that set him unmistakably apart from the rustic boys who lived a little farther west. Spelling, punctuation, and issues of syntax remained rough and idiosyncratic through his teens, but improved significantly by his twenties.

Washington's biographers, desperate for documents embodying some scrap of the elusive humanity of their subject, have combed through the 218 pages of school exercises that survive from Washington's tenth through thirteenth year. Most of the manuscripts are exercises in mathematics and surveying. Twenty-one of the pages are legal forms—bills of sale and exchange, contracts, conveyances, deeds, leases, and even wills—which young Washington copied and saved, doubtless to serve him as models when, as an adult, he would have routine need of such documents. There is also a recipe "To Keep Ink from Freezing or Moulding" and two scraps of verse—thirty lines entitled "On Christmas Day" and seventeen devoted to "True Happiness." As with the ink recipe, these poetic scraps were almost certainly copied from some source, now unknown.

Within this youthful literary and autobiographical desert is one tantalizing manuscript entitled "Rules of Civility & Decent Behaviour In Company and Conversation," a collection of 110 maxims of gentlemanly, ethical, and polite conduct, in which Washington's early admirers and biographers rejoiced to have found a window into the youthful development of a man of great and heroic character. The very first maxim, for example, seems to lay the very foundation of a noble public man: "Every Action done in Company, ought to be with Some Sign of Respect, to those that are Present." And others also set high the bar of becoming self-restraint, of good conduct, and of sound morality:

17th Be no Flatterer, neither Play with any that delights not to be Play'd Withal.

19th let your Countenance be pleasant but in Serious Matters Somewhat grave.

21st Reproach none for the Infirmaties of Nature, nor Delight to Put them that have in mind thereof.

22d Shew not yourself glad at the Misfortune of another though he were your enemy.

23d When you see a Crime punished, you may be inwardly Pleased; but always shew Pity to the Suffering Offender.

25th Superfluous Complements and all Affectation of Ceremonie are to be avoided, yet where due they are not to be Neglected.

35th Let your Discourse with Men of Business be Short and Comprehensive.

40th Strive not with your Superiers in argument, but always Submit your Judgment to others with Modesty.

44th When a man does all he can though it Succeeds not well blame not him that did it.

48th Wherein you reprove Another be unblameable yourself;

for example is more prevalent than Precepts.
[4]9 Use no Reproachfull Language against any one neither Curse nor Revile.
[5]0th Be not hasty to believe flying Reports to the Disparag[e]ment of any.
56th Associate yourself with Men of good Quality if you Esteem your own Reputation; for 'tis better to be alone than in bad Company.
58th Let your Conversation be without Malice or Envy, for 'tis a Sig[n o]f a Tractable and Commendable Nature: And in all Causes of Passion [ad]mit Reason to Govern.
59th Never express anything unbecoming, nor Act agst the Rules Mora[l] before your inferiours.
67th Detract not from others neither be excessive in Commanding.
89th Speak not Evil of the absent for it is unjust.
109th Let your Recreations be Manfull not Sinfull.
110th Labour to keep alive in your Breast that Little Spark of Ce[les]tial fire Called Conscience.

Some of the maxims are considerably more homely:

4 In the Presence of Others Sing not to yourself with a humming Noise, nor Drum with your Fingers or Feet.
5th If You Cough, Sneeze, Sigh, or Yawn, do it not Loud but Privately; and Speak not in your Yawning, but put Your handkercheif or Hand before your face and turn aside.
6th Sleep not when others Speak, Sit not when others stand, Speak not when you Should hold your Peace, walk not on

when others Stop.
7th Put not off your Cloths in the presence of Others, nor go
out your Chamber half Drest.
8th At Play and at Fire its Good manners to Give Place to
the last Commer, and affect not to Speak Louder than
Ordinary.
9th Spit not in the Fire, nor Stoop low before it neither Put
your Hands into the Flames to warm them, nor Set your
Feet upon the Fire especially if there be meat before it.
10th When you Sit down, Keep your Feet firm and Even,
without putting one on the other or Crossing them.
11th Shift not yourself in the Sight of others nor Gnaw your
nails.[3]

Yet even in this admixture of the profound and the trivial the biographer may find something to admire. Here is evidence that, from an early age, George Washington regarded every aspect of conduct as important to character, as if greatness of character were a continuum that ran seamlessly from resisting the urge to bite your nails to keeping the spark of conscience alive within your breast.

Then came a later generation of scholars, apparently determined to wipe the smiles from the faces of the early Washington biographers. The later writers were not content simply to assume that young George either wrote the maxims himself or, at the very least, pored over books to compile them personally. In his scholarly edition of *George Washington's Rules of Civility and Decent Behaviour in Company and Conversation*, historian Charles Moore pointed out that the maxims Washington wrote out had already been in use in France for a century and a half, and in England for a century.[4] Prior to Moore, in 1891, a scholar named Moncure D. Conway traced the origin of the maxims to *Bienséance de la Conversation entre les Hommes,* a treatise written in 1595 for the benefit of the French Jesuit College of La Fleche. A Father Perin subsequently translated the maxims into Latin, adding a new chapter on table manners, and published the work at Pont-a-Mousson in 1617. The book was popular enough to be republished at Paris in 1638 and at Rouen in 1651. Then it became an international bestseller, with translations into Spanish, German, and Bohemian. A French-language edition appeared in Paris by 1640, and an English version was printed in London the same year. Interestingly, the marketing-conscious London publisher advertised the work as having been written by an eight-year-old child prodigy.

The 1640 English edition is crude and, although it resembles Washington's manuscript, the young Virginian certainly did not copy this version. Could he, then, have translated the 1640 French version? As we shall see in chapter 7, Washington's lack of French would get him into deep trouble and even bring an accusation of treacherous homicide against him. So we know that he did not translate his maxims from the French.

Moncure Conway believed that the maxims were translated from the French by one Reverend James Marye, a Jesuit-educated Anglican who came to Virginia in 1735 with the first Huguenot Colony as pastor of St. George's Parish, Spotsylvania County. He lived just eight miles from Fredericksburg. Could Marye, as Conway believed, have been Washington's teacher and given him his translation to copy? Possibly. But there is no evidence of this, as, indeed, there is no evidence (beyond common-sense speculation) that he went to school at Fredericksburg as opposed to having been tutored privately at Ferry Farm. In any case, more recent scholarship suggests that Washington copied the maxims from a version published by Francis Hawkins in England. Like the cruder English edition, the Hawkins translation was published about 1640. It appeared in ten other editions between 1646 and 1672. The Hawkins volume may or may not have been commonly available in the colonies, but it is certainly possible that Augustine, Lawrence, or Austin might have brought the book back from England.

There is still some scholarly dispute over the origin of the material Washington copied as well as the circumstances under which he copied it. No one, however, seriously disputes that the maxims were indeed copied—presumably in 1744 and, most likely, as an extended exercise in penmanship.

Does this mean, then, that their content is essentially without meaning?

Not at all. To begin with, the maxims were preserved along with other items of Washington's school work that proved useful to him: mathematical exercises and notes relevant to surveying (which, as we are about to see, became the young man's first profession), legal forms, and even an ink recipe. The obvious implication is that he and his family thought the maxims sufficiently useful to preserve as well. Even more important, American schoolmasters from the colonial era through the nineteenth century typically ensured that reading and penmanship assignments did double duty. The material the student copied had to be more than mere pen fodder. It needed as well to be useful and valuable. This was the very principle William Holmes McGuffey would apply in the first of his celebrated *Readers* in 1836, little less than a hundred years after Washington copied the maxims. As the McGuffey volumes were intended to teach reading while also imparting religion, morality, and ethics, so colonial-era copybook exercises taught both penmanship and the modes of behavior that reflected the ideals of contemporary society. Although not original, the *Rules of Civility* are hardly meaningless; they tell us what values young George Washington was expected to learn, to absorb, to practice, and, indeed, to embody.

What we cannot say for certain about the *Rules of Civility* is how deeply they actually engaged—or failed to engage—George Washington. Those early biographers, who assumed that the youngster had invented the rules himself, could also assume that the maxims had a personal connection with him. Although we can see the maxims as expressions of social norms, expectations, and ideals, we cannot simply assume that they had special significance for the boy Washington. What we *do* know is that he was deeply enthralled by another school subject, mathematics, especially as it was applied to surveying.

In Lawrence and the other gentlemen and ladies who frequented Mount Vernon, Washington certainly saw the rules of civility in action, but, even more vividly, he became aware of the ubiquity of surveying. As Lawrence and his circle discussed the acquisition of new lands and the possibility, through a renegotiated Indian treaty and the favorable resolution of the Fairfax claims, that the "Ohio country"—the western wilderness—would be opened to settlement, they spoke always of the necessity of survey. And when the new Treaty of Lancaster, concluded on July 4, 1744, did indeed open white settlement beyond the Blue Ridge, and when Lord Fairfax did emerge victorious in his dispute with royal colonial authorities early in 1745, the talk of surveys became even more urgent.

If it seemed to George that the surveyor was a man of singular importance and power in the world, he was not mistaken. At this time in Virginia, a hard-working frontier surveyor could earn about a hundred pounds per year, an income substantially greater than what most middling planters earned and surely better than that of any tradesman. Moreover, this income was only from surveying fees. The work of a surveyor also put him in position to patent choice tracts for himself, thereby acquiring substantial acreage for even more profit. So far as his fellow Virginians were concerned, a surveyor was a professional deserving of the respect accorded to a physician, a clergyman, or a military officer. Surveying was no mere trade, but a calling worthy of a gentleman.

As George awaited his mother's final decision on his going to sea, he made himself familiar with the surveying tools his father had left. He applied his mathematical education to them, and by August 1747—when he was just fifteen—neighbors and relatives began hiring him to run simple surveys. The first recorded payment he received was for a set of surveys run in early October 1747, for which Washington earned £2 3s., a substantial amount of money. He enjoyed the work, and he enjoyed the money, so that when his mother finally handed down her verdict on the seagoing life—she would not give her permission—George was hardly upset. He had found something better to do, something interesting in and of itself and something that promised not just a good living, but the possibility of real wealth.

George William Fairfax was a most worthy son to Colonel William Fairfax. He had been born in the Bahamas and educated in England. When he joined his father in Virginia, he rose quickly in public life, becoming a justice of the peace and, in 1748, at age twenty-three, a Burgess as well. Colonel Fairfax decided to dispatch a surveying party to plat out the Fairfax holdings along the South Branch of the Potomac, a tract far into the frontier. Either George William or his father invited sixteen-year-old George to join this party. George well understood that not only would this give him an opportunity to serve on an expedition in company with so fine a gentleman as the younger Fairfax, it would also allow him to observe and to assist James Genn (or Glenn), the commissioned surveyor of Prince William County. George was excited by the invitation, but he knew that there was still the obstacle of his mother to be overcome. Perhaps because she had just withheld her blessing from the boy's maritime future, she seems to have yielded without a struggle in the case of the survey expedition. George was free to go.

The party set out from Mount Vernon and nearby Belvoir on March 11, 1748, making forty miles on the very first day. George brought with him a blank book in which he recorded "A Journal of my Journey over the

Mountains began Fryday the 11th. of March 1747/8." The journal, each
passing day dutifully dated, reveals the youth's orderly approach to the
expedition but also betrays, as some historians and biographers have complained, a paucity of imagination:

*Saturday March 12th. This morning Mr. James Genn the
surveyor came to us. We travel'd over the Blue Ridge to
Capt. Ashbys on Shannondoa River. Nothing remarkable
happen'd.*

To be sure, the boy was not quite dead to all that surrounded him:

*Sunday March 13. Rode to his Lordships Quarter about 4
Miles higher up the River we went through most beautiful
Groves of Sugar Trees & spent the best part of the Day in
admiring the Trees & richness of the Land.[5]*

Gratified as we are that George could appreciate beauty and spend "the
best part of the day" admiring the trees and the rich land, we are nevertheless disappointed that no more profound comment accompanies the
adventure of traveling "over the Blue Ridge" than "Nothing remarkable
happen'd." Yet perhaps this very absence of imagination is a salient clue to
the young man's evolving character. In his novel *Lord Jim*, Joseph Conrad
called imagination "the enemy of men, the father of all terrors." It is
imagination, a quality most of us prize, that proves the undoing of

Conrad's young hero, destroying his courage, prompting him to an act both he and others deem cowardly, and driving him to redeem himself through ultimately fatal heroism. From his very first battle on the eve of the French and Indian War to his final victory at Yorktown in the American Revolution, George Washington exhibited a calm, uncannily matter-of-fact courage. Perhaps this is proof that he, unlike Lord Jim, was not afflicted by "the father of all terrors." Perhaps Washington's was a courage born of an absence of imagination—as if, whether at age sixteen in 1748, twenty-one in 1753, or forty-three in 1775, Washington saw only the reality of what was immediately before him, picturing in his mind no terror behind it. Perhaps it was the absence of imagination that would make him so inspiring a combat leader. For whatever reason, when on March 23 the surveyors saw "thirty odd Indians coming from War with only one Scalp," George was entirely unafraid. "We had some Liquor with us," he noted in his journal, "of which we gave them Part it elevating there Spirits put them in the Humour of Dauncing of whom we had a War Daunce." Nor did this appear fearsome to him, but, rather, "most comicle."[6]

That he was unafraid on the frontier did not mean that George Washington was fully content there. Put up for the night of March 15 in the house of one Captain Isaac Pennington, the young man was "Lighted in to a Room & I not being so good a Woodsman as the rest of my Company striped my self very orderly & went in to Bed as they call'd it when to my Surprize I found it to be nothing but a Little Straw—Matted together without Sheets or any thing else but only one Thread Bear blanket with double Weight of Vermin such as Lice Fleas &c. I was glad to get up (as soon as the Light was carried from us) & put on my Cloths & Lay [fully clothed] as my Companions. Had we not have been very tired, I am sure we should not have slep'd much that night." On the 26th, he remarked of supper at the house of Solomon Hedges ("one of his Majestys Justices of the Peace for the County of Frederick"), "there was neither a Cloth upon the Table nor a Knife to eat with." And on April 4, he wrote of being "attended by a great Company of People Men Women & Children" as the survey party tramped through the woods. "I really think they seem to be as Ignorant a Set of People as the Indians." Although he lived on the cusp of the frontier, young Washington had never before seen the people at the heart of the frontier. Now that he saw them, he was unimpressed—and harbored no romantic illusions as to their native nobility.[7]

By the time the expedition returned on April 13, George Washington and his companions had spent thirty-three days on the frontier. By the standards of the day, this was hardly a marathon achievement, and the surveying party had not been exposed to the true extremity of an unexplored wilderness. Yet the experience was valuable to the young man. By his own admission, he was not a natural frontiersman, but he had held his own out-of-doors. He discovered no affinity for frontier folk, whom he regarded as uncouth, but he had found—in his matter-of-fact manner—stirring beauty in the frontier lands. Of most immediate importance, he had gained practical experience as a frontier surveyor. He had taken a hand in running lines through a trackless wilderness. In the short term, this experience would launch him on a career as a professional surveyor—a profession profitable in itself, but especially so for a youngster not yet out of his teens. In the longer term, the practical proof that he could master the wilderness through the precise measurement of it must have had a formative impact on George Washington. Surveying was a powerful force in every aspect of colonial life: economic, political, cultural, and emotional. It brought to the wilderness human order—or, more precisely, an order born of European traditions of rational thought. It was, therefore, a form of cultural conquest, and it must have shaped Washington's attitude toward the western lands into which he would soon venture when the lines drawn by the Anglo-Americans conflicted with those drawn by the Franco-Americans. At his brother's Mount Vernon house, military talk mixed freely with the talk of surveys. George Washington, who would soon become a soldier, began as a surveyor.

The impulses toward both professions were, for him, inextricably linked.

By the age of sixteen, Washington had learned to pass the time—when he was not traipsing through the frontier—in reading, eagerly devouring *The Spectator*, the stylish and chatty magazine imported from London, and in a more desultory manner reading works of English history. By the fall of 1748, he had acquired a taste for billiards and cards, including whist and loo. He enjoyed making these games interesting with wagers that were more than mere tokens. As Lawrence dressed well, so did George. As Lawrence conversed with skill and courtesy—and danced nicely, too—so did George.

The only cloud on this sunny horizon concerned Lawrence as well. His health began to fail—so much, that in December 1748 he secured a leave of absence from the House of Burgesses and sought convalescence at Mount Vernon. In the spring of 1749, Lawrence was feeling worse, racked by a cough, which made him think that he should leave Virginia in search of some healthier climate. He attended the House of Burgesses when it convened but, once again, in May, had to secure a leave. His gloom deepened with the deaths of his children—three in all by 1749.

As for George, he managed to rise above the prevailing anxiety and sorrow when, in July 1749, he was appointed the official surveyor of Culpepper County at the age of seventeen, thanks to his connection with Lord Fairfax and his son William. It was an auspicious professional start for so young a man, and for the next three years, from July 1749 to October 1752, he performed numerous surveys not only in Culpepper, but also beyond the county, in the farther reaches of the Fairfax proprietorship. It was a life that demanded and developed personal strength and endurance, as well as strong leadership; Washington required the services of assistants—"chainmen"—who were often of a most rough-and-ready sort. In addition to these qualities, running a survey called for a calm, clear, and nimble mind. Washington needed to use a circumferentor—a surveying compass with sights, mounted on a tripod—to determine the boundary line bearings. This done, he would send his chainmen to measure off the line precisely in the direction his circumferentor reading determined. The chainmen carried a surveying chain consisting of eight-inch wrought-iron links totaling thirty-three feet ("2 poles") in length, with which they measured off the lines, notching trees as they proceeded to indicate the run of the line. It was hard and painstaking work that required continual monitoring and correction, and when the fieldwork was completed, Washington had to reduce the data to a finished survey, complete with a formal description of the boundaries of the land surveyed and a neatly drafted plat. Young though he was, he put a high value on his work. The Virginia Assembly had fixed a fee of £1 11*s.* per 1,000 acres for surveys in the frontier counties. Washington charged more, £2 3*s.*—the maximum permitted in counties along Virginia's fall line (the drop in the level of the land, as demarcated by waterfalls in the colony's parallel rivers). No one seems ever to have challenged his premium fee—perhaps because of Washington's Fairfax connections, and perhaps, too, because he did his work efficiently and accurately. Over the three years in which he worked as a professional surveyor, Washington must have realized about £400 in fees. During this time, he also acquired 2,315 acres of choice Shenandoah Valley land for himself.

Just as George was embarking on his surveying career, Lawrence set out for London on a double mission. He meant to find a physician who could diagnose and cure his lung ailment, and he wanted to pursue an extraordinary business opportunity. After several months, Lawrence returned from London undiagnosed, let alone cured, but he had closed the deal that founded the Ohio Company. On March 16, 1749, King George II granted 200,000 acres to this syndicate of British and American traders and speculators. There was, however, a stout string attached: within seven years, the company had to plant a settlement of 100 families and build a fort for their protection or forfeit the land. However, if Lawrence and his partners could attract a sufficient number of settlers by that time, the Ohio Company would be granted an additional 300,000 acres.

The Ohio Company project would shape George Washington's early military career and, indeed, by bringing Anglo-American fortunes into direct conflict with Franco-American fortunes, would in large measure determine the destiny of North America. At the moment, however, George saw the grand scheme as highly theoretical, whereas Lord Fairfax had just handed him something real: his first major surveying assignment, in Frederick County. In the spring of 1750, even as his half-brother mentally wrestled with suspicious Indians and vague French threats, both of which were slowing the progress of the Ohio Company, George was riding over the Blue Ridge and into the Shenandoah Valley. Here he not only executed surveys, but invested a large portion of his collected fees in acquiring land—the first of the tracts that would amount to 2,315 acres by the fall of 1752. When he returned to Mount Vernon near the beginning of winter, he found that Lawrence and Nancy Washington had a new child, a baby girl named Sarah, which surely cheered his half-brother, but did not entirely lift from him the burden of the Ohio Company's difficulties. Although he had returned from London with no medical enlightenment, his health had improved in proportion to the excitement he felt over the Ohio Company venture. Now that company matters were becoming increasingly frustrating, his health was once again in decline. He traveled to the Warm Springs seeking a cure, but toward the end of March 1751 he resolved to try something different. He would not chance another winter in Virginia. At the time, Barbados was widely seen as a haven for those afflicted in the lungs. Yet it seemed unwise for Lawrence, in his present condition, to make the trip alone. Nor was it practical for Nancy and newborn Sarah to come along. It is a measure of George

Washington's love for Lawrence that he eagerly volunteered to accompany his brother, even though that meant giving up the profitable autumn surveying season—as well as several months' opportunity to buy more of the dwindling supply of bargain-priced Shenandoah lands. There is no evidence that George gave so much as a second thought to the matter. All his life, Lawrence had given unstintingly to him, and now Lawrence needed his companionship. Besides, it *would* be an adventure.

❧

The two set sail on September 28, 1751, and were settled for the night at a Bridgetown tavern on November 3. On the very next day, even before they found long-term lodgings, Lawrence called on Dr. William Hilary, who specialized in treating lung sufferers seeking health in the gentle climate of Barbados. Dr. Hilary gave Lawrence something neither the physicians of Virginia nor those of London could give: hope. He assured him that his disease was capable of being cured—provided that the brothers stay in the country, where the air was healthier than in town. Accordingly, Lawrence and George rode out in search of a rural place to live. The commandant of Fort James opened his house to them—at the nearly stratospheric price of £15 a month. As far as George was concerned, however, he would have paid even more. The fort was ideally located—in the country, near the water, but only about a mile outside of town—and provided a prospect of Carlisle Bay "and all the shipping" on it, as Washington noted in the diary he began to keep. Around him, the spectacle of tropical growth—especially the abundance of fruits—was nearly overwhelming, but what interested George most was Fort James itself. His diary entries describing the place could have been written by a seasoned military engineer of the period: "It's pretty strongly fortified and mounts about 36 guns within the fortifications, but [has] two fascine batteries mg. 51"—that is, two batteries mounting cannon that fired 51-pound balls. Fort James was the first fort George Washington had ever seen, yet he appraised its defenses as if he had been born a general.[8]

George Washington's Barbados idyll cracked on November 17 when he came down with a high fever, headache, and severe body pains. Within three days, he was covered in red spots, which blossomed into ugly papules. There was no mistaking it: Washington had smallpox—a disease all dreaded but few escaped in the eighteenth century. There was nothing exceptional about the course the disease took in the young man. To be sure, smallpox could be fatal, but in one as strong as Washington this was not the expected outcome. By November 28, he was clearly on the mend. Like most men and women of his time, he would bear for the rest of his life the pockmarks of a survivor, but like those others, he knew that he would carry lifelong something more as well: immunity to the disease—a disease all too common in armies and in the places armies most commonly go. Conversation, school exercises, surveying, a tour of a Caribbean fort, and now even illness all prepared Washington for the career he did not yet know would be his.

*

The fate of men is partly what they themselves make of it, but partly in other hands. George Washington survived smallpox and won future immunity from it. Lawrence Washington, despite Dr. Hilary's optimism, did not so much decline as he failed to get better. By December 1751, he was thinking about seeking different air. The air of Mount Vernon was bad for him—he knew that—but the air of Barbados was proving ineffectual. Perhaps the Bermudas would offer a breeze more salubrious. He decided to give those islands a try. But already, George must have recognized, Lawrence was anticipating failure there as well, for he went on to speak of what he would do if the climate of the Bermudas made no improvement. He would return to Virginia and try the air of Frederick County, which, higher than that of Mount Vernon and environs, was also drier. In any case, Lawrence told George to return now to Virginia without him and get on with the career he had interrupted.

So George Washington took ship alone on December 21, 1751, and landed at Yorktown on January 28 of the following year. Before traveling to Mount Vernon to bring Nancy news of her husband, the young man hired a horse and rode to Williamsburg to introduce himself to Robert Dinwiddie. Technically, Dinwiddie was Virginia's lieutenant governor—the royal governor was ensconced in England—but, in practical terms, he was *the* governor of the colony and was always addressed as such. As it happened, when Washington called on him, Dinwiddie was away, visiting Green Spring six miles off, but such was the young man's standing in the colony that he was invited to return later in the day when the governor was expected back. In the meantime, Washington diverted himself with what few attractions the capital offered.

Little is known of George Washington's first visit with Governor Dinwiddie, the man who would send him on his first military mission—a mission that would result in two battles—one a victory, the other a defeat—battles that launched what historians have often called the first *world* war. The pair dined together, and the governor inquired after Lawrence's health. Beyond these two bare facts, anything more speculation.

On the day after his dinner with the governor, George returned to Yorktown, where, with a Colonel John Lewis, he watched a cockfight—and not just any cockfight, but a "great main of cocks," a battle royal among prize barnyard gladiators on whom the finest gentlemen of the neighborhood laid substantial wagers—typically five pistoles per bout, but as much as a hundred pistoles on some.[9]

After a stay with the colonel in his home, George began the journey to Mount Vernon, which he reached on February 5 or 6. He then picked up his surveying career where he had left it, tramping through the frontier of Frederick County and making a fair amount of money, despite a dispute with the College of William and Mary over commissioning fees due that institution. George also added to his land holdings in Frederick County. He returned from the surveying expedition, however, with a nasty case of pleurisy, which kept him from pursuing the affections of the sixteen-year-old daughter of William Fauntleroy, Elizabeth—"Betsy"—with whom George was smitten.

She was not his first love. In 1749 or 1750, George had addressed a letter to "Dear Friend Robin"—who may have been his cousin, Robert Washington (born 1729)—telling him of "a very agreeable Young Lady," with whom he might "pass my time very pleasantly," were "my heart disengag'd." Alas, disengaged Washington's heart was not, for spending time with the young lady was "only adding Fuel to fire." Her company, he wrote, only "makes me the more uneasy" because it "revives my former Passion for your Low Land Beauty." Seventeen or eighteen at the time, Washington testified to Robin that "was I to live more retired from youn[g] Women I might in some measure eliviate my sorrows by burying that chast and troublesome Passion in the grave of oblivion or etarnall forgetfulness for as I am very well assured that's the only antidote or remedy that I ever shall be releivd by . . ." He wrote at this time an almost identical letter to "Dear Friend John"—probably another cousin—complaining that the "conversasions of an agreeable young Lady" were "only nourishment to my former Affa[ir] for by often seeing her brings the other into my remembrance . . ." The agreeable young lady of these letters was probably Mary Cary (1733–1781), the younger sister of Sally Cary, the beautiful wife of George William Fairfax, but the identity of Washington's unforgettable "Low Land Beauty" has never been guessed. Intriguing is a letter from this same period addressed to "Dear Sally"—not Sally Cary, but an otherwise unidentified young woman—in which George confessed himself "almost discouraged from Writing to you as this is my fou[r]th [letter] to you since I receivd any from yourself." He hoped that she would "not make the Old Proverb good out of sight out of Mind," because "one of the greatest Pleasures I can yet foresee . . . [is] often hearing from you hope you'l not deny it me." Having said this, Washington continued—perhaps coyly—"I Pass the time of much more agreabler than what I imagined I should as there's a very agreeable Young Lady lives in the said house where I reside." Presumably, she was the same young lady—perhaps Mary Cary—Washington mentioned to Robin and John. She "in a great Measure chears my sorrow and dejectedness tho. not so as to draw my thoughts altogether from your Parts." Washington continued: "I could wish to be with you down there with all my heart but as it is a thing almost Impractakable shall rest my self where I am with hope's of shortly having some Minutes of your transactions . . ." Could this apparently unresponsive correspondent be George's "Low Land Beauty"? We do not know.[10]

Three poetic fragments in Washington's hand survive from this time, one of which seems surely to embody the anguish of young love unrequited:

Oh Ye Gods why should my Poor Resistless Heart
Stand to oppose thy might and Power
At Last surrender to cupids feather'd Dart
and now lays Bleeding every Hour
For her that's Pityless of my grief and Woes
And will not on me Pity take
Ill sleep amongst my most Inviterate Foes
And with gladness never wish to Wake
In deluding sleepings let my Eyelids close
That in an enraptured Dream I may

In a soft lulling sleep and gentle repose
possess those joys denied by Day [11]

Most of the handful of scholars who have commented on this piece
conclude that its polished verse, correct spelling, and proper syntax cannot have been composed by Washington, whose letters and diary entries
at this age exhibit the clumsy sentence structure and idiosyncratic spelling
of someone who had, after all, received little formal education. Yet even
the fact that Washington chose to copy it (if that is what he did; no
source has ever been identified) suggests his state of mind: that of a
lovesick teenager who is far from becoming the marble monument
known to history.

George Washington was seventeen or eighteen when he wrote these
letters and wrote or copied this piece of verse. In 1752, he was twenty,
and in the spring of that year he met, at Naylor's Hole in Richmond
County, Betsy Fauntleroy. He made overtures to her, was spurned,
resolved to try again, but fell ill with pleurisy. He wrote to Betsy's father,
William Fauntleroy, on May 20:

> *I shou'd have been down long before this but my business in*
> *Frederick detain'd me somewhat longer than I expected and*
> *immediately upon my return from thence I was taken with*
> *a Violent Pleurisie which has reduced me very low but pur-*
> *pose as soon as I recover my strength to wait on Miss Betcy,*
> *in hopes of a revocation of the former, cruel sentrence, and*
> *see if I can meet with [any alter]ation in my favour. I have*
> *inclos'd a letter to her which i shou'd be much obligd to you*
> *for the delivery of it . . .* [12]

The "inclos'd" letter has never been located, but Betsy apparently responded to it with a negative even more vehement than before, where-upon Washington surrendered, and the girl's name never again appears in any of his papers.

Whatever unhappiness Betsy's rejection produced was nothing compared with his growing anxiety over Lawrence. His half-brother's letters from Bermuda were grim. He felt, he said, "like a criminal condemned," adding faintly: "though not without hopes of reprieve." His Barbados doctor prescribed a milk diet and much riding in the fresh air, warning that a precipitate return to Virginia would "most certainly destroy" him. By the time he wrote his next letter, Lawrence's hopes had clearly diminished: "The unhappy state of health which I labor under makes me uncertain as to my return. If I grow worse I shall hurry home to my grave; if better, I shall be induced to stay here longer to complete a cure." When, therefore, sometime before June 16, Lawrence arrived at Mount Vernon, there was no mistaking the meaning of his early return. On June 20, he feverishly drew up and signed his last will and testament. His will made, he died little more than a month later, on July 26, 1752, aged thirty-four or thirty-five.[13]

For George Washington, it was an end and a beginning. He was the principal executor of his half-brother's estate, chiefly responsible for sorting out the hastily composed and almost hopelessly confusing will, and entirely responsible for arranging the funeral and seeing to the construction of a burial vault. Whatever grief he felt would have to make room for the completion of these duties. Most of Lawrence's estate, including his stock in the Ohio Company, went to his wife, Nancy, and his infant daughter, Sarah. George would share equally in real estate that would go to Lawrence's brothers in the event that Sarah should die childless. Further, upon Nancy's death—and if Sarah died without issue—George would inherit Mount Vernon, together with all of his half-brother's other Fairfax County real estate. More immediately for George Washington— and for the rest of his life—there was the shining legacy of Lawrence

Washington's example of Virginia manhood: martial skill and valor combined with a dauntless speculative faith in the future of the country.

2

OF EMPIRES AND SELF-INTEREST

When John Washington decided to leave *The Sea Horse of London* in 1657, Europeans had already been making a new start in America for more than 150 years. For a century and a half, it had been regarded as a place for new starts, so much so that the early European explorers, settlers, or invaders thought of the New World as paradise, another Eden, perhaps even the Old Testament Eden itself. As Columbus wrote to Isabella and Ferdinand in 1500 after his third voyage, "I believe that this land which your Highnesses have commanded me to discover is very great, and that there are many other lands in the south of which there have never been reports." Sail a little farther south in the New World, Columbus wrote, and "I believe that the earthly Paradise lies here." Although his first voyage, in 1492, had landed him well north of what he later speculated was Eden, his earlier rapturous descriptions of the landscape and the people of the Caribbean island he called Hispaniola also evoke images of the earthly paradise: a place of lush valleys, infinite fertility, delicious climate, and a people so innocent that "They do not have arms, and they are all naked, and of no skill in arms."[1]

The native people Columbus first encountered were as welcoming, pleasant, and helpful as they were beautiful. Yet this Eden seemed to invite from the Spaniards nothing more powerfully than the urge to despoil it. The logbook Columbus kept of his first voyage is known to history only through a combination transcription and redaction made by Bartolomé de las Casas. Born in Seville in 1484, Las Casas sailed at age eighteen to the New World, where he participated in the conquest of Cuba. Witnessing an orgy of destruction there, Las Casas was spiritually transformed. He became a priest and dedicated himself to protecting the Indians from his countrymen. In 1542, he wrote *A Short Account of the Destruction of the Indies*, which he addressed to Philip II of Spain in the hope that, duly informed of his subjects' crimes, the monarch would intervene to stop them. In his later general *History of the Indies*, Las Casas depicted Columbus's own struggle to rein in the rapacity of his men on lovely Hispaniola: "The Indians were so open and the Spaniards so greedy and disorderly," Las Casas wrote, "that it was not enough for them that for a lace-end, and even for bits of glass and of pottery and other things of no account, the Indians give them all they want; but even without giving the Indians something, the Spaniards want to have and take everything . . ."[2]

Columbus did have difficulty controlling his men on the first voyage. Of his three ships, the famous *Niña, Pinta,* and *Santa Maria,* the *Santa Maria* ran aground in a storm, and the *Pinta,* under the wayward captaincy of Martín Alonso Pinzón, set off on its own in November 1492. The ship would reappear late in January, but Columbus was not aware of that when he decided to return to Spain on January 16, 1493. Unable to pack everyone into the little *Niña,* he built on Hispaniola the fortress settlement of La Navidad, complete with a European-style tower, fort, and moat, and left there thirty-nine Spaniards, charging this garrison with gathering gold, finding the source of more gold, and stockpiling a store of spices, which were, by weight, even more valuable than gold.

Columbus returned to Hispaniola on his second voyage, in November

1493, only to discover that all of the garrison had been killed by the "innocent" Taino natives. After much inquiry, he discovered further that no sooner had he left for Spain than the garrison set about picking the countryside clean, raping the native women, and stealing the Indians' food and other stores. One night, as the Spaniards slept, the Tainos killed them. Those who awoke and ran, they hunted down and killed later. It was the first recorded war in Eden. There would be many more.

By the time George Washington was coming of age, the New World had long been a battlefield. In addition to countless wars among the Indian tribes—most of which, unrecorded, are unknown to history—there had been numerous wars between whites and Indians. As early as the sixteenth century, the Spanish Conquistadors battled the Native Americans of the Southwest, and in Virginia, for twenty years, between 1622 and 1644, colonists had fought with what they called the Powhatans, a collection of at least thirty-two Indian tribes initially under the control or influence of the "paramount chief" (or mamanatowick), Wahunsonacock (ca. 1550–1618), whom the English knew by his throne name, Powhatan. At the very beginning, the Powhatans took pity on the struggling colonists and helped them to survive their first terrible winters, but as colonial tobacco cultivation took hold, creating an ever greater colonial demand for land, relations between the English and the Powhatans deteriorated. By 1610, after the colonists appropriated cleared Indian fields for tobacco farming, the Powhatans alternately fought against and traded with the English. In 1613, Samuel Argall, mariner and colonist, abducted not Powhatan, but his daughter Pocahontas, whom Virginia's governor decided to hold hostage as a means of extorting good behavior from the Indians. An extraordinary young woman, Pocahontas behaved more as an ambassador than a hostage. She learned English, thoroughly ingratiated herself with the colonists, and ultimately married John Rolfe, one of the most prominent planters among them. This marriage, combined with Powhatan's desire to continue profitable trading with the English, doubtless played a role in bringing about a truce in 1614.

Despite the pressures created by the tobacco growers' increasing hunger for land, an uneasy peace endured between the settlers and the Powhatans until the death of the old chief in 1618. Opechancanough, Powhatan's half-brother, succeeded him, and although he pledged continuing friendship with the English, he was never committed to it. When in 1622, a planter known to history only as Morgan ventured inland to trade with the Indians and was never heard from again, two colonists (on the flimsiest of evidence) accused a prominent Powhatan, Nemattanow (or Nematanou), of having ordering Morgan's murder. They exacted revenge by murdering Nemattanow, for which Opechancanough, in turn, vowed vengeance. Hearing the chief's threats, the other colonists made threats of their own, which—surprisingly—elicited from Opechancanough a renewed pledge of eternal friendship. As if to demonstrate his goodwill, on March 20, 1622, the chief personally served as guide to a group of planters traveling through the woods. Two days later, on Good Friday, came further gestures of apparent amity. To English settlements all along the James River, Captain John Smith later wrote, the Indians "as at other times . . . came unarmed . . . with Deere, Turkies, Fish, Fruits, and other provisions to sell us, yea in some places sat downe at breakfast with our people, whom immediately with their owne tooles slew most barbarously, not sparing either age or sex, man woman or childe, so sudden in their execution, that few or none discerned the weapon or blow that brought them to destruction."[3]

It was a brilliant and ruthless campaign of surprise attacks coordinated by Opechancanough. By the end of this Good Friday, 347 settlers had been killed—fully a third of the colony. Only the intervention of an Indian boy called Chanco, the Christianized servant of a colonist named Mr. Pace, saved Jamestown from total annihilation. When the boy's brother had ordered him to murder Pace, Chanco instead told his master of the plot. Pace in turn alerted Governor Francis Wyatt, who proclaimed the English colony's new policy: "It is infinitely better to have no heathen among us, who were but as thornes in our sides, than to be at peace and league with them."[4] War continued, at first steadily and then sporadically, for the next two decades.

Up north, in the Connecticut Valley in 1637, another alleged murder triggered war between the colonists and the Indians. In 1634, the ship of Captain John Stone, a disreputable "trader" (who was really more of a pirate), rode at anchor in the mouth of the Connecticut River. Indian raiders, most likely western Niantics, a satellite or "client" tribe of the Pequots, attacked and killed Stone. According to one Pequot version, Captain Stone had kidnapped a party of Indians, and was killed by another group of Indians seeking to rescue the captives. Another Pequot variant held that the raid had been nothing more or less than a case of mistaken identity. The killers, commissioned by the Pequots, thought that they were attacking Dutch traders who had murdered a tribal sachem named Tatobam. The conflicting stories notwithstanding, the Pequots, though they had not killed Stone, recognized that a member of a tributary tribe had. Having no desire to provoke war with the English, they moved quickly to placate colonial authorities, and on November 7 signed the Massachusetts Bay-Pequot Treaty, whereby the Pequots agreed to hand over those guilty of Captain Stone's murder, to pay an exorbitant indemnity, to relinquish rights to any Connecticut land that the English might wish to settle, and to trade exclusively with the English. Although a portion of the promised indemnity was duly paid, the Pequots never produced Stone's killers. For two years, the English did nothing about this; then, on June 16, 1636, a Plymouth trader reported a warning he had received from Uncas, chief of the Mohegans, that the Pequots, fearing the colonists were about to attack them, intended to make a preemptive strike. In July, acting on this information, Connecticut and Massachusetts Bay officials convened a conference with representatives of the Western Niantics and Pequots at Fort Saybrook, on the Connecticut River. The colonists reasserted the demands of the 1634 treaty. The Indians apparently promised to comply, but a few days after the meeting word reached colonial authorities that another trading captain, John Oldham, together with his crew, had been killed off Block Island. This time, the perpetrators were Narragansetts or members of a tribe subject to them. The Narragansett sachems hastened not only to condemn the murder, but volunteered reparations. This notwithstanding, the colonists launched a vigorous war against the Pequots and Narragansetts, which resulted in the virtual annihilation of the Pequot tribe and the reduction of the Narragansetts.

The next major war between whites and Indians also occurred in New England. Massasoit, chief of the Wampanoags and longtime friend of the English (it was through his aid that the Pilgrims survived their first terrible winter in the New World) died in 1661 at the age of 81. His son Wamsutta succeeded him and continued the tradition of friendship with the English. However, under Wamsutta, the Wampanoags divided their loyalty between two competing English colonies, Rhode Island and Plymouth. The Plymouth Colony's militia major (later governor), Josiah Winslow, seized Wamsutta at gunpoint and took him to Duxbury to answer conspiracy charges and prove his loyalty to Plymouth by selling land to that colony rather than to Rhode Island. During his captivity, Wamsutta contracted a fever and died. His twenty-four-year-old brother, Metacom or Metacomet, whom the English called King Philip, succeeded him as sachem and, like a number of other Wampanoags, suspected that Winslow had not merely abducted Wamsutta, but had poisoned him. Relations between the colony and King Philip deteriorated, and early in 1671 Philip, outraged that the new Plymouth settlement of Swansea flagrantly encroached on his land, staged an armed display to intimidate the town's citizens.

On April 10, 1671, he was summoned to Taunton, Massachusetts, to apologize and to surrender his people's arms. By the end of September he was haled to Plymouth, where he stood trial for failure to abide by the Taunton agreement. Fined £100, the sachem was further humiliated by a requirement that he henceforth obtain colonial permission in all matters involving the purchase or sale of land; he was also forbidden to wage war against other Indians without authority from the colonial government.

For three years after this, Philip quietly forged anti-English alliances with the Nipmuck Indians and his tribe's former rivals, the Narragansetts. Then, in January 1675, came another revelation of Wampanoag designs against the English. John Sassamon—or Saussaman—a Christianized Indian who had been King Philip's confidant, alerted the English to the sachem's plotting. On January 29, Sassamon's body was found on the ice of a frozen pond. Philip was accused of complicity in the murder and was again haled into court, but won release for lack of evidence. On June 11, just three days after other Indians were executed for the murder, word of Wampanoags arming near Swansea and Plymouth Town reached authorities. They also heard of scattered incidents of cattle killed and houses looted in outlying settlements. Already, settlers were beginning to desert some towns: Swansea, adjacent to Wampanoag country, was the first to be partially abandoned, and Indians began appropriating property left behind. An outraged settler shot a looter: the first blood of the war. Now Massachusetts, Plymouth, and Rhode Island joined forces to mobilize an army, which was mustered during June 21 through 23, 1675. By the time the resulting war ended in October 1676, half of the region's English towns had been badly damaged and a dozen destroyed completely. The fragile colonial economy suffered devastating blows, both as a result of the direct cost of the war—some £100,000—and because of the disruption of the fur trade with the Indians and the virtual cessation of coastal fishing and the West Indies trade. Not only did the war siphon off the manpower customarily devoted to these industries, but many men never returned to their peacetime occupations; one in sixteen colonists of military age died. Many others—men, women, children—were also killed, captured, or starved. Among the Indians, at least 3,000 perished, and many of those who did not die were deported and sold into slavery. In proportion to New England's white population of 30,000, King Philip's War was the costliest in American history.

There were other conflicts as well between whites and Indians, including, in Virginia, Bacon's Rebellion of 1676, in which a demagogue named Nathaniel Bacon led a popular revolt against Governor William Berkeley even as Bacon and his followers also waged unauthorized warfare against Susquehannock and Occaneechi Indians. Bacon had actually employed the Occaneechi as proxy warriors to fight the Susquehannocks on his behalf. When the Occaneechi war party returned victorious with Susquehannock prisoners and a cache of captured pelts, Bacon attempted to seize the furs and enslave a group of Manikin Indians, who had fought as allies of the Occaneechi. When the Occaneechi refused to relinquish either the pelts or their Manikin allies, Bacon turned on them. It was a small-scale example of what, by the end of the seventeenth century, would be repeatedly enacted in progressively larger contexts: not merely warfare between Indians and colonists, but the involvement of Indians in disputes between colonial powers.

The world into which George Washington had been born was increasingly torn by warfare between the two greatest North American colonial rivals, France and Britain, conducted substantially through Indian proxies. Whereas the wars between colonists and Indians were almost exclusively provoked by land disputes, those between the colonial powers certainly put territorial control at stake, but they were also extensions of European conflicts. They constituted, in effect, the New World theater of Old World wars. If Columbus and many of those who came after him "contaminated" with conflict what they saw as Eden, the French and Indian War of 1754–1763 and the three major colonial wars that preceded it did much more than taint the earthly paradise. They transplanted—whole—Old World enmities and power struggles to the New, transforming America into a battlefield on which Europe sought to resolve its conflicts. While the Washingtons and their French colonial counterparts saw America as a place of new beginnings, the leaders of their mother countries enacted upon it some very old blood disputes.

❦

The first of the major conflicts leading up to the French and Indian War was dubbed King William's War. It was named for Britain's William III, who, shortly after he ascended the throne, formed with the League of Augsburg and the Netherlands the Grand Alliance on May 12, 1689. This coalition opposed France's Louis XIV, who had invaded the Rhenish Palatinate on September 24, 1688. In Europe, the war that broke out was an eight-year conflict known as the War of the League of Augsburg. The Palatinate was a very long way from North America, but the European conflict nevertheless exacerbated the chronic hostilities between the French and English colonists. As King William's War, the conflict pitted the French and Abenaki Indians (of northern New England and south-eastern Canada) against the English colonists and their Iroquois allies.

In the Europe of the seventeenth, eighteenth, and even nineteenth centuries, war was really a deadly simple business of numbers. Except in rare instances of great military genius or great military stupidity, the side with more men won, as enemy armies essentially arrayed themselves opposite one another and opened fire. The army that could produce the most fire the fastest—that is, the bigger army—generally killed more men and therefore emerged victorious. The aggressive governor of New France (as the French American colonies were styled), Louis de Buade, comte de Frontenac, desperately wanted to descend upon New York from Canada, but he knew that he did not have the required numbers for such a conventional invasion. Not to be thwarted, he proposed instead to fight a new, unconventional kind of warfare, which he called "la petite guerre," a little war. It was a phrase that would eventually metamorphose into *guerrilla war*, which aptly describes the nature of combat Frontenac introduced. It was a tactical approach that sought to compensate for a shortage of troops by exploiting what military resources were available in

an America of woods and wilderness: small, stealthy bands of woodsmen
and skilled Indian warriors, all "soldiers" who could fight a war consisting
not of battles in the formal European manner, but of ruthless ambush
murders, committed without warning or mercy in isolated frontier outposts and settlements. Nor would it be a war of army against army. This
new breed of "soldier" did not distinguish between combatants and civilians. All alike were targets. La petite guerre, though small in scale, was
"total warfare," as the profoundly influential military theorist Carl von
Clausewitz would define it in his seminal early nineteenth-century essay,
On War. It was combat that engulfed entire peoples. If Europe brought its
Old World conflicts to the New, there were at least some New World
leaders willing to fight those traditional conflicts with tactics departing
radically from tradition.

In earlier colonial wars, the Indians had been the enemy. Now shrewd
colonial leaders such as Frontenac enlisted them as allies. Many Indian
tribes were desperate to preserve their lands and the resources of their
lands against white incursions. As more and more Europeans came to
North America—and had children here—the Indians became aware that
they would inevitably be overwhelmed. But they also observed that the
Euro-Americans were anything but a united lot. Many tribes were willing
to exploit the conflicts they saw between the groups of trespassers. In
places where the English were seen as a threat—not only to Indian home-
lands, but also to profitable trading relationships with the French—tribes
tended to ally themselves with the French. Where French incursions
threatened Indian holdings as well as trade with the English, the Indians
allied themselves with the English.

In King William's War, the French made use, first and foremost, of the
Abenakis, whom they induced and encouraged to terrorize the English
settlements throughout Maine and New Hampshire. Indeed, the French
as well as the English looked to their Indian proxies to employ combat
practices, including clubbing, burning, and various other forms of lethal
torture in which European commanders and soldiers normally did not

engage. (Scalping, a war practice long associated with many Indian tribes, was also widely practiced by Europeans—albeit not normally by soldiers in regular European armies—and historians have engaged in a long debate over whether the Europeans learned the practice from the Indians or vice versa.) Colonists on both sides tended to view Indians, especially Indian warriors, as savages, and English as well as French commanders exploited this fear to wield the warriors as weapons of terror.

Through the summer of 1689, Abenaki raids on far-flung English settlements had become so destructive that the English were forced to abandon all their outposts east of Falmouth, Maine. Boston authorities responded to the crisis by mustering and dispatching to the north an army of six hundred, but what little training this militia force had was in conventional European march-form-stand-shoot warfare, and it had little effect against Indian guerrillas. Another military convention Frontenac flouted was the traditional suspension of combat in the winter. At the onset of the season, Frontenac assembled a combined force of 160 Canadians and some one hundred Indians to mount a three-pronged assault from Montreal into New York, New Hampshire, and Maine. If a winter campaign was hard on the victims of the attack, it was also brutal on the attackers, and after reaching the Hudson via a frozen trek down Lake Champlain to the southern tip of Lake George, the exhausted leaders of the assault force decided to attack Schenectady, which was closer than Albany. On the afternoon of February 8, 1690, after marching across frozen swampland, they reached the vicinity of the settlement. Attacking after nightfall, they met with no resistance from a village that was "guarded" by nothing more formidable than a pair of snowmen. In the span of two hours, the French and Indians ravaged Schenectady, killing sixty men, women, and children, most of them as they slept in their beds.

On March 27, another segment of Frontenac's forces attacked Salmon Falls, New Hampshire, killing thirty-four settlers, and in May, they hit Fort Loyal (Falmouth, Maine), taking the lives of nearly a hundred English colonists. At about this time—on May 1, 1690—delegates from

Massachusetts, Plymouth, Connecticut, and New York convened at
Albany to plan an invasion of Canada, which, they hoped, would choke
off the raids at their source. Sir William Phipps would be in overall command of a pair of land forces from New York and New England, which
were to be supported by a naval force sailing up the St. Lawrence River.
On May 11, 1690, Phipps's ships captured Port Royal, Acadia (present-
day Annapolis Royal, Nova Scotia), but the overland component of his
expedition soon bogged down. Worse, by November, Phipps's army
encountered the scourge to which George Washington would become
immune as a young man. It was decimated by smallpox and compelled to
withdraw. With the failure of Phipps's army, the French evicted the
English from their Hudson Bay outpost at the mouth of the Severn River
by the end of 1690 and, in 1691, retook Port Royal.

Despite the English setbacks, Frontenac's "petite guerre" produced
nothing but little victories. While the guerrilla actions wrought much terror, they accomplished nothing of enduring strategic value. Worst of all
for the French, the powerful Iroquois, five allied Northeastern tribes—the
Cayuga, Mohawk, Oneida, Onondaga, and Seneca—remained loyal to
the English and fought alongside them.

In September 1691, Benjamin Church, superannuated hero of King
Philip's War, was called out of retirement to lead three hundred militiamen to Saco, Maine, an English outpost that had been the target of
repeated attacks. Church won no single decisive engagement, but he did
sufficiently wear down the Abenakis to bring several sachems to peace
talks in October. On November 29, 1691, these leaders concluded a
treaty in which they agreed to release captives, to report to the English
any French plots against them, and to refrain from hostilities until May 1,
1692. Yet no sooner was the treaty signed than the Abenakis generally
violated their pledge, joining with French Canadians to attack York,
Maine, on February 5, 1692. At the beginning of June, Wells, Maine, fell
under the hatchet, followed by Deerfield, Massachusetts on June 6. In
January 1693, a French and Indian force raided Mohawk villages in New

York, capturing three hundred Mohawks, most of them women, children, and old men. Worse, many other Mohawks fled to the Caughnawaga mission in Canada. The Caughnawagas were Mohawks who had coverted to Catholicism and were therefore allied not with the Protestant English, but with the Catholic French. The Euro-American wars were thus beginning to tear apart ancient tribal solidarities.

It was not events in America that ended King William's War; rather, it was the conclusion of the Treaty of Ryswick in Europe in September 1697. This document brought the War of the League of Augsburg to an end and, with it, King William's War as well—although frontier violence continued spasmodically until a new war flared in 1702.

Like King William's War before it, Queen Anne's War was the American theater of a larger European conflict. England, Holland, and Austria, fearful of an alliance between France and Spain, formed in 1701 a new anti-French Grand Alliance a year after King Charles II of Spain, a Hapsburg, died, having chosen a Bourbon as his successor. The French supported Charles's nominee, Philip of Anjou, a grandson of Louis XIV, whereas England, Holland, and Austria favored the second son of Hapsburg emperor Leopold I, an obscure Bavarian archduke named Charles. The War of the Spanish Succession was declared in Europe on May 4, 1702. In America it took its name from that of the reigning queen of England and began on September 10, 1702, when the South Carolina legislature authorized an expedition to seize the Spanish-held fort and town of St. Augustine, Florida. After a British naval expedition plundered the town, a force of five hundred colonists and Chickasaws attacked the fort in December. Failing to breach it, they turned to further pillaging, then put St. Augustine to the torch. The sack of St. Augustine and the surrounding area brought a series of Indian raids in retaliation, to which James Moore, former South Carolina governor, responded by leading a mixed force of militiamen and Chickasaws in ravaging the territory of the Appalachee tribe of western Florida during most of July 1704. Moore's men killed or captured the inhabitants of seven villages, virtually wiping out the Appalachee. They also destroyed thirteen of fourteen Spanish missions in the country. These were not the small-scale raids typical of colonial warfare, but rather a juggernaut of ruin that had profound strategic effect, opening a path into the heart of the French Louisiana territory, including the French settlements along the Gulf of Mexico.

The French responded by feverishly recruiting allies among the southern tribes, courting the Choctaws, Cherokees, Creeks, and Chickasaws. The Chickasaws refused to budge from their pro-English stance, and the Cherokees managed to remain neutral. Some Creek bands sided with the French, but France's most effective ally proved to be the Choctaws, who intercepted Moore's relentless advance and checked him before he could penetrate Louisiana.

In the meantime, up north, the French commanded much more extensive Indian alliances. In large measure, this was less the result of aggressive French recruitment of allies than it was a product of the prevailing English colonial attitude, which typically treated Indians with contempt, in effect sending them into the arms of the French. On August 10, 1703, a party of settlers broke into and plundered the Maine house belonging to the son of Jean Vincent de l'Abadie, baron de St. Castin. Because his mother was the daughter of an Abenaki chief, St. Castin was likewise considered a chief, and the attack on his house provoked retaliatory Indian raids along some two hundred miles of the northern New England frontier.

Farther north, in Nova Scotia, the English hero Benjamin Church, now so old that he had to be assisted over fallen logs in his path, led 550 men into Acadian French territory, where he wrought terror upon the settlements of Minas and Beaubassin during July 1704. Between August 18 and 29, in Newfoundland, a mixed force of French and Indians operating out of Placentia destroyed the English settlement at Bonavista in a series of raids in retaliation for the devastation of Minas and Beaubassin.

The pattern of raid and counterraid continued in the north as well as the south. In 1710, hoping to break this ruinous cycle with a decisive victory, the British colonies sent a delegation of Mohawk chiefs across the Atlantic to the court of Queen Anne. It was a visit elaborately orchestrated to win sympathy and material support for the colonial plight. The chiefs, dressed in magnificent "savage" attire—designed by a London theatrical costumer—made a sensation at court, and Queen Anne immediately authorized a large contingent of English forces to sail to the colonies, with troops under the command of Colonel Francis Nicholson and transports and warships under Admiral Sir Francis Hobby. The land and sea components of this expedition reduced and captured Port Royal, Nova Scotia, by October 16, 1710. The conquest of all French Acadia soon followed. Inspired by victory, Hobby's subordinate, Sir Hovendon Walker, led a naval expedition against Quebec, but was shipwrecked at the mouth of the St. Lawrence River, losing more than 1,600 men. The next year, another assault against the French Canadian capital was mounted but, grossly mismanaged, had to be aborted. Queen Anne's War looked as if it would be another indecisive colonial conflict, but at about the time of the Walker disaster, France's Louis XIV, burdened by debt and weary of war, indicated his readiness to end the conflict in the New World as well as the Old. Moreover, in the course of the eleven-year struggle, Archduke Charles, the Bavarian candidate supported by the Grand Alliance, had died, leaving Louis's grandson Philip of Anjou to ascend the Spanish throne by default. Thus the original source of the war, the issue of the Spanish succession, was moot. Fate and nature having in effect sided with Louis, he signed the Treaty of Utrecht on July 13, 1713, ceding to the English Hudson Bay and Acadia, but retaining Cape Breton Island and other small islands in the St. Lawrence. Still unsettled, however, were the boundaries between French Canada and the English colonies to the south. As for the Abenakis and other French-allied Indians, they signed a treaty with the New Englanders, pledging to become loyal subjects of Queen Anne.

After making peace in Queen Anne's War, Britain and Spain concluded the *asiento,* essentially a contract that permitted the English to trade with the Spanish colonies in goods and slaves. British traders freely abused the privileges granted by the asiento, provoking a Spanish crackdown on smugglers. One English sea captain, Robert Jenkins, claimed that Spanish coast guards cut off his ear during an interrogation. There is no doubt that Jenkins was missing an ear, but it is most likely that he had lost it in a barroom brawl and not to a Spaniard's blade. No matter; Jenkins's countrymen believed the Spanish capable of anything, and in 1739 Britain and Spain began the "War of Jenkins's Ear." Within less than a year, this conflict merged with a much greater war, called in Europe the War of the Austrian Succession (1740–1748), in which Lawrence Washington had fought—or *would* have fought, had British general Thomas Wentworth allowed the "provincial" regiments to leave their ships and participate in combat ashore.

The War of the Austrian Succession had been provoked by the death of Holy Roman Emperor Charles VI in 1740, which brought a number of challenges to the succession of his daughter Maria Theresa as monarch of the Hapsburg lands. Eager to advance a claim to the Hapsburg territories, King Frederick the Great of Prussia invaded Silesia. France, Spain, Bavaria, and Saxony aligned themselves with him, while Britain came to the aid of Maria Theresa. When the fighting, as usual, spread to the North American colonies, it was called King George's War, after King George II of England.

Reflecting the European hostilities, Georgia's founder James Oglethorpe led an invasion of Spanish-held Florida in January 1740. Aided in the west by the Creeks, Cherokees, and Chickasaws, Oglethorpe captured Fort San Francisco de Pupo and Fort Picolata, both on the San Juan River. From May through July, he laid siege to St. Augustine, but withdrew when Spanish forces menaced him from behind. After repulsing a Spanish counterattack on St. Simon's Island, Georgia, in the Battle of Bloody Marsh on June 9, 1742, Oglethorpe made a second attempt to capture St. Augustine. When this failed in 1743, he withdrew from Florida.

In the north, neither the Anglo-Americans nor the Franco-Americans prosecuted the war with much vigor until the French attempted to recapture Port Royal late in 1744. This occasioned the only conventional European-style battle of King George's War, the British siege of Louisbourg on Cape Breton Island, Nova Scotia. After a siege of forty-nine days, the fort there fell on June 16, 1745, to a force of 4,200 Massachusetts militiamen. It was a formidable prize, boasting the greatest concentration of cannon in North America and guarding the approach to the St. Lawrence River. Apart from this engagement, however, King George's War was like the other colonial wars before it, consisting not of sieges and "set-piece" battles, but of guerilla warfare, much of it carried out by Indians. This time, however, the English were much more aggressive about recruiting Indian "auxiliaries." William Johnson, a prominent English colonist, had spent years cultivating close relationships with various Indian tribes and personally financed a series of Mohawk raids against French supply lines and similar objectives. Although each raid was in itself modest, this series of attacks had a significant impact on French logistics and threatened many Franco-American colonists with the prospect of a ruinous war of attrition.

Not that the French stood idle during this onslaught. French-allied Indians made lightning raids on many New England settlements. On November 28 and 29, 1745, French and Indian troops captured and burned Fort Saratoga, New York, and all through 1746, Abenakis raided many New England towns. On August 20, 1746, Fort Massachusetts, at the western foot of Hoosac Mountain, fell to an attack by French and Indians, laying open Deerfield to repeated Indian raids.

Despite English efforts, most of the Indians who fought in King George's War were allied with the French. Among the most effective Indian allies of the English, however, were the fierce and disciplined Mohawks. Although the other Iroquois tribes struggled to maintain neutrality, they nevertheless inclined toward the English. Their official neutrality nominally extended to the many Iroquois-dependent tribes in the Ohio country frontier, the most important of which were the Shawnee. Nevertheless, in November 1747, a delegation of Ohio-country warriors, principally Shawnee, came to Philadelphia to ask authorities there for arms to fight the French. Their motivation was trade, and, indeed, the English colonies had come to learn that trade was their strongest inducement to alliance. Toward the end of the war, during August and September 1748, Pennsylvania and Virginia commissioned Conrad Weiser, a trader, to treat with the Ohio tribes. Weiser persuaded the Wyandots, who lived just north of the Shawnees, to join what Pennsylvania called its "Chain of Friendship," a trade-based alliance between the colony and a number of Indian tribes. A few months earlier, on July 20, 1748, the Miamis (also called Twightwees, a name derived from the cry of the crane), who lived in present-day Indiana and western Ohio, had joined the chain. Such alliances were important, and although King George's War gained little for either the British or the French in North America, it did establish certain enduring alliances with Indian tribes and factions. By the end of the war, the Iroquois tribes (especially the Mohawks) had grown closer to the English, while many of the non-Iroquois, Algonquian-speaking tribes sided with the French—and did so, typically, with more enthusiasm than the Iroquois showed for the British. When the Treaty of Aix-la-Chapelle was signed on October 18, 1748, ending both the War of the Austrian Succession and King George's War, no great territories had been won or lost. The peace that resulted was, in fact, little more than a protracted truce, a prelude to the epochal French and Indian War, in which young George Washington would play a catalytic role.

King William's War, Queen Anne's War, and King George's War, collectively the prelude to the French and Indian War, were fought primarily east of the Blue Ridge Mountains. The French and Indian War would have a much wider field, and it would begin not in the settled East, but at the frontier, the Ohio River Valley—the threshold of the greater West and the heart of the territory claimed by the Ohio Company.

Lawrence Washington died in 1752, satisfied that the Ohio Company, in which he was a principal stockholder (and, as of 1751, its president), had obtained a royal grant of 200,000 acres. Yet he also died in anxiety and frustration over Indian troubles and, even more, over the possibility that conflict with French claims would cost his company physical possession of its granted lands, resulting in their forfeit as well as that of the additional 300,000 acres promised once the company had successfully settled the original grant. Nevertheless, by the time of Lawrence's death, the Ohio Company had set up trading posts and rude forts throughout the Ohio valley as the nuclei around which settlements were to be established.

After Lawrence's death, control of the Ohio Company passed to Governor Robert Dinwiddie, another major stockholder. As a citizen of Virginia, George Washington owed allegiance to his governor. Because the Washington family was heavily invested in the Ohio Company, George shared with Dinwiddie the even more tangible—and perhaps more urgently compelling—common cause of fortune. That Washington was a British colonial patriot cannot be doubted. But by the mid-eighteenth century in America, patriotism was more than an abstract political and spiritual conviction. It was also a matter of wealth, which was an issue of land, which in turn was the future of oneself, one's family, and, of course, one's country.

ERRAND INTO THE
WILDERNESS

Most of us today would readily assent to the proposition that "nothing is more important than family." It is, in fact, a statement so noncontroversial as to be a bland commonplace, not really worth a second thought. But give it a second thought. If nothing is more important than family, why do we sneer at the mediocre man of business who is touted as a success story because he has just become the CEO of "the family firm"? To be sure, in the sphere of personal relationships, nothing is more important than family, but today, personal relationships typically occupy a sphere quite distinct from that of career. We are expected to "make it on our own," which means to "make it on our merits," and the maxim "It's not what you know, but who you know that counts" is uttered with disapproval and derision. There is the sphere of family, and there is the world of vocational advancement and professional achievement—and we like to think of these as being separate. It is only right. It is only fair.

Our currently pervasive model of self-made success is rooted in the mythology of democracy, which, in turn, is grounded in the mythology of the frontier. In origin, all American success is self-made, we believe. Ours is a nation carved out of the wilderness, and the wilderness was a place where men and women either survived and prospered on their own, or they died—regardless of who their father or mother might have been. As American civilization developed, we believe, this "frontier spirit" drove certain individuals to success in business, commerce, and government. In our collective national mythology, the archetypal Americans are Daniel Boone on the frontier and Benjamin Franklin in the city. They made their way by grit and brains in a country that presented formidable dangers but potentially limitless rewards.

Myth is not a synonym for *untruth*. The power of mythology is in the vast truth it contains. Yet neither is myth a synonym for fact. We have chosen Boone and Franklin (and Lincoln, Ford, and Edison, along with a veritable roster of other Horatio Alger heroes) as the archetypes of the American success story, but the fact is that when America was getting started, for every Boone and Franklin—truly self-made men who confronted the actual or the urban frontier on their own—there was a Fairfax, a Dinwiddie, or a Washington: men who believed in the deepest way possible that nothing was more important for success in America than family.

The American colonies had governments and corporate enterprises of various sorts, but the most important and pervasive unit of social, political, and economic structure was the family. The eighteenth-century colonies had their Franklins and their Boones, but these self-made men had yet to transform their lives into mythology. At this time and in this place, the paradigm for making one's way in the world was based on family ties. Nothing was more important. So when a succession of Washington men ingratiated themselves with the leading families of Virginia and made marriages with the daughters of those families, they were not craven social climbers looking for an easy alternative to their own hard work and initiative. They were Americans of the eighteenth-century mainstream. It was fine for a Boone to carve out a settlement in the wilderness or a Franklin to set up as a Philadelphia printer and then go on to greater fame and fortune, but it was far more common for one Washington after another to unite his family with others in order to create the social, political, and economic power structure of Virginia.

Thanks to his half-brother Lawrence, George Washington had been introduced to the Fairfaxes and Governor Dinwiddie. Like Lawrence Washington, Dinwiddie was a principal of the Ohio Company, which was, perforce, the bond between the Washington and Dinwiddie families. Officially, Lawrence had been president of the company and a stock-holder. On Lawrence's death, the presidency passed to Dinwiddie, and the stock to Lawrence's wife and infant daughter.

Lawrence Washington had also held another important office, adju-tant general of the Virginia colony.

By colonial law, every free white Virginian over the age of twenty-one was obligated to serve in the militia when called or to provide a substitute at his own expense. In 1728, the governor and Council of Virginia cre-ated the office of adjutant general. The officeholder, on whom was conferred the militia rank of major, was responsible for raising the required number of militiamen when notified by the governor. The adju-tant also had the responsibilities of organizing the militiamen into companies and for training them for service. Lawrence Washington was appointed to the position in 1743, but his tenure had always been, in effect, nominal. He had never been required to call up the militia, let alone organize, train, or lead it. Ultimately, his chronic illness prompted him to turn over most of his actual military duties to a deputy adjutant, George Muse.

None of this mattered to twenty-year-old George Washington. Given that his half-brother had held the post and that the Washingtons and the Dinwiddies were united by a mutual interest in the Ohio Company, George believed himself entitled to become the new adjutant general— never mind that he had never been a soldier himself (as Lawrence was), let alone commanded troops (as Lawrence had). When we understand that reliance on family connections was natural and expected in a young man seeking advancement, George Washington's lobbying Governor Dinwiddie for the adjutancy seems less presumptuous than it otherwise might. But it is also apparent that Washington was emboldened by even more than Lawrence's incumbency in the position. As a child, he had heard much talk of war, and he had hung on his half-brother's every word about military service in Cartagena. In Barbados, he was attracted to the fort, which (as we saw) he analyzed with the eye of a veteran—even though he had never before set foot inside a military installation. George Washington must have felt a natural affinity for military leadership, and it seemed to him simply inevitable that he should inherit his half-brother's military office.

As early as March or April 1752, Dinwiddie had been holding discussions about dividing the unwieldy Virginia adjutancy into three more manageable districts, each to be commanded by a different officer. George therefore knew that even if he succeeded in capturing one of the districts for himself, his position would be less exalted than Lawrence's had been. This being the case, he set his sights on obtaining the plum among the three districts, the adjutancy of the Northern Neck. This district was not only near Washington's home, it encompassed the wealthiest part of the colony. Washington wished to command, to the greatest extent possible, *his* kind of people. But he knew that William Fitzhugh, the son of the prominent George Fitzhugh of Stafford County, wanted Northern Neck for himself. He was also aware that Fitzhugh had the right family connections, added to which was his bona fide military experience—in Cartagena, with Lawrence. Moreover, he was already a political figure of some importance, representing Stafford County in the House of Burgesses. Nevertheless, Washington knew also that Fitzhugh had just married Ann Frisby Rousby of Calvert County, Maryland, and that the couple was to live there in Rousby Hall. By June, therefore, some doubt arose as to whether Fitzhugh, now a Marylander, would be able to accept the adjutancy of Northern Neck, Virginia.

What happened next says much about young Washington. Although

he felt entitled to the adjutancy by virtue of his late half-brother's occu-
pancy of the office—as well as whatever natural aptitude for it he might
have sensed in himself—Washington did not passively await Dinwiddie's
decision or, for that matter, Fitzhugh's. On June 10, 1752, he wrote the
governor: "Being impatient to know Colo. Fitzhugh's result; I went to
Maryland . . ." He spoke there with Fitzhugh and informed Dinwiddie
that the colonel "is willing to accept of the Adjutancy of the Northern
Neck, if he can obtain it on the terms he proposes." Presumably, these
terms included the privilege of serving as a Virginia adjutant while living
not in Virginia, but Maryland. Concerning the prospects of Fitzhugh's
obtaining the adjutancy, Washington editorialized for Dinwiddie's benefit:
"he hardly expects [those terms] will be granted Him." Moreover,
Fitzhugh gave Washington a letter (now lost) to deliver to Dinwiddie.
Either Fitzhugh informed Washington of its contents or the young man
sneaked a peek, for Washington noted his belief that the letter "inform's
of his intention" and then continued in considerable detail:

> *He told Me, he would, when conveniency admitted, build a*
> *House in Virginia, at which he should sometimes reside. If I*
> *could have the Honour of obtaining that [the Northern*
> *Neck district], in case Colo. Fitzhugh does not, or either of*
> *the other two [districts]; should take the greatest pleasure in*
> *punctually obeying from time, to time, your Honours com-*
> *mands; and by a strict observance of my Duty, render myself*
> *worthy of the trust reposed in Me . . .*[1]

In his remarks, Washington sought to plant doubt in Dinwiddie's
mind about the suitability of Fitzhugh, a Marylander, for the post of
Northern Neck adjutant. Beyond this, he also sought to reserve his place

next in line, should Fitzhugh finally decline the offer of the adjutancy. And he even covered himself should Dinwiddie offer and Fitzhugh accept the Northern Neck position, declaring that either of the other two districts would be acceptable—indeed, more than acceptable, giving him the "greatest pleasure in punctually obeying . . . your Honours commands."

Washington may have felt entitled to certain things by virtue of his family connections, but he did not passively wait for them to fall into his lap. He acted aggressively—yet with socially appropriate deference—to obtain them. Washington's eagerness to obtain the adjutancy suggests a natural inclination toward a military career, but if his sense of entitlement to that post came in part from some notion of his possessing a military destiny, Washington would not quietly await the arrival of that destiny. He actively sought it.

On November 6, 1752, the Council of Virginia decided to divide the adjutancy not into three, but into four districts. Fitzhugh was awarded the Northern Neck—which he did ultimately decide to accept—and Washington was offered the post of adjutant for the Southern District. He took the oath of office on February 1, 1753, some three weeks before turning twenty-one. The £100-per-annum post was a rare distinction for so young a man, much as the position of county surveyor had been for a seventeen-year-old. Yet what happened next suggests that George—son of a second-tier Virginia landowner but linked, through his late half-brother, to one of the finest families of Virginia—did not simply *feel* entitled to such honors, he *understood* himself to be so entitled. Indeed, he understood himself to be entitled to much more.

At about this time, on November 4, 1752, Washington was initiated as an Entered Apprentice in the Fredericksburg Masonic lodge, which had held its very first meeting little more than two months earlier, on September 1. Much has been written about the role of the Freemasons in American history and, in particular, the American Revolution. In his classic 1937 history of lodges and clubs in America, *Fifty Million Brothers,* Charles W. Ferguson went so far as to call Washington's Continental

Army—the federal army of the American Revolution—"a Masonic convention," and Gordon Wood, in his Pulitzer Prize-winning *The Radicalism of the American Revolution* (1993), declared that "It would be difficult to exaggerate the importance of Masonry for the American Revolution. It not only created national icons that are still with us; it brought people together in new ways and helped fulfill the republican dream of reorganizing social relationships. For thousands of Americans, it was a major means by which they participated directly in the Enlightenment." Although some more recent historians have suggested that the influence of the Freemasons on American history, including the independence movement, has in fact been exaggerated, the first American lodge was founded as early as April 13, 1733, and many more followed, especially by midcentury, so that there were scores of American lodges by the eve of the Revolution. Although some writers have disputed the facts, it is generally believed that Benjamin Franklin, Samuel Adams, James Otis, Richard Henry Lee, James Madison, and Alexander Hamilton were all Masons. Other founding fathers, including Thomas Jefferson, Thomas Paine, John Adams, and Patrick Henry, were not, and even Washington was reportedly ambivalent about his membership, perhaps going so far in about 1780 as to call Freemasonry "Childs Play."[2] Yet in 1752, unquestionably, the most prominent men of both emerging and established American communities were flocking to initiation. Being a Freemason was both a means of gaining influence and of certifying one's properly influential position in colonial society. Whatever he may have thought about Freemasonry in later life, Washington had been willing to part with a hefty initiation fee of £2 3s. (the premium price he himself demanded for a survey) and then rose rapidly in the Fredericksburg lodge, passing from Apprentice to Fellow Craft on March 3, 1753, and to Master Mason—the highest of the traditional Masonic orders in colonial America—on August 4, 1753, just ten months after having been initiated. Whatever this says about Washington's early commitment to the Craft, it suggests that his fellow Masons, presumably well-connected and locally prominent men, regarded him socially as "one of us."

And that certainly describes how George Washington regarded himself. Appointment to the adjutancy of the Southern District was both remunerative and an honor. It also gave this young man, who had no military experience, supervision over some of the colony's best militia companies (not that this was saying a great deal, given the generally poor quality of the Virginia militia at midcentury). Yet, having accepted the post, Washington *still* wanted the Northern Neck and, what is more, felt entitled to it. He did not hesitate to inform the Council of Virginia of his wishes. When the Council president chided in reply, pointing out that two others were "strongly recommended" for the post, Washington persisted—and his persistence paid off. After just a few months in office, Fitzhugh resigned, and the Council of Virginia named George Washington adjutant of the Northern Neck.

🌿

As he celebrated his twenty-first birthday, the traditional passage into full adulthood, George Washington had reason not merely to believe himself fairly launched in life, but even to feel that he had, to a significant degree, already arrived. He was a prosperous county surveyor *and* an adjutant of the best district in Virginia—twice over a colonial official—entitled to be addressed as "Major." He was also a Freemason, the owner of ten or more slaves, and the proprietor of 4,291 acres (including 2,000 in the highly promising Shenandoah Valley). Well connected with the Fairfaxes and Governor Dinwiddie, he was a tall and healthy young man, immune to smallpox, accustomed to the outdoors yet perfectly at home in the finest of Virginia drawing rooms.

By no means was his new office as adjutant strictly honorific. By law, all Virginia men over twenty-one were obliged to render militia service if called. For years, however, the law had been neglected, and Governor Dinwiddie, keenly aware of the growing threat from the French and their Indian allies, decided that it was high time to knock the rust off the legislation. He called for the first general muster of the Virginia militias to commence in September 1753, in preparation for which he informed his district adjutants that they should first gather the county militia officers and ensure that these men were ready to drill the companies once they had been assembled.

It was a prudent plan, flawed only, in the case of Washington, by the young man's total absence of military experience. Aware of this deficiency himself, Washington grasped that before he could train the county officers who had to train the men of the militia, he had to train himself. There were a variety of drill manuals available in colonial Virginia, ranging from such dated but still widely consulted British works as *Directions for Musters*, printed by Thomas Buck in 1638, Henry Hexham's *The Principles of the Art Militarie* (1639), and *Militarie Discipline, or The Young Artilleryman* (1643), by William Barriffe. We know, too, that many of the British regiments that came to North America during the French and Indian War carried their own manuals with them—for example, *Exercise for the Foot, with the Differences to be Observed in the Dragoon Exercise,* published in 1757 by order of Prince William Augustus, Duke of Cumberland, and George Grant's *The New Highland Military Discipline*, also published in 1757.

Doubtless, in 1753, Washington could lay his hands on the earlier books or on books similar to those published during the French and Indian War. Although military historians have called the *Memoirs of Benjamin Church,* published in 1716 by a son of the hero of King Philip's War (1675–1676), the first American military manual, there is no evidence that Washington read it. And that is a pity; for Church had developed the "ranger" concept, the special combat unit that combined white frontiersmen with friendly Indians to carry out strikes against hostile Indians in frontier or wilderness environments unsuited to conventional militia forces. Church kept notes on his tactics and operations, which were published in the 1716 volume. Washington, however, was not interested in creating a "ranger" unit—if he was even familiar with the term—but in learning (so that he could in turn teach) the basics of marching and weapons handling. Doubtless, whatever concept of combat he may have had at this point was strictly conventional—a matter of deploying a firing line of three ranks of men, the front-most of which fired a disciplined volley against the enemy, then moved behind what had been the third rank while the second rank (now up front) fired, then moved behind what had been the first rank, which was now in the arduous process of reloading. And so it would go, a front rank always firing while the middle rank prepared to do so, and the third rank reloaded. The object of this three-rank firing line was to maintain a rapid and continuous series of volleys, and the best-drilled soldiers were those who had sufficient discipline to stay in their ranks as they faced opposing fire, who could discharge their weapons effectively, who could then move in a smart and orderly fashion to the rear rank, and who could reload quickly and without error, then repeat the entire procedure for as long as the battle lasted. Discipline, rapidity of fire, and efficiency of weapons handling were the heart and soul of standard eighteenth-century military tactics.

In conventional European combat, opposing commanders arrayed their forces in lines opposite one another, and the side with the most men and the most thoroughly drilled men, who could pour more volleys against the other side while sustaining fewer losses than the other side, was the side that prevailed. It was a grim calculus of combat. Did Washington understand and appreciate it? We don't know. Clearly, his half-brother had regaled him with tales of the Cartagena expedition—but Lawrence Washington and his regiment had never even been permitted to leave their ship.

In any case, more immediately grim was the dismal quality of the militia troops available to the Virginia companies. While the ultimate goal of

eighteenth-century military drill was to produce a nearly mechanical efficiency of fire to be maintained *under* fire, the more immediate object was
to inculcate the most basic level of discipline, to transform a rabble into a
body of men with at least the appearance of soldiers. It was Washington's
job, as adjutant, to instruct his subordinate officers sufficiently so that
they could achieve in the men under their command basic as well as combat discipline. Did Major Washington succeed in this? Again, we do not
know. No record survives of his meeting with the militia officers under his
supervision, and, indeed, no record suggests that he even visited any of
the counties under his jurisdiction during 1753. To be sure, he may have
visited them, but if he did, no county magistrate thought to record the
fact, and Washington himself made no such notes in his diaries or letters.
For that matter, none of his letters or diary entries during this period so
much as mentions military matters or his military responsibilities.

The Treaty of Aix-la-Chapelle, which ended both the War of the Austrian
Succession and King George's War on October 18, 1748, said much, as
treaties usually do, but was completely silent on the most momentous
issue in North America at the time: the claim to the Ohio country. At
war's end, both Britain and France asserted possession, a circumstance
that virtually guaranteed the outbreak of another war.

Even during intervals of relative peace, there was between the French
and English in North America a well-founded mutual suspicion. The
French suspected that the English intended to occupy the Ohio country
in order to drive a wedge between French Canada and Louisiana. After
all, "divide and conquer" had been a maxim of strategy since ancient
Rome. As for the English, they believed that the French clearly meant to

undermine them from the rear, claiming the western region of the continent from north to south, thereby confining the future of British North America to the East Coast.

For the likes of Dinwiddie and Washington, the French threat had at least three levels, all menacing. First, it was an assault on the British empire; second, an assault on Virginia; and, third, it was an assault on family fortunes—because French possession of the Ohio country would nip the Ohio Company in the bud.

Already, the pinch was being felt, in that the French had largely usurped the fur trade. Beaver pelts were a form of currency on the frontier. Trade, especially with the Indians, was typically calculated not in coin but in skins—so many for a blanket, for gunpowder, for a hunting shirt. The pelts, which were in great demand in North America as well as Europe (where fashion increasingly demanded beaver hats, beaver collars, beaver cuffs, and beaver boot tops), had all the liquidity of cash. At one time, beaver were universally plentiful, even on the coast, but in a remarkably short time, they had been hunted virtually to extinction in the Tidewater regions. The peltries moved steadily westward, and Indians and white trappers moved westward with them. By the mid-eighteenth century, the richest harvest was to be had in the Ohio country. Thus, whoever controlled that region laid claim not only to the future—of country and of family fortune—but to the present as well. With the peltries of the Ohio country came wealth, liquidity, and control over the Indians who, much as they resented white incursions into their homeland, also craved profitable trade.

On June 26, 1749, less than a year after the end of King George's War, Roland-Michel Barrin, marquis de La Galissonière, governor of New France, sent Captain Pierre-Joseph Céleron de Blainville with 213 men on an expedition into the Ohio country. He carried two items of cargo with him. The first was a message to all of the Indians he encountered (he traveled as far west as Logstown, site of modern-day Ambridge, Pennsylvania, on the right bank of the Ohio River, eighteen miles northwest of

Pittsburgh): *The English want to rob you of your country. I am warning them to stay away.* The second item he carried was a load of lead plates, each inscribed with the French emperor's claim to sovereignty, which Céleron buried at intervals along his round trip of some 3,000 miles.

In August 1749, La Galissonière was replaced as governor by Jacques-Pierre de Jonquière, who decided that it would take more than a few words to the Indians and a bundle of lead plates to secure the Ohio country against the English. He built Fort Rouillé at the location of modern Toronto with the purpose of severing trade between the northern Great Lakes and Oswego, the British stronghold on the south shore of Lake Ontario in New York. Jonquière also built up and augmented the French fortifications at Detroit, then launched a raid against the Shawnee, who were the most powerful and flagrant of the tribes who did business with the few English traders working the Ohio country. Jonquière's move against the Shawnee was not big enough to inflict decisive damage or even to intimidate them. If anything, it was a strategic error, which served only to drive the Shawnee more deeply into the English fold.

While Jonquière jockeyed for position in the Ohio country, British colonial authorities encouraged English traders to be aggressive. They authorized the acquisition (by purchase) of more western land from the Indians and, during May–July 1752, they negotiated the Treaty of Logstown between the Six Iroquois Nations (Oneida, Onondaga, Seneca, Cayuga, Mohawk, and Tuscarora tribes), the Delaware, the Shawnee, and the Wyandot Indians on the one side, and Virginia as well as the Ohio Company on the other. By the Treaty of Logstown, the colony and the company secured a quitclaim to the entire Ohio country.

The French did not fail to respond. While delegates from the Miami tribe were negotiating at Logstown, news reached them that French-led Indian forces had raided Pickawillany (present-day Piqua, Ohio), the Miami "capital," on June 21, 1752. The town had been razed, obliterated. By way of response to the raid, Tanaghrisson, a much-venerated Seneca chief known to the English as the Half-King, asked the Virginia delegates at Logstown to tell their government to build a fort at the Forks of the Ohio (the confluence of the Ohio and Monongahela rivers, site of present-day Pittsburgh), the better to defend the Senecas and other western tribes (including the Miamis) against the French and their Indian allies.

Doubtless, the delegates gave the Half-King the answer he sought—but the Virginia authorities did not rush to build the fort, nor did they respond in any way to the attack on Pickawillany. This was all too typical of the English colonial attitude toward the Indians. Whereas the French courted their Indian allies and generally developed a relationship of quid pro quo, the English and the English colonists usually treated them with contempt, making promises they never intended to keep. In this case, the failure to march in force to the Forks of the Ohio and build a fort sent the Miamis into the arms of the French—an event that rapidly unraveled the Logstown treaty and drove English trade out of the Ohio Valley altogether.

The sudden collapse of the Logstown treaty presented a golden opportunity to Ange Duquesne de Menneville, marquis Duquesne, who had replaced La Jonquière as governor of New France on July 1, 1752. Duquesne ordered the construction of new forts in a chain from Montreal down to New Orleans. It was, in effect, a chain drawn across the Ohio country, closing that territory to the English—and not only closing it to them, but thoroughly intimidating the Iroquois, thereby neutralizing the most important Indian ally the English had. With the Iroquois shaken, the smaller English-allied tribes throughout the Ohio country also folded, one by one. Those few that wished to remain loyal, and therefore appealed to the English for help in resisting the French, were usually met with indifference or even turned away.

With French forts sprouting in the Ohio valley and Indian allies falling away, if not driven away, the summer of 1753 was in general a low point for English prospects on the frontier. More particularly, the times bode ill for the Ohio Company, which brought to self-assured men like Dinwiddie and Washington—men who believed their fortunes were tied to land and that they were entitled to their fortunes—an unexpected and unwelcome dimming of their personal horizons. The situation was unacceptable.

It was unacceptable far across the ocean as well. In August 1753, even as England's few precious Indian alliances were disintegrating, Lord Halifax, a principal booster of Britain's North American empire, was prodding the royal cabinet toward a declaration of war against France. He cited the 1713 Treaty of Utrecht (ending both the War of the Spanish Succession and Queen Anne's War), which stipulated the status of the Iroquois as *British* subjects. Halifax also dug up allusions to certain deeds drawn up between the English and Iroquois from 1701 to 1726. Based on the treaty-defined status of the Iroquois as British subjects and a fistful of deeds, Halifax asserted the English right to a vast expanse of Iroquois lands, including those the Iroquois had originally claimed by conquest— that is, the Ohio valley. Having made his case, Halifax drew the cabinet to what seemed to him a self-evident conclusion: the French, by trading throughout the Ohio country, had invaded Virginia—clearly an act of war. Taking Halifax's point, cabinet and crown authorized Governor Dinwiddie to do whatever he deemed necessary to evict the French from the Ohio country.

Although some historians and Washington biographers have written that the first thing Dinwiddie decided to do was call on Adjutant Major Washington to journey to the Ohio country to warn the French away, the initiative for this mission was actually Washington's, not Dinwiddie's. Colonial newspapers, including the *Virginia Gazette,* were full of stories about the arrival of some 1,500 French regulars in the spring of 1753 and of the construction of French forts. Washington understood just as clearly as Dinwiddie what this meant. Beyond the newspaper accounts, Washington was almost certainly privy to the government dispatches that passed through Colonel Fairfax's hands. Perhaps Fairfax even told him that the governor was planning to send a warning to the French interlopers.[3] In any case, as usual, Washington did not passively await the development of events. He saw a need for action—and an opportunity to take charge of that action—and therefore set out for Williamsburg, unsummoned and on his own initiative, arriving on or about October 26, 1753.

The first time Washington had visited colonial Virginia's capital, in order to introduce himself to the governor after his return from Barbados in January 1752, he had found the town a sleepy place with little to amuse a young man. Now, however, Williamsburg was bustling. The burgesses were gathering for a special early session of the assembly to determine how best to counter the French "invasion." In August, Dinwiddie had written to the government of the mother country, calling for men, materiel, and funding to build, garrison, and equip forts against the French. He received by way of response a communication signed by King George III himself, instructing him to safeguard the Ohio country and promising military aid. The idea of sending a preliminary warning to the French—an eviction notice, as it were—was not Dinwiddie's, but the British government's. It was included in the communication that arrived over the signature of the king.

As early as May 1753, Dinwiddie had asked Governor George Clinton of New York to make inquiries as to why the French were sending troops into English territory, and somewhat later Dinwiddie sent the traders William Trent and William Russell to find the French outposts and warn the commanders there that they were treading on English territory. Clinton, however, delivered no useful information, and neither Trent nor Russell ventured west of Logstown. Clearly, the governor was in a bind. He knew the French were out there, but he did not know exactly where they were, and he had even less idea of their numbers. For although he was aware that 1,500 French regulars had arrived on the southern shore of Lake Erie in the spring, he also knew that their ranks had been swept by disease, leaving fewer—but just how many fewer?—to man the forts. Not only did Dinwiddie urgently need reliable reconnaissance, he also needed to deliver the warnings mandated by King George III himself.

And here, suddenly, was young Major Washington, unbidden, offering his services as scout, emissary, and messenger. An entry for October 27, 1753, in the journal of the Council of Virginia records: "The Governor acquainted the Board that George Washington Esqr. Adjutant General for the Southern District, had offered himself to go properly commissioned to the Commandant of the French Forces, to learn by what Authority he presumes to make Incroachments on his Majesty's Lands of the Ohio."[4] What is important about this entry, aside from its recording the historical fact of Washington's having volunteered for the mission, is the notation of what was clearly Washington's insistence and stipulation that he be "properly commissioned." On one level, of course, this was only prudent. He did not want to approach a French officer without the full and absolute authority of the governor. But it also suggests that whatever else motivated Washington—love of country and zeal to protect the family fortune—he craved *official* sanction and the standing within colonial government and society that sanction conferred. Already a county surveyor and a Virginia adjutant, he wanted certification as a royal emissary.

The council swiftly approved Washington's appointment, drawing up a letter to be delivered to the "Commandant of the French Forces on the Ohio" and issuing Washington's commission on "Wednesday the 31st. of October 1753," the morning of the very day he "set out on the intended Journey." Dinwiddie's commission was dated October 30, the day before it was handed to the major, and appointed Washington as the governor's "express Messenger," authorizing and empowering him "to proceed hence with all convenient & possible Dispatch, to that Part, or Place, on the River Ohio, where the French have lately erected a Fort, or Forts, or where the Commandant of the French Forces resides, in order to deliver my Letter & Message to Him; & after waiting not exceeding one Week for an Answer, You are to take Your Leave & return immediately back." The commission was accompanied by more detailed instructions, which directed Washington to proceed first to Logstown and there "address Yourself to the Half King, to Monacatoocha & other the Sachems of the

Six Nations; acquainting them with Your Orders to visit & deliver my
Letter to the French commanding Officer; & desiring the said Chiefs to
appoint You a sufficient Number of their Warriors to be Your Safeguard,
as near the French as You may desire, & to wait Your further Direction."[5]

The Half-King, it was known, had already warned the French that
they were trespassing on Indian lands in the Ohio country.
Monacatoocha, more familiarly known to the English as Scarouady, was
an Oneida chief who ranked in prestige just below the Half-King and
who, like him, had played an important role in the Logstown treaty.
Governor Dinwiddie wanted his emissary to be protected, but he also
wanted to demonstrate to the Indians that he was looking out for their
interests against the French. He left up to Washington's judgment just
how close to bring the Indians to the French commandant, as if he were
unsure whether their presence would enhance or diminish Washington's
apparent authority. Should the French commandant be made to see that
the English had powerful sachems on their side? Or was it better for the
Indian escort to be kept in the background, so that the mission would
appear to be that of a royal British envoy communicating with a French
official? Dinwiddie left it to Washington to decide. He was, however,
explicit that the mission was not purely diplomatic:

> You are to take Care to be truly inform'd what Forts the
> French have erected, & where; How they are Garrison'd
> [manned] & appointed [fortified], & what is their Distance
> from each other, & from Logstown: And from the best
> Intelligence You can procure, You are to learn what gave
> Occasion to this Expedition of the French. How they are like
> to be supported, & what their Pretentions are.[6]

Yet Dinwiddie was careful to instruct Washington not to behave like a spy. After "the French Commandant has given You the requir'd & necessary Dispatches," the governor instructed Washington to "desire of him that, agreeable to the Law of Nations, he wou'd grant You a proper Guard, to protect You as far on Your Return, as You may judge for Your safety, against any stragling Indians or Hunters that may be ignorant of Yr Character & molest You."[7] It was a bold stroke on the governor's part, asking the target of espionage to safeguard the spy sent against him. But Dinwiddie understood that doing so effectively proclaimed Washington's mission (at least for the benefit of the French) as strictly diplomatic in nature—an official embassy.

In addition to the written instructions, Governor Dinwiddie also verbally instructed Washington to ask the French commandant pointedly why the French had arrested and taken prisoner British subjects trading with Indians in the Ohio country, and in particular why they had driven John Frazier (or Fraser), a Pennsylvania gunsmith and Indian trader, from his trading post at Venango—a settlement the French now occupied. Additionally, Dinwiddie instructed Washington to call on Christopher Gist at Wills Creek, which was on the way to Logstown, handing him a written request from Dinwiddie and the Council of Virginia that Gist serve as the major's guide. This was not intended to undermine Washington's authority, but to give him the benefit of a very prominent trader who knew the Ohio frontier better than just about any other colonist. He had been an explorer and surveyor, and had been commissioned by the Ohio Company in 1750 to explore the Ohio region as far as the mouth of the Scioto River. The following year, he pushed his explorations as far south as the Great Kanawha River and was so highly respected that, in 1752, he represented the Ohio Company at the council that produced the Treaty of Logstown.

Washington was fortunate that Dinwiddie had thought to solicit Gist's assistance. Venturing into the far frontier was always a hazardous undertaking. Doing so in November, when days were growing short and rains, frequent and heavy, were turning to ice and snow, was especially arduous. Traveling this country when it was occupied by increasingly hostile Frenchmen and their Indian allies multiplied the dangers as well as the hardships. Urgent as the expedition was, Washington nevertheless took time to determine his other personnel requirements. He needed men to tend the horses and the baggage, and he needed an interpreter with fluency in the local Indian tongues and another interpreter who could speak French. Finding frontiersmen to do the menial labor of the expedition was not difficult, Washington knew, and he also had a firm idea of who to tap as a French interpreter. Hiring a Frenchman was out of the question—such a person, under the circumstances, could hardly be trusted—and he knew of no British colonist fluent in French, but he was aware that, near Fredericksburg, there lived a young Dutchman named Jacob van Braam, who spoke his native Dutch, of course, as well as enough French to have emboldened him to advertise himself, in Annapolis in 1752, as a teacher of French. English was something of another matter. It was his *third* language, and that is the way he spoke it. Yet Washington decided to make do because van Braam had been a lieutenant in the Dutch army and was therefore accustomed to military discipline.[8] When he reached Fredericksburg on November 1, Washington located van Braam and hired him on the spot.

From Fredericksburg, Washington and van Braam set off for Alexandria, where they purchased some of the supplies and equipment necessary for the expedition. This done, they headed through Vestal's Gap to Winchester, where Washington purchased horses and various supplies, including a tent. From here, the pair headed northwest and across the Potomac to Wills Creek, which they reached on November 14. There they located the cabin of Christopher Gist, to whom Washington delivered Dinwiddie's letter. Gist read it and agreed to accompany the young major to the Ohio. Washington then left Gist to prepare himself for the trip while he went out to recruit what he called "servitors"—four men to do the heavy lifting. Barnaby Currin was a Pennsylvania Indian trader;

John MacQuire (or McGuire or McGuier), also an Indian trader, had been a soldier in Fairfax County; William Jenkins often served Governor Dinwiddie as a messenger; and Henry Steward was known to have a good working knowledge of the frontier. These men were sorely needed, because the expedition was by now loaded down with some formidable freight. There were weapons, powder, and ammunition, of course, as well as a tent, food stocks, and wampum—strings of shell beads that were useful as a kind of currency in dealing with Indians, but that were even more important as the ritual means of establishing goodwill and solemnizing agreements with them. In addition to the wampum, Washington also carried various other items to give as presents to the Indians; presents were absolutely necessary to demonstrate friendly intent and secure cooperation. Additionally, the expedition carried a stock of medicines and plenty of tobacco, as well as what was described as "Indian dress" for Major Washington, should he begin to find his conventional dress uncomfortable in the wilderness.

The party of seven men set out from Wills Creek on November 15, bound for John Frazier's new trading post at the junction of the Monongahela and Youghiogheny rivers, the first major stopping place on the way to Logstown. From Winchester to Wills Creek was some forty miles. Frazier's trading post was about sixty-four miles beyond this, and Logstown another thirty miles farther on. None of them would be easy miles. There was something of a trail through the thick woods, but mostly it was little more than scratches in the ground leading fourteen miles almost due west and steeply up to an elevation of about 3,000 feet in the Alleghenies. From here, Washington's party would turn to the northwest and head for the "Great Crossing" of the Youghiogheny, a ford some twenty miles farther. Those twenty miles would be even harder than the previous fourteen because of the many ridges to be crossed, the hardest of which was Laurel Ridge. Adding to the difficulty of this journey, there would be rain, constant and icy. In sum, it would be an epic of hardship—yet quite typical of any wilderness journey of the time.

❧

At the end of the very first day's march, November 15, the party camped at George's Creek, having made just over eight miles. A messenger, breathless, came into camp and presented Gist with a letter from one of his sons. The young man had fallen ill while en route home from the country of the Cherokee. He was now camped, ailing, at the mouth of the Conegocheague River, which was a half-dozen miles southwest of present-day Hagerstown, Maryland. He asked his father to come to his aid, believing that only he had the medical knowledge to help him.

Gist was a man of about forty-seven, whereas Washington had just turned twenty-one. Nevertheless, Gist appealed to the major, who, though less than half his age, was the commander of the expedition. What should he do? His son needed him. Should he leave the expedition?

Washington did not order Gist to stay, but he told him in no uncertain terms that his place was with the expedition. It was an embassy of great importance to Virginia and to England.

Gist agreed—apparently without argument. Using materials he had brought with him, he compounded a remedy and gave it, along with a letter to his son, to the messenger. The boy would have to treat himself.

The incident says as much about Washington as it does about Gist. Clearly, Gist's sense of duty was profound. He understood and accepted that his public mission trumped his private need. Washington, too, was driven by a commitment to duty and to the mission. Yet one cannot help feeling that, in Washington's case, the commitment was not entirely altruistic. If Gist left, the mission might fail, which meant that he, George Washington, would fail—fail in his very first assignment for the governor and the king. He would not let that happen, not even to save the son of Christopher Gist. Moreover, whereas the situation confronted Gist with a choice between family and duty, there was no such dilemma for George

Washington. In carrying out this public mission on behalf of England, Virginia, *and* the Ohio Company, Washington also served his family.

Whatever Washington's motives in persuading him to remain with the expedition, it was a very good thing that Gist did decide to stay. During his first venture to the frontier, as a young surveyor in 1748, Washington had dismissed the backwoods folk as an "Ignorant . . . Set of People," but he now discovered that the frontier also attracted men like Christopher Gist, who were loyal, brave, resourceful, and marvels of endurance. Gist was comfortable in his dealings with Indians—who called him Annosanah—yet he was also a well-educated white man. Judging from the quality of his letters, his command of grammar, syntax, and vocabulary was superior to that of Washington. In his dealings with Washington, he seems to have been a combination mentor (especially in matters of Indian culture and basic woodcraft) and adviser, yet was also a natural diplomat; he never presumed to *tell* his youthful commander what to do, but sparingly made suggestions. Washington was not ungrateful. Years later, in a letter of May 30, 1757 to John Robinson (speaker of the Virginia House of Burgesses), he praised Gist as a man who "has had extensive dealings with the Indians, is in great esteem among them, well acquainted with their manners and customs, is indefatigable and patient . . . As for his capacity, honesty and zeal, I dare venture to engage."[9]

By November 17, Washington and his party had reached Laurel Hill and had climbed its 2,400-foot height, then descended about seven hundred feet to a wide and boggy plateau, which was distinguished from the surrounding country by the comparative thinness of its forest growth. Gist told Washington that the clearing was known as Great Meadows.

They paused here to contemplate the next leg of the journey. They would have to ascend another set of mountains, Chestnut Ridge, which was west and northwest of Great Meadows. If, from here, they continued due west, they would reach the Monongahela River, which would take them to the Ohio—and the French commandant. The problem was that neither Washington nor even the far more experienced Gist knew whether that part of the Monongahela was navigable by canoe. Moreover, the trek over Chestnut Ridge and then down to the Monongahela was far more difficult than simply proceeding north from Great Meadows and marching overland to the Ohio. Therefore, they decided to strike out in a northerly direction—only to be greeted the next day, November 18, by the first substantial snowfall of the season. They rested at what Gist described as his "new settlement," a rude outpost consisting of a twenty-by-thirty-foot house and a few small outbuildings located between the Youghiogheny and Monongahela. They had, by this time, traveled just about seventy miles from Wills Creek.

Snow or no snow, Washington led his men the next day on a twenty-mile march north across the Youghiogheny to a place known as Jacobs Cabins, an abandoned settlement presumably named after a Delaware chief called Captain Jacobs. Here the party spent the night as the snow turned to freezing rain. When Washington awoke the next morning, he discovered that some of the expedition's horses had wandered off. In the driving, drenching, icy rain, the men tracked the horses, recovering them by eleven o'clock. This accomplished, they set off again, now turning toward the northwest, roughly following the Youghiogheny. Gist bagged a deer, and the party refreshed itself on venison. The feast did not stop the rain, of course, but it surely made the weather more bearable.

On November 22, the expedition reached the Monongahela at the mouth of Turtle Creek, which was near the settlement of John Frazier, the gunsmith and Indian trader whom the French had driven out of Venango. Washington must have passed Governor Dinwiddie's question on to Frazier: Why had the French forces evicted him? There is no record of Frazier's narrative of this event, but we know that he did give Washington some bad news and some good. The bad was that the Half-King had delivered to him a string of wampum together with a message for Governor Dinwiddie warning that three tribes, or nations, of French-allied Indians had "taken up the hatchet" (declared war) against the English. As if to solemnize this message, Frazier presented Washington

with the wampum. The other piece of news was more hopeful. French
troops had indeed been advancing from Lake Erie toward the Ohio River;
however, the principal column was intercepted by mounted messengers
who delivered the news that the so-called "general" of French forces,
Pierre Paul de la Malgue, Sieur de Marin, had suddenly died. The news
had been sufficient to prompt the withdrawal northward of most of the
Ohio-bound French army. Yet even this "good" news was mixed with bad;
for although it was a good thing that the French had withdrawn from
English territory, Washington was left to wonder just how far he would
now have to travel to find the French commandant.

The prospect of having to go any farther than necessary was hardly
inviting. As winter rapidly approached, each day brought colder
weather—yet not nearly cold enough to hard-freeze the streams, which
had been swollen by ceaseless rainfall. "The Waters," Washington
observed in his diary, "were quite impassable, without Swimming our
Horses." Therefore, he secured the "loan of a Canoe from Mr. Frazer" and
sent "Barnaby Currin & Henry Steward down Monongahela, with our
Baggage" while he and the rest of his party rode unencumbered to "the
Forks of Ohio," where they would meet up with Currin, Steward, and the
expedition's equipment. Washington reached the rendezvous before the
waterborne portion of his party, and therefore "spent some Time in view-
ing the Rivers, & the Land in the Fork, which I think extremely well
situated for a Fort; as it has absolute Command of both Rivers." The next
day, however, Washington's "Curiosity led me to examine" the situation
"more particularly," and he now concluded that putting a fort precisely at
the Forks was not as good an idea as putting one along the Ohio itself,
which would still command both the Ohio and the Monongahela, yet be
cheaper to build and better protected from enemy artillery attack.[10] These
were detailed and thoughtful observations—especially coming from a
young man who had only seen a single fort, at Barbados, and who had no
formal military training, let alone training in the art of fortification.
While Washington may have second-guessed himself about where

precisely to locate a fort, he had no doubt whatsoever about the necessity of building one—*somewhere*—near the Forks of the Ohio. He well knew that whoever controlled this great confluence of waters controlled the gateway to all of the west, which was accessible via the river.

After successfully rendezvousing with Steward, Currin, and the expedition's baggage, Washington contemplated completing the journey to Logstown, where he would meet the Half-King. But first, apparently acting on the advice of Gist, he decided to call on Shingas, principal chief of the Turkey or Unalachtigo tribe of Delaware Indians. At this time, Shingas was a friend of the English, and he lived on the site of a fort planned for the Ohio Company. Washington was given to understand that prudent politics dictated his inviting Shingas to accompany the expedition to meet with the Half-King at Logstown. Shingas agreed and, in company with a lesser chief, Lowmolach by name, he (as Washington wrote in his diary) "attended us to Logstown, where we arriv'd between Sunsetting & Dark, the 25th: Day after I left Williamsburg." He continued, laconically: "We travel'd over some extream good & bad Land to get to this Place."[11]

❧

Once he had reached Logstown, Washington was loath to waste time. Discovering that the Half-King was "out at his hunting Cabbin on little Bever Creek, about 15 Miles off," he approached Monacatoocha, the English-allied Oneida chief also known as Scarouady, "& inform'd him, by John Davison Interpreter that I was sent a Messenger to the French General, & was ordered to call upon the Sachems of the Six Nations, to acquaint them with it." Giving Monacatoocha a string of wampum to certify the importance of his message and mission, along with the gift of "a twist of Tobacco," Washington asked "him to send for the Half King; which he promis'd to do by a Runner in the Morning, & for other Sachems."[12]

The first visitors Washington received the next day, November 25, were not the Half-King and his entourage, but four or five men in faded and stained French uniforms, led by a British trader named Brown. The Frenchmen were deserters. The young major summoned his interpreter, van Braam, and began closely interrogating them. What he learned confirmed the darkest rumors of French intentions.

The men explained that they had been part of a force of 100, which had been sent up the Mississippi to rendezvous at Logstown with another 100 French troops and then, together, advance farther up the Ohio River, deeper into the territory of the Ohio Company. Presumably, Washington asked them why the French were doing this, but he recorded no answer. Perhaps these lowly deserters did not know the answer. Washington, however, was certain that *he* knew. The 200 French soldiers were bound up the Ohio to build a fort at the fork he himself had just left. Of all the French forts being built in the Ohio country, this was the most strategically threatening.

Washington now drilled deeper. He asked how many men the French had on the Mississippi and how many forts. There were four small forts, he was told, each garrisoned with thirty to forty men, complete with cannon, located between New Orleans and the "Black Islands"—which was van Braam's translation of what he heard as "Isle Noires," but which must have been Illinois, an obscure reference to a western Indian tribe entirely unknown to van Braam or Washington. In the course of the interrogation, Washington was to make out the names of other western tribes, also unknown to him: Obiash (Wabash) and Chawanon (Shawnee).[13] His growing sense must have been that the French were recruiting a truly vast Indian alliance, poisoning the West against the English, yet he betrayed no alarm at the odds mounting against the English, the Ohio Company, and, for that matter, the tiny expedition he led.

The deserters continued. At New Orleans, they said, there were "35 Companies of 40 Men each, with a pretty strong Fort, mounting 8 large Carriage Guns," while at the other end, "at the Black Islands," there were "several Companies, & a Fort with 6 Guns."[14]

We do not know precisely how long the interrogation went on, but it did not last beyond three in the afternoon, which is the hour at which Washington recorded the arrival of the Half-King. In deference to the Seneca sachem's lofty station, Washington called on *him* at his cabin "& invited him & Davison privately to my Tent." There he "desr'd him to relate some of the Particulars of his Journey to the French Commandant, & reception there, & to give me an Account of the Way & Distance."[15]

The Half-King began by delivering the hard news that "the nearest & levelest Way was now impassable, by reason of the many large miry Savannas; that we must be oblig'd to go by Venango," which was some fifty miles northeast of Logstown, at the confluence of French Creek and the Allegheny River. From there, it was another thirty miles to Fort LeBoeuf, lodgment of the French commandant. The Half-King cautioned that he would "not get near to the Fort under 5 or 6 Nights Sleep, good Traveling." Once there, the sachem continued, Washington should not expect a pleasant reception, for he himself had been "receiv'd in a very stern Manner."[16]

Washington meticulously recorded the Half-King's recitation of his speech to the French commandant as well as his account of the reply he had received. "Fathers," the Half-King had said to the Frenchman, "I am come to tell you your own Speeches, what your own Mouths have declar'd."

FATHERS You in former Days set a Silver Bason before us wherein there was the Leg of a Beaver, and desir'd of all Nations to come & eat of it; to eat in Peace & Plenty, & not

to be Churlish to one another; & that if any such Person
shou'd be found to be a Disturber; I here lay down by the
Edge of the Dish a rod, which you must Scourge them with;
& if Me your Father shou'd get Foolish in my old Days, I
desire you may use it upon me as well as others.
NOW FATHERS it is you that is the Disturber in this
Land, by coming & building your Towns, and taking it
away unknown to us & by Force. FATHERS We kindled a
Fire a long Time ago at a Place call'd Morail, where we
desir'd you to stay, & not to come & intrude upon our Land.
I now desire you may dispatch to that Place; for be it known
to you Fathers, this is our Land, & not yours. FATHERS I
desire you may hear me in Civilness; if not, We must handle
that rod which was laid down for the Use of the obstropu-
lous. If you had come in a peaceable Manner like our
Brothers the English, We shou'd not have been against your
trading with us as they do, but to come Fathers, & build
great Houses upon our Land, & to take it by Force, is what
we cannot submit to.[17]

Washington knew that there was much to admire in this speech. Its style
was worthy of a sachem, and its reasoning was that of a wise man. It
demonstrated clearly that the Half-King perceived the French as invaders
and the English as trading partners. All of this was good for Washington,
for the English, and for the Ohio Company. We cannot know, of course,
if Washington pondered the implications of the speech beyond these
points, but the fact is that it also demonstrated both the sophistication of
Iroquois politics and the desperate state of the Indian situation. On the
one hand, the Half-King clearly set forth what the Indians saw as the basis
of any white-Indian alliance: the Indians exploited divisions between

whites with the purpose of using one white faction to help drive another from their land. On the other hand, if the Half-King truly believed that only the French intended to "build great Houses" on Indian land, whereas the English intended to do no more than trade, he was deluding himself. But what the Half-King said next suggests that he harbored no illusions about the permanence of white-Indian alliances:

> *FATHERS Both you & the English are White. We live in a Country between, therefore the Land does not belong either to one or the other; but the GREAT BEING above allow'd it to be a Place of residence for us; so Fathers, I desire you to withdraw, as I have done our Brothers the English, for I will keep you at Arm's length. I lay this down as a Tryal for both, to see which will have the greatest regard to it, & that Side we will stand by, & make equal Sharers with us: Our Brothers the English have heard this, & I come now to tell it to you, for I am not affraid to discharge you off this Land.*[18]

The land between that of the French (to the west) and the English (to the east) was ordained by the "GREAT BEING" as Indian land. That, the Half-King declared, was the permanent and proper state of things, and for that reason, he has desired the French to withdraw, "as I have done our Brothers the English." He told the French commandant that he had laid down this proposition as "a Tryal for both" the French and the English, "to see which will have the greatest regard to it, & that Side we will stand by, & make equal Sharers with us." Whichever side, French or English, came closest to abiding by the permanent and proper state of things, the Half-King would side with—the implication being that the alliance would last only as long as the ally continued to abide by what the Great Being had decreed.

It was a subtle diplomacy, sophisticated as it was fragile, and the French commandant's reply simply crushed it underfoot. Whereas the Half-King addressed the commandant and his compatriots with the customary title of respect—"Fathers"—the commandant replied with a title of contempt, addressing the Half-King as "my child":

> *NOW MY CHILD I have heard your Speech. You spoke first, but it is my Time to speak now. Where is my Wampum that you took away, with the Marks of Towns in it? This Wampum I do not know, which you have discharg'd me off the Land with; but you need not put yourself to the Trouble of Speaking for I will not hear you: I am not affraid of Flies or Musquito's; for Indians are such as those; I tell you down that River I will go, & will build upon it according to my Command: If the River was ever so block'd up, I have Forces sufficient to burst it open, & tread under my Feet all that stand in Opposition together with their Alliances; for my Force is as the Sand upon the Sea Shoar: therefore here is your Wampum, I fling it at you. Child, you talk foolish; you say this Land belongs to you, but there is not the Black of my Nail yours, I saw that Land sooner than you did, before the Shawnesse & you were at War: Lead was the Man that went down, & took Possession of that River; it is my Land, & I will have it let who will stand up for, or say against it. I'll buy & sell with the English (mockingly). If People will be rul'd by me they may expect Kindness but not else.*[19]

Indians were mosquitoes or flies, whereas the French were a force as numerous as "Sand upon the Sea Shoar." This land belongs to *you?* Not so much as the dirt beneath my fingernail belongs to you! By virtue of the lead plates Pierre-Joseph Céleron de Blainville had buried in 1749, the land you claim is French.

Dinwiddie charged Washington with discovering the fate of two English traders taken prisoner by the French. The Half-King had, in fact, asked the French commandant about them "& receiv'd this Answer": "CHILD You think it is a very great Hardship that I made Prisoners of those two People at Venango, don't you concern yourself with it we took & carried them to Canada to get Intelligence of what the English were doing in Virginia."[20]

Now Washington had a clear idea of what manner of man the French commandant was, and he also had knowledge of a clear provocation to war: the French had made prisoners of two peaceful traders. The Half-King supplied other valuable intelligence as well: that the French had built "two Forts, one on Lake Erie, & another on French Creek," and he furnished Washington with "a Plan of them of his own drawing." [21]

That night, the young major digested all that the Half-King had said and reported, and, the next day, he "met in council at the Long House" with the assembled sachems. He was careful to address them neither as "fathers" nor as "children," but, pointedly, as *brothers:*

> *BROTHERS I have call'd you together in Council, by*
> *Order of your Brother the Governor of Virginia, to acquaint*
> *you that I am sent with all possible Dispatch to visit &*
> *deliver a Letter to the French Commandant of very great*
> *Importance to your Brothers the English: & I dare say to you*
> *their Friends & Allies. I was desir'd Brothers, by your*
> *Brother the Governor, to call upon you, the Sachems of the*
> *Six Nations, to inform you of it, & to ask your Advice &*

Assistance to proceed the nearest & best Road to the French.
You see Brothers I have got thus far on my Journey. His
Honour likewise desir'd me to apply to you for some of your
young Men to conduct and provide Provisions for us on our
Way: & to be a Safeguard against those French Indians,
that have taken up the Hatchet against us. I have spoke this
particularly to you Brothers, because His Hon. our Gov-
ernor, treats you as good Friends & Allies, & holds you in
great Esteem. To confirm what I have said I give you this
String of Wampum.[22]

Washington recorded that the sachems considered his speech for
"some Time" before "the Half King got up & spoke": "NOW MY
BROTHERS. In Regard to what my Brother the Governor has desir'd of
me, I return you this Answer. I rely upon you as a Brother ought to do, as
you say we are Brothers, & one People. We shall put Heart in Hand, &
speak to our Fathers the French, concerning the Speech they made to me,
& you may depend that we will endeavour to be your Guard."[23]

This reply must have both greatly relieved and gratified Washington.
Young and inexperienced though he was, he had, in his first important
speech to the most powerful and influential sachems, won their cooperation. He dutifully recorded what the Half-King said next:

BROTHER, as you have ask'd my Advice, I hope you will be
ruled by it, & stay 'til I can provide a Company to go with
you. The French Speech [wampum] Belt is not here, I have
it to go for to my hunting Cabbin likewise the People I have
order'd are not yet come, nor can 'til the third Night from
this, 'till which Time Brother I must beg you to stay. I

> *intend to send a Guard of Mingoes, Shawnesse, &*
> *Delawar's, that our Brothers may see the Love and Loyalty*
> *We bear them.*[24]

On one level, this was simply counsel from the older and wiser man to
be patient. Washington recorded his reply: "As I had Orders to make all
possible Dispatch, & waiting here very contrary to my Inclinations; I
thank'd him in the most suitable Manner I cou'd, & told that my Business
requir'd the greatest Expedition, & wou'd not admit of that Delay."[25]

This would not be the last time George Washington rejected the
advice of the Half-King. Perhaps the rejection was the product of the restless young major's inexperience, or perhaps Washington sensed an ulterior
motive in the Half-King's reluctance to move expeditiously. Perhaps he
dimly suspected that this reticence reflected some unspoken division
among the sachems. Certainly, Washington took note of how his own
eagerness greatly displeased the Half-King, and he took care to record
Davison's translation of the Half-King's further words to him: "this is a
Matter of no small Moment, & must not be enter'd into without due
consideration," the Indian cautioned. Did Washington think that these
words betrayed some misgiving on the part of the Half-King or the other
sachems? We cannot know. But whatever else he may have suspected (or
failed to suspect), Washington understood that, much as he wanted to, he
could not leave immediately "without affronting them in the most egre-
gious Manner"; therefore, "I consented to stay."[26]

Almost certainly hoping to end the council on a more positive and
decisive note, Washington then returned to the sachems the "String of
Wampum" he had received at Frazier's cabin, the wampum they intended
to accompany conveyance of their speech warning Governor Dinwiddie
that "three Nations of French Indians, (vizt.) Chippaway's, Ottaway's, &
Arundacks, had taken up the Hatchet against the English." Offering this

wampum, Washington invited the sachems to repeat the speech now so
that he could deliver it to Governor Dinwiddie exactly as they wanted
him to. This invitation, Washington had every reason to believe, would be
accepted as a sign of his high regard for the sachems and what they had to
say; for, among Indians, speech on important matters was an object of
great value, symbolized and solemnized by the wampum. How disappointed Washington must have been, then, when the sachems replied that
they wanted to postpone repeating the speech "'til they met in full
Council with the Shawnesse, & Delawar Chiefs."27 Why the delay? Why
the need for another council? If Washington suspected that this further
demonstration of reticence boded ill, he made no note of it.

The next day, November 27, came and went without incident, but on
the twenty-eighth, the Half-King, together with "Monacatoocha & two
other Sachems" entered Washington's tent "& beg'd . . . to know what
Business we were going to the French about." For Washington's earlier
speech had given no details. "This was a Question I all along expected,"
he recorded in his diary, "& [I] provided as satisfactory Answers as I cou'd,
which alay'd their Curiosity a little." For whatever reason, Washington did
not think it wise to share the particulars of his mission with his "brothers." Although whatever vague answer he may have given appeared to
allay the Indians' curiosity, it also seems to have prompted Monacatoocha
to report some sinister news concerning the French. A "few Days ago," he
said, an Indian from Venango had brought word that a Captain
Joincaire—the French "Interpreter in Chief, living at Venango, & a Man
of Note in the Army"—had "call'd all the Mingo's, Delawar's &ca.
together . . . & told them that [the French] intended to have been down
the River this Fall," but postponed their advance until spring, when they
would come into the country "with a far greater Number." When they
did come, Joincaire cautioned, the Indians had better be "quite Passive, &
not intermeddle, unless they had a mind to draw all [the French] force
upon them; for that they expected to fight the English three Years . . . in
which Time they shou'd Conquer."28

Up to this point, Monacatoocha seemed to imply that the English had best share all information with their allies, for all—English and Indians—were much threatened by the French. Yet, as he continued, the implication became more sinister: Joincaire had told the Indians that "shou'd [the English] prove equally strong [as the French], that they & the English wou'd join to cut [the Indians] off, & divide the Land between [the English and the French]: that . . . there was Men enough to . . . make them Masters of the Ohio."[29] Whereas Washington attempted to persuade the sachems that the French were the common enemies of the English and the Indians, the French were apparently implying that, if necessary, they would unite with the English against the Indians.

Did Monacatoocha's speech give the major pause, hinting as it did at a wealth of suspicion and doubt lurking beneath the unity conveyed in the Half-King's reply to Washington's earlier speech? Again, we have no answer because Washington recorded no doubts. Yet, on the twenty-ninth, he was approached by the Half-King and Monacatoocha very early in the morning. Although the Half-King had promised that the escort would be ready to leave on that day, the two sachems "beg'd me to stay one Day more."[30]

Surely this should have alarmed Washington. Instead, he accepted the Half-King's explanation that the Shawnee chiefs had not yet sent him their wampum and that Shingas (who was to form part of the escort) had not yet assembled his warriors and had also been detained by the sickness of his wife. As Washington understood Indian customs, possession of the wampum was important, because returning it to the French would signify that whatever agreements existed between the tribes and the French were officially terminated. Giving back the wampum, Washington wrote, "was shaking of[f] all Dependence upon the French"; therefore, "I consented to stay, as I believ'd an Offence offer'd at this Crisis, might have been attended with greater ill Consequence than another Day's Delay."[31]

Before the sun set on the 29th, the Half-King regaled Washington with a new speech telling him how he would firmly and fiercely warn the

French to vacate their lands. He also showed Washington various strings of wampum, which were intended to underscore the seriousness of the warnings. One large string of black-and-white wampum, Half-King explained, was especially significant. If the French spurned the warning on this occasion, the great string of wampum would be passed along from one Six Nations tribe to another, a signal to all for immediate action against the French.

Filled with speeches and displays of wampum, Major George Washington retired for the night and slept soundly. When he awoke the next morning, November 30, he was introduced at last to the promised escort. It consisted of an old chief named Jeskakake, another called by the English White Thunder, one young hunter (whose job would be to kill game for the expedition), and the Half-King. Three men, in addition to himself, were all this venerated sachem, full of lofty speech and laden with wampum, had been able to muster.

If Washington was dismayed, he made no note of it in his diary. Rather, he recorded only the Half-King's explanation—for the Half-King was never without explanation—that the other chiefs in council had determined that "a greater Number might give the French Suspicion of some bad Design, & cause them to be treated rudely." Washington left no comment on the absurdity of this justification. Based on the reception the French commandant had already accorded the Half-King, and given the nature of the party's mission, what other manner of reception could be expected, whatever the size of the delegation? Yet it is clear that he did not swallow the excuse: "I rather think they cou'd not get their Hunters in," he wrote.[32]

That the Half-King, the most reliable ally of the English, could not persuade the other sachems to muster their hunters or warriors in an effort to drive off invaders who menaced Englishman and Indian alike would surely have filled a more experienced emissary with much doubt if not frank fear and trembling. Washington could hardly have been happy about being attended into hostile territory by no more than three old men and a youthful hunter, yet all he wrote in his diary was this: "We set out about 9 o'Clock, with the Half King, Jeskakake, White Thunder, & the Hunter; & travl'd on the road to Venango."[33] Major George Washington meant to carry out his mission, with the aid of many and strong or few and feeble.

4

LE BOEUF

To the eight men of his original party, including himself, Washington now added three old Indian chiefs and a youthful hunter. This constituted the whole of an embassy that was intended to overawe the French commandant, impressing him with the majesty of British colonial might. If the young major had any misgivings, he did not betray them, but simply directed Christopher Gist to lead on. Perhaps Washington was naïve, or perhaps his ambitious desire to accomplish his mission blinded him to the reality of just how little a dozen men in the American wilderness amounted to. Or perhaps Major Washington, at twenty-one years of age, leading his maiden command, already possessed what every great general possesses: a strong will, a habit of mind that conceives the future tense as the equivalent of accomplished fact.

Perhaps he was motivated by all of these things—naïveté, ambition, a born commander's indomitable will—or perhaps the example of young George Washington teaches us that the will of a great general is founded on just the right combination of naïveté and ambition.

"We set out about 9 o'Clock," Washington recorded in his diary for November 30, "& travel'd on the road to Venango . . . an old Indian

Town, situated on the Mouth of French Creek on [the] Ohio [River]. . . about 60 Miles from the Logstown"—although, as Washington wearily observed, it was actually "more than 70 [miles by] the Way we were oblig'd to come." In his typically laconic manner, Washington recorded that they arrived at Venango on December 4 "without any Thing remarkably happening, but a continued Series of bad Weather."[1] We are left only to imagine, then, what these twelve men actually felt, making their way through terrain so difficult that it obliged them to stretch sixty straight miles into seventy roundabout ones, and always riding through the icy and miserable gloom of a rapidly gathering winter.

Washington did not record each laborious day: how the first night, after a fifteen-mile slog, was spent in a place called Murthering (or Murdering) Town, a predictably cheerless place, whose name was doubtless intended to memorialize some dark wilderness event long forgotten. Washington would see more of this settlement on his return from the French commandant, but for now, whatever its sinister associations may have been, it represented nothing more than a night's rest and a place to trade for dried meat and parched corn—staple rations of armies and others who must march through strange countries.

Whether the party was refreshed by the sleep and the food Murthering Town had to offer or whether they were inspired to distance themselves from that dismal locality, they made what Washington estimated to be a full thirty miles on the next day, December 1. They bedded down for the night, then woke on December 2 to a renewed siege of grim weather, an icy rain that retarded their progress but gave the young Indian hunter time to bag a brace of bucks, the meat of which must have revived the party's spirits considerably that evening.

December 3 was a brighter, drier day, and the expedition made twenty-two miles before the men pitched camp at what Christopher Gist said was a head branch of the Great Beaver Creek. Some later authorities who have attempted to trace Washington's progress conclude that they had actually reached Sandy Creek, a tributary of the Allegheny River, which put them near the site of the modern town of Raymilton—some eight miles off course (to the west) for anyone heading toward Venango. Christopher Gist knew this country better than any other English colonist, but his knowledge was far from perfect. In mid-eighteenth-century America, *marching* through the wilderness was little different from *wandering* in the wilderness.

Venango lay another fifteen miles north, where the French Creek emptied into the Allegheny. When Washington and his men reached it on December 4, the major wrote, "We found the French Colours hoisted at a House where they drove Mr. Frazer an English Subject from."[2] Of course, Washington had known that Venango was in French hands, but the sight of the fleur-de-lis flying over a "House" built on ground from which an Englishman had been driven marked this unmistakably as his first encounter with the enemy.

Yet there was still hope for the English. Washington was careful to describe the French military headquarters at Venango as a "House," not a *fort*. Most likely, the structure was what frontier people called a "strong house"—essentially an ordinary dwelling that had been hardened to a degree and stocked with arms and ammunition, but by no means genuinely fortified. It was a place from which trade could be conducted and a defense against an attack mounted. It was undeniably the precursor of a fort, and its presence here meant that the French were inexorably progressing in their occupation of the Ohio country, but perhaps not quite as quickly as Dinwiddie had feared.

Washington wasted no time in confronting the enemy. He "immediately repair'd to [the "House"] to know where the Commander resided: There was three Officers, one of which, Capt. Joncaire, inform'd me, that he had the Command of the Ohio, but that there was a General Officer at the next Fort, which he advis'd me to for an Answer."[3]

Here was a degree of subtlety new in the experience of young Washington. On the one hand, Captain Philippe Thomas de Joncaire, Sieur de Chabert, boldly and provocatively identified himself as being in

"Command of the Ohio"—the principal artery by which the Ohio Company and the English colonies would either grow or wither—yet he simultaneously identified himself as subordinate to another commander and, in an apparently friendly manner, suggested that Washington deliver Governor Dinwiddie's message to him.

Joncaire presented himself with undue modesty. He was, in truth, a very important figure in this part of the Ohio country. The son of a Seneca mother and a French officer, he was the ideal frontiersman, partaking as he did of the heritage of the Indian and the European alike. He prospered as a trader and, as a soldier for France, held the title of Chief Interpreter for the Six Nations. Joncaire was a principal conduit between the French and the Indians. Why did he demur when Washington offered him Dinwiddie's letter? Perhaps he genuinely felt that he lacked sufficient authority to accept it. Perhaps, too, he wanted to impress Washington with the strength of the French in the region. In contrast to the strong house at Venango, Fort Le Boeuf, the military facility on Lake Erie, was a bona fide fort headquarters of a general. Moreover, the trip of some forty or fifty more miles would serve to show Washington something of the breadth of territory the French now controlled. Sent to overawe the French, Washington now found himself the subject of Joncaire's campaign to overawe him.

Yet Joncaire went about it all with the utmost cordiality. Apparently, he did not believe that it was necessary to be impolite to one's enemy. Joncaire "invited us to Sup with them, & treated [us] with the greatest Complaisance," Washington noted in his diary.[4] With significant perspicacity and prudence, Washington accepted the dinner invitation on behalf of Jacob van Braam, John Davison, Christopher Gist, and himself—but purposely excluded the Indians. He may have assumed that Joncaire's invitation was to be understood not to include them but, more likely, it was Washington who did not want them included. Joncaire was a half-breed who exerted great influence over Indians, and Washington did not want to give him an opportunity to make unwanted suggestions that might poison their minds.

As to the meal, Washington recorded (with, one imagines, a certain glee) how the French "dos'd themselves pretty plentifully" with wine, which "soon banish'd the restraint which at first appear'd in their Conversation, & gave license to their Tongues to reveal their Sentiments more freely." Given the full and precise nature of Washington's notes, we can assume that either he took care not to "dose" himself similarly or that his capacity was greater than that of his hosts. In any event, the Frenchmen told Washington that "it was their absolute Design to take Possession of the Ohio, & by G____ they wou'd do it, for tho' they were sensible, that the English cou'd raise two Men for their one; yet they knew their Motions were too slow & dilatory to prevent any Undertaking of theirs."[5]

And there was more. Washington discovered that the French operated from a conviction that the Ohio country was theirs by a right that derived from "a Discovery made by one La Sol [LaSalle] Years ago." Joncaire frankly informed Washington that the French "Expedition" into the Ohio country was "to prevent [the English from] Settling on the [Ohio] River or Waters of it, as they have heard of some Families moving out in order thereto."[6]

Washington seemed to think that this conversation was valuable intelligence obtained through the agency of wine. Perhaps it was the product of alcohol-induced indiscretion, but Joncaire was an experienced trader, soldier, and frontier diplomat, and it is doubtful that he ever spoke without purpose. More than likely, he *wanted* Washington to know that the French were in the Ohio country to stay, that they had beaten the English to the territory, and that they did not intend to relinquish what was clearly theirs by virtue of prior claim.

The same diary entry that records Joncaire's revelation of French intentions goes on to provide detailed information about the numbers and disposition of French troops on and near the Ohio. Washington refers to this information as "the best Intelligence [he] cou'd get," an ambiguous phrase that does not specify where he got the information. Was it at table, from Joncaire and his companions? If so, the level of detail provided went far beyond any kind of intentional propaganda aimed at intimidating the English or undermining their morale and suggests that the Frenchmen really did overimbibe. However, it is also possible that Washington obtained the intelligence separately. In either case, what he gathered was that the French had had 1,500 men east of Lake Oswego, but after the death of General Paul Marin de la Malgue, more than half were recalled, leaving just "6 or 7 Hundred . . . to Garrison four Forts, 150 or there-abouts in each" extending across all the key passages to the Ohio. Washington noted in his diary various other details concerning the forts, their garrisons, and their disposition.[7] In joining what he had learned about French motives on the one hand and actual French military assets on the other (whether Joncaire told him this at table or Washington gathered it elsewhere), the major was able to provide a remarkably complete picture of the current French threat to Virginia and the Ohio Company. Dinwiddie had sent him, young and relatively inexperienced though he was, into the wilderness in large part to seek intelligence critical to the future of Britain in America. It was a tall order, yet even if Washington had decided to turn back at once, his mission would have been worthwhile, performed well and successfully. He had ascertained that the threat was real, but not yet overwhelming. It was invaluable first-hand information.

But Washington well knew that his mission was not yet at an end. He had a letter to deliver. Joncaire, who had been so polite, continued to oblige. He promised to provide Washington with a French escort to ride to Fort Le Boeuf. Washington accepted.

And it was now that Captain Joncaire began to work his wiles. On December 5, the day after the dinner with the French, a hard, icy rain began again to fall. Perhaps Washington could have continued his journey to Fort Le Boeuf despite the inclement weather, had he not been encumbered by the horses and supplies of his French escort; however, the augmented expedition would have to wait for drier conditions to negotiate the road along French Creek. Joncaire did not have it within his power to control the weather, but he could—and did—exploit it to delay Washington's journey. This had two advantages for the French. First, it gave them that much more time to continue the build-up of their forces. Second, it gave Joncaire an increased opportunity to undermine Washington's relations with his Indian companions.

As for those companions, they added another reason for delay. The Half-King and his two fellow chiefs met in council with their allies the Delawares, who lived in the vicinity of Venango. The Half-King passed on to the Delaware chief Kustaloga (or one of his designated braves) the wampum Shingas had presented him to return to the French as a seal on the renunciation of any alliance between them and the Indians. He was stunned when Kustaloga refused to accept the wampum belt. The Delaware chief protested politely that because Shingas had sent no speech, he could not accept the belt to present to the French, because he could not presume to make a speech for another chief. If the wampum were to be returned, the Half-King would have to do it himself. This was not exactly a renunciation of the alliance between the Iroquois and the Delaware, but it was an act that distanced the Delaware from the Iroquois decision to sever relations with the French. It was not a favorable development for the English.

As if the disappointing response from Kustaloga were not a sufficiently adverse development in Washington's mission, the time consumed by the Iroquois-Delaware council gave Joncaire the opportunity to approach the Indians. He innocently inquired of Washington why he had not brought the chiefs to dinner. The major replied that he had been uncertain whether or not Joncaire wanted them there, adding that he had heard Joncaire "say a good deal in dispraise of Indians in general."[8] As if by way of correcting this perception, Joncaire promptly ordered one of his soldiers to invite the chiefs to visit with him right away.

He greeted them with a solicitude as extravagant as de Marin's earlier reception of the Half-King had been rude and offensive. Whereas de Marin had dismissed the Half-King as a "child," Joncaire made overtures of deep respect, friendship, and alliance, offering presents and brandy. Much brandy. Washington looked on helplessly as the increasingly inebriated Half-King failed to say anything to Joncaire about his desire that the French leave the Ohio country, let alone make any move to return the wampum belt to him.

It was now clear to Washington that a new objective had been added to his mission. He had to keep "his" Indians out of the clutches of the French. In this contest, Washington had to admit that he had just lost the first skirmish, but never mind; they would all be on their way tomorrow.

❦

Tomorrow—December 6—found the Half-King at the entrance to Washington's tent first thing in the morning. He was, Washington recorded, "quite Sober," and also, quite ashamed of himself. To expiate that shame, he "insisted very much that I shou'd stay & hear what he had to say to the French." He intended to put his foot down to Joncaire and repeat to him what he had said to de Marin: that the French must leave the country of the Ohio. Washington confided to his diary, "I fain wou'd have prevented his speaking any Thing 'til he came to the Commandant." The major feared that Joncaire would erode the chief's newfound resolution with merely another flask of brandy to which were added sugared words nearly as intoxicating. But, alas, Washington "cou'd not prevail." The Half-King insisted that Joncaire was the man to be dealt with, that "at this Place Council Fire was kindled," that here "all their Business with these People were to be transacted, & that the Management of the Indian Affairs was left solely to Monsieur Joncaire."[9]

Did Washington fully grasp what Joncaire had already succeeded in doing? To Washington, the Frenchman had disclaimed final authority over French forces in the region, directing him to the commandant at Fort Le Boeuf. But to the Half-King, he presented himself as the *sole* manager of Indian affairs. In this, Joncaire had skillfully begun to separate English from Indian interests. The Half-King and Washington might march together, but the object of Washington's journey lay miles away (according to Joncaire), whereas the Half-King and his brethren had already arrived at just the right place. In any event, Washington was suffi-ciently savvy to agree to yet another day's delay before starting for Fort Le Boeuf: "As I was desirous of knowing the Issue of this [the Half-King's meeting with Joncaire], I agreed to stay." Yet the major hedged his bet by sending "our Horses a little Way up French Creek, to raft over & Camp" so as to have a head start on December 7. For he was by this time familiar enough with Indian speeches to know that the council would not be ended until "near Night."[10]

"About 10 o' Clock they met in Council," Washington wrote. After what were doubtless many pro-forma preliminaries, solemn and interminable, "the [Half] King spoke much the same as he had done to the General [de Marin], & offer'd the French Speech Belt which had before been demanded, with the Marks of four Towns in it."[11] The build-up proved anticlimactic, however, as Joncaire, who had presented himself as sovereign in Indian affairs, now blithely declined to accept the wampum belt. In contrast to de Marin, there was no trace of bluster, threat, or contempt in this demurral, but, rather, a polite though sudden change of direction. The belt, he told the Half-King, should be presented to the commandant at Fort LeBoeuf.

The upside of this turn of events was that Joncaire had been backed into a corner, forced to step back from the authority he had claimed to possess. That was good, because it distanced him from the Half-King and the other chiefs. However, the downside was that the return of the belt had yet to be accepted, which meant that the connection between the French and the Six Nations, along with the Delawares, remained intact. Worse, Joncaire dragged out the council, doing all he could to detain the Indians, presumably so that he could renew his seduction of them.

As Washington had predicted, the council did not end until near nightfall, whereupon all returned to their respective quarters. After waiting a while, Washington sent for the Indians. They sent a reply that they could not come to see him just now because they needed to call on Chief Kustaloga to ascertain more fully his reasons for not agreeing personally to give up the belt to the French. Thoroughly suspicious now, Washington ordered his Indian interpreter, John Davison, to go to the Indians and "strictly charg'd [him] not to be out of their Company," lest some unknown mischief be hatched.[12]

On the morning of December 7, George Washington was greeted at his tent by a man he had probably met at Joncaire's table, Michel Pepin, universally known among the French as Commissary La Force, a highly influential figure in French-Indian relations who would soon assume great importance in Washington's early military career. With La Force were three French soldiers. The four of them, he announced, would have the honor of escorting the major and his men to Fort Le Boeuf. La Force further announced that they were ready to leave—immediately. It is not clear whether this was a bald attempt to induce Washington to leave without the chiefs, but in any case, the major was not tempted. He explained that he and his white companions were ready, but that the Indians were not present. Presumably anxious to avoid offending the chiefs by seeming to prod, Washington refrained from immediately sending for them, but instead waited before finally dispatching Christopher Gist to bring them to the trail.

The morning waned. Finally, at about eleven, Gist arrived with the three chiefs and the hunter. He reported to Washington that he did have considerable trouble prying them from the embrace of Joncaire, who "did everything he could to prevail on our Indians to stay behind us.[13] But at long last, united—at least in physical presence—the white men and Indians continued their journey.

La Force pointed out that French Creek flowed in an arc fifty miles to Fort Le Boeuf. Fortunately, he knew a shortcut, roughly along the chord of that arc, which would reduce the journey by some fifteen miles— although the way would be difficult, especially since the incessant rains had swollen the many branches intersecting the rough trail. Much time was lost felling trees to improvise fords over rushing, icy streams. Nevertheless, rain, cold, and the necessity of this extension of the journey did not diminish Washington's appetite for promising real estate. He was a soldier on a military mission, but he was also every inch the land specu- lator, and he took note of "several extensive & very rich Meadows, one of which was near 4 Miles in length, & considerably wide in some Places."[14] For Washington—as for Dinwiddie—the diplomatic, political, and mili- tary errand into the wilderness was inextricably linked to the land on which a family's fortunes depended.

*

In the twilight hours of December 11, after four days on the trail, the eight Englishmen, four Indians, and four Frenchmen reached the eastern bank of the creek just opposite Fort Le Boeuf, which was perched on the western bank. Washington sent his interpreter van Braam across the creek to announce his arrival. A short time later, a group of French officers rowed over in a canoe and formally invited Washington and his party to the fort.

More than likely, nothing beyond military formalities and miscellaneous pleasantries were exchanged that evening. It was agreed that official business would wait until morning. Accordingly, as Washington recorded on December 12, "I prepar'd early to wait upon the Commander, & was receiv'd & conducted to him by the 2d. Officer in Command." The commander, the Sieur Legardeur de St. Pierre de Repentigny—called more manageably Legardeur de St. Pierre—was, Washington noted, "a Knight of the Military Order of St: Lewis, & . . . an elderly Gentleman," who nevertheless had "much the Air of a Soldier."[15] He was, in fact, a hardened veteran of frontier battle, having served as a lieutenant in warfare against the Chickasaws during 1739, and experienced in wilderness exploration, having led expeditions through much of France's western claims. He bore as evidence of his long service a patch concealing the loss of an eye. A seasoned frontier hand, he was nevertheless new to Fort Le Boeuf, having assumed command just a week earlier as a replacement for the deceased General de Marin.

"I acquainted him with my Business," Washington wrote, "& offer'd my Commission & Letter," only to have Legardeur de St. Pierre politely decline to accept them, pending "the Arrival of Monsieur Riparti, Capt. at the next Fort, who was sent for & expected every Hour."[16] ("Captain Riparti" was almost certainly Captain de Repentigny, a relative of Legardeur de St. Pierre.)

By this time, George Washington had grown accustomed to the French penchant for infinite delay, but he used the interval to study the fort, which he did earnestly until shortly after two in the afternoon, when he was told that Riparti (or de Repentigny) had arrived from the fort at Presque Isle (modern Erie, Pennsylvania), and that the two commanders were now prepared to receive Washington's commission and letters. The officers accepted the documents "& adjourned into a private Apartment for the Captain [Riparti/de Repentigny] to translate, who understood a

little English." This done at length, "the Captain desir'd I wou'd walk
in & bring my Interpreter to peruse & correct [the translation], which
I did."[17]

By the standards of diplomatic language of the day, Dinwiddie's letter
was firm—abrupt, even. "Sir," it demanded—

> *The lands upon the Ohio River in the western parts of the
> colony of Virginia are so notoriously known to be the prop-
> erty of the Crown of Great Britain that it is a matter of
> equal concern and surprise to me to hear that a body of
> French forces are erecting fortresses and making settlements
> upon that river within H. M.'s Dominions.*
>
> *The many and repeated Complaints I have received of
> these acts of hostility, lay me under the necessity of sending
> in the name of the King my Master, the bearer hereof,
> George Washington Esq., one of the Adjutants-General of
> the Forces of this Dominion; to complain to you of the
> encroachments thus made, and of the injuries done to the
> subjects of Great Britain in open violation of the law of
> nations now existing between the two Crowns.*
>
> *If these facts are true and you shall think fit to justify your
> proceedings I must desire you to acquaint me by whose
> authority and instructions you have lately marched from
> Canada, with an armed force and invaded the King of
> Great Britain's territories in the manner complained of, that
> according to the purport and resolution of your answer I
> may act agreeably to the commission I am honoured with
> from the King my Master.*
>
> *However, Sir, in obedience to my instructions it becomes
> my duty to require your peaceful departure; and that you*

> *would forbear prosecuting a purpose so interruptive of the*
> *harmony and good understanding which His Majesty is*
> *desirous of cultivating with the most Christian King.*
>   *I persuade myself you will receive and entertain Major*
> *Washington with the candour and politeness natural to your*
> *Nation; and it will give me the greatest satisfaction if you*
> *return him with an answer suitable to my wishes for a very*
> *long and lasting Peace between us. . . .*[18]

After van Braam reviewed and approved the French translation of the document, Major Washington asked for the commandant's answer. He replied that he would call a council —which Washington pointedly called a "Council of War"—to formulate an answer. That council apparently consumed much of December 13, time Washington used to resume his detailed study of "the Dimensions of the Fort, & making what Observations I cou'd." Although he "cou'd get no certain Account of the Number of Men here," he estimated that there were "an Hundred exclusive of Officers, which are pretty many." Washington ordered his companions "to take an exact Account of the Canoes that were haled up, to convey their Forces down in the Spring"; they counted "50 of Birch Bark, & 170 of Pine; besides many others that were block'd out, in Readiness to make."[19] Clearly, an invasion fleet was being assembled.

On December 14, Washington still awaited the commandant's reply. It was probably on this day that Legardeur de St. Pierre made the extraordinary suggestion to him that, instead of settling for a reply to Dinwiddie's letter from the mere commandant of Fort Le Boeuf, he should push on to Quebec to present the letter to the governor of Canada. This, a journey of some 800 miles one way, would have occupied young Washington for quite some time, almost indefinitely delaying his report to Governor Dinwiddie. More important, it would have more or less permanently separated Washington from the Half-King and the other chiefs. Washington was not about to allow either eventuality, and he replied to the suggestion by pointing out that his orders were to deliver the letter to the French commandant and to no one else. Moreover, as he noted with dismay that the "Snow increased very fast" and "our Horses daily got weaker," he decided to send "them off unloaded, under the Care of Barnaby Currin & two others, to make all convenient Dispatch to Venango, & there wait our Arrival, if there was a Prospect of the Rivers Freezing, if not, then to continue down to Shanapin's Town at the Forks of Ohio, & there wait 'til we came to cross Allegany."[20] Washington had secured from the commandant the loan of two canoes. He awaited the commandant's reply to Dinwiddie's letter and news from the Half-King concerning the commandant's reply to the return of the wampum belt. As soon as that matter was settled, Washington intended to use the canoes to rendezvous as quickly as possible with Currin, the two others, and the horses (assuming they survived), then to speed back to Williamsburg.

Bad weather, starving horses, and loss of time were not Washington's only problems as he was forced to tarry at Fort Le Boeuf. "I found many Plots concerted to retard the Indians Business, & prevent their returning with me," he noted. Determined to do "all in my Power to frustrate [the French] Schemes," he urged the Half-King to get on with the return of the wampum belt. Obliging him, the Half-King and his comrades "pressed for admittance this Evening, which at length was granted them privately with the Commander, & one or two other Officers." Later, the Half-King reported to Washington "that he offr'd the Wampum to the Commander, who evaded taking it, & made many fair Promises of Love & Friendship; said he wanted to live in Peace & trade amicably with them." As a proof of this, Legardeur de St. Pierre said "he wou'd send some Goods immediately down to Logstown for them."[21]

The report confirmed Washington's worst fears about French intentions to seduce the Indians away from him. Additionally, he suspected that the real aim of the proposed French expedition was not so much to deliver goods, as it was to "bring away [take prisoner] all of our stragling traders they may meet with." After all, the expedition was to include "an Officer, &ca.," and when Washington asked Riparti/de Repentigny "by what Authority he had taken & made Prisoners of several of our English Subjects," the captain replied blandly that "the Country belong'd to them, that no English Man had a right to trade upon them Waters; & that he had Orders to make every Person Prisoner that attempted it on the Ohio or the Waters of it."[22]

All of this was sufficient evidence of the aggressive intentions of the French. Washington pressed the captain on the particular case Dinwiddie had mentioned, of an English boy who had been captured. Riparti/de Repentigny "acknowledg'd that a Boy had been carried past [captured]," then he continued, more sinisterly, that he had seen some Indians with "two or three white Scalps"; however, he "pretended to have forgot the Name of the Place that the Boy came from." Washington also inquired into the fate of two Pennsylvania traders taken prisoner, "John Trotter, & James McClocklan," and was told that "they had been sent to Canada, but were now return'd Home."[23]

This exchange with the captain was but a prelude to the evening, when Washington finally received the commandant's answer to Dinwiddie's letter:

As I have the honor of commanding here in chief, Mr. Washington delivered me the letter which you wrote to the commander of the French troops.

I should have been glad if you had given him orders, or he had been inclined, to proceed to Canada to see our General, to whom it belongs, rather than to me, to set forth the evidence and the reality of the rights of the King, my master, to the lands situated along the Belle Riviere, and to contest the pretensions of the King of Great Britain thereto.

I am going to send your letter to the Marquis Duquesne [the governor of Canada]. His reply will be a law to me, and, if he should order me to communicate it to you, Sir, I can assure you that I shall neglect nothing to have it reach you very promptly.

As to the summons you send me to retire, I do not think myself obliged to obey it. Whatever may be your instructions, I am here by virtue of the orders of my General, and I entreat you, Sir, not to doubt for a moment that I have a firm resolution to follow them with all the exactness and determination which can be expected of the best officer.

I do not know that anything has happened in the course of this campaign which can be construed as an act of hostility, or as contrary to the treaties between the two Crowns; the continuation of which interests and pleases us as much as it does the English. If you had been pleased, Sir, to go into detail regarding the deeds which caused your complaints, I should have had the honor of answering you in the most positive manner, and I am sure that you would have had reason to be satisfied.

I have made it a particular duty to receive Mr. Washington with the distinction owing to your dignity, his position, and his own great merit. I trust that he will do me justice in that regard with you, and that he will make known to you the profound respect with which I am, Sir, Your most humble and most obedient servant.[24]

Once he handed Washington his reply, Legardeur de St. Pierre seemed suddenly eager to send him on his way, even as he continued his attempts to lure the Indians into remaining with him. To Washington and the white men, the commandant presented "a plentiful Store of Liquor, Provisions & ca. to be put on board our Canoe." Washington understood that while this Knight of St. Louis "appear'd to be extremely complaisant, . . . he was plotting every Scheme that the Devil & Man cou'd invent, to set our Indians at Variance with us, to prevent their going 'till after our Departure. Presents, rewards & every Thing that cou'd be suggested by him or his Officers was not neglected to do."[25]

For the first time during the entire expedition into the wilderness, Washington confessed to being afraid:

> *I can't say that ever in my Life I suffer'd so much Anxiety as I did in this affair: I saw that every Stratagem that the most fruitful Brain cou'd invent: was practis'd to get the Half King won to their Interest . . . I went to the Half King and press'd him in the strongest Terms to go. He told me the Commander wou'd not discharge him 'till Morning . . .*[26]

If the Half-King's reply to Washington had been truthful, Legardeur de St. Pierre's approach to the Indians was evidently progressing from persuasion to an outright assertion of authority over them. The commander "wou'd not discharge him"! What gave Legardeur de St. Pierre the authority to hold or discharge a chief of the Six Nations? On the other hand, if the Half-King were fabricating this reason for delay, the implications were even worse, suggesting that he was indeed slipping into the clutches of the French commander.

Washington decided to act as if the Half-King's account were perfectly accurate and honest, and he therefore "went to the Commander & desired him to do their Business, & complain'd of ill Treatment; for keep-

ing them, as they were Part of my Company was detaining me, which he
promis'd not to do . . ." By way of reply, Legardeur de St. Pierre
"protested he did not keep them but was innocent of the Cause of their
Stay." This disclaimer notwithstanding, Washington "soon found . . . out"
the cause: "He had promis'd them a Present of Guns, &ca. if they wou'd
wait 'till Morning." In great frustration, Washington consented to the
Indians' request to wait one more day "on a Promise that Nothing shou'd
hinder them in the Morning."[27]

On the sixteenth, Washington wrote: "The French were not slack in
their Inventions to keep the Indians this Day also"; however, they were
constrained by the promise to give the guns, and they knew that, once
that present was given, the Indians would be on their way. According to
Washington, the Frenchmen once again "endeavour'd to try the Power of
Liquor; which I doubt not wou'd have prevail'd at any other Time than
this, but I tax'd the [Half-]King so close upon his Word that he refrain'd,
& set off with us as he had engag'd."[28] Into the canoes they piled, white
men and Indians. Not a shot had been fired. But from this, his first battle
with the French, George Washington had emerged the victor, albeit by
the very narrowest of margins.

5

MURTHERING TOWN

George Washington had delivered the governor's letter and secured the French reply. He had also ascertained the French intentions and gathered a wealth of intelligence concerning the state of their military preparedness. Yet none of these achievements would mean anything until he returned to Williamsburg to report to Dinwiddie, and with the French preparing major military action, a speedy return was critical.

The Indians were in one canoe, the whites in the other. Shortly after the party left Fort Le Boeuf, the Indians, who had delayed so long, seemed suddenly impatient, paddling with such vigor that they quickly outdistanced Washington and the other white men. Rounding a bend in French Creek, they disappeared. Washington did not see them all through the day of December 16. On the next day he spotted their canoe. Ordering his men to row to shore, he entered their camp, but found no one there. Never one to panic, Washington assumed that they had gone hunting and decided he would wait for them. In due course, three of the four Indians did return, lugging with them the meat from three bears, which they shared out with the white men that evening. As to the fourth Indian—White Thunder—he had somehow become separated from the other three and did not return that night, nor the next morning.

That was a big problem. The Indians would not continue homeward until their comrade had found his way to them. Washington may have expressed sympathetic understanding in this situation, but his sole objective was to return to Williamsburg without delay. His sense of urgency was heightened by the changing weather. The icy rain and snow had ceased, and with the end of the precipitation came a rapid drop in the level of French Creek. Soon, it would either freeze solid or simply be too low to float the canoes. Washington therefore decided to leave the Indians behind. They knew where he was headed, and they could probably catch up with him after the belated hunter returned.

The major's fears concerning the condition of the creek were well-founded. "We had a tedious & very fatiguing Passage down the Creek," he recorded in his diary, "several Times we had like to have stove against Rocks, & many Times were oblig'd all Hands to get out, & remain in the Water Half an Hour or more, getting her over the Shoals." As the teenage Washington had shown a natural affinity for fortifications and other military matters, so now, when he was obliged to ply the waters in a canoe, did he naturally adopt the language of an old salt, writing of nearly getting "stove" against rocks and being obliged to call out "all Hands" to float the canoe over the shallows.[1]

In one bend of the river, reached on December 21, "the Ice had Lodg'd & made it impassable by Water; therefore we were oblig'd to carry our Canoe across a neck [of] Land a quarter of a Mile over."[2] This impromptu portage meant emptying the canoe, carrying its contents overland to less thickly frozen water around the bend, carrying the canoe there as well, and then reloading. The time required for the effort had one advantage. It slowed Washington sufficiently to allow the Indians to catch up. They paddled easily through the channel Washington and his men had cleared for themselves through the thinner ice—not just one canoe, but four. The Half-King, White Thunder, and the other Indians were in one, and the other three canoes were jammed with Frenchmen.

Washington had just moved heaven and earth to pry the Indians from the embrace of the French at Fort Le Boeuf, and here they were, once again, in the company of the enemy. The sight must have caused him considerable frustration and anxiety. These emotions were somewhat relieved the next day, December 22, when the major watched the canoes maneuver sharply in a rocky and icy shallow. Suddenly, one of the overcrowded French boats overturned. Indeed, Washington soon learned, this was the *second* French boat that had been upset. They had set out from Fort Le Boeuf in four, but one capsized before the party had caught up with Washington, forcing all the Frenchmen to jam themselves into the three remaining craft. Doubtless, the major was pleased that the Indians had seen the French embarrassed not once, but twice, and he was probably even more delighted that, among the cargo they had lost, was a load of brandy and wine—French seductions that he was eager to keep out of Indian hands.

Washington reached Venango on December 22. The horses and the men he had earlier sent down from Fort Le Boeuf were waiting for him, but he could not have been pleased by the condition of the animals. They had already been in want of food as the winter closed in, and he had gambled that adequate feed could be found at Venango. In fact, the horses now looked weaker than ever, and Washington concluded that keeping them at this French outpost would not fatten them up. The only option, he decided, was to start off right away and hope for the best. That left open the question of what the Indians would do. Washington hoped that they would choose to accompany him overland to Logstown, but the French were offering their canoes—and their company. The major sent for the Half-King and asked: Will you come with us? He answered that White Thunder had been so badly injured during the hunt that he was "unable to walk" and therefore they had no choice but to travel by canoe.[3]

By this time, Washington knew better than to take at face value any statement involving relations between the French and Indians. Quite possibly, what the Half-King said was true. White Thunder might be too

badly hurt to travel overland. Yet it was just as likely that his condition
made for nothing more than a convenient excuse. It was not that
Washington feared some grand plot was being hatched between the
Indians and the French, but that the Half-King and the others were willing to forsake Washington and the English alliance wherever and
whenever the French offered the prospect of alcohol and gifts.
Washington concluded that it was far more important for him to return
to Dinwiddie quickly than it was to linger in an effort to protect the
Indians from French blandishments. Besides, whereas the problem on the
outward trip had been losing the loyalty of the Indians in the midst of
French-controlled territory, the return trip was taking the Indians closer
and closer to English-controlled territory, which therefore reduced the
magnitude of the danger. Nevertheless, the major took the Half-King
aside and cautioned him that Joncaire would make wild promises, would
say anything to win the chief's loyalty. The Half-King protested that he
was all too familiar with the value of French promises and was not about
to be taken in by them.

    The Indian chief gave Washington more than this assurance. He said
he would try to send the trader Joseph Campbell to meet him at the forks
of the Ohio to deliver a speech intended for the ears of Governor
Dinwiddie. Furthermore, if Washington liked, he would ask Campbell to
accompany him for a time to obtain provisions for his party. According to
the highly respected trader George Croghan, Campbell was no great bargain; he had an unsavory reputation as "a bad man . . . corrupted by the
French."[4] Was the Half-King trying to introduce a French sympathizer
into Washington's party? Probably not on purpose. All evidence suggests
that the Indian chief had conceived a certain respect and affection for
George Washington. After all, it was at this time, if not earlier, that he
bestowed upon Washington the Indian name of Caunotaucarius, which
meant Taker of Towns. This impressive name was a double honor, inas-
much as the Six Nations had originally bestowed it upon Washington's
great-grandfather. Thus it was intended not only to suggest the esteem in

which the Half-King held him, but also to convey a long-standing alliance that transcended both Washington and the chief. Most likely, his proposal to send Campbell to him was made with the best of intentions and was a misreading of the trader's character rather than a deliberate set-up. In any event, Campbell never showed up.

Washington and the other white men set off on December 23, bound for Murthering Town. After only five miles, it became apparent to the major that the horses were giving out. He called a halt for the night, then in the morning decided that "Our Horses were now [too] weak & feeble" to carry all the party's heavy baggage as well as riders. Doubtless with a heavy sigh, Washington "& others (except the Drivers which were oblig'd to ride) gave up our Horses for Packs, to assist along with the Baggage." With riders dismounted, the baggage could be divided up among more of the horses. Washington donned the "Indian walking Dress"—a deerskin hunting shirt—he had brought with him and pushed on.[5]

All Christmas Eve, the men tramped along an icy, snow-covered trail. Christmas Day offered more of the same, and when he awoke the day after Christmas, Washington discovered that three of his men were severely frostbitten. Not only were the horses growing "less able to travel every Day," the frostbitten members of the party were almost totally incapacitated. "The Cold," Washington wrote in his diary, "increas'd very fast, & the Roads were getting much worse by a deep Snow continually Freezing; And as I was uneasy to get back to make a report of my Proceedings to his Honour the Governor, I determin'd to prosecute my Journey the nearest way through the Woods on Foot."[6] He instructed his men to build a temporary shelter, where the three disabled travelers could rest and recover while awaiting more moderate weather. He proposed to Christopher Gist that he accompany him southwest to Murthering Town, where they would rest and then, leaving the trail, make their way directly for the cabin of John Frazier, traveling southeast through the woods. There they could get fresh horses and continue the journey with greater speed.

Gist was not happy. He did his best to impress upon Washington just how hard it was to walk many miles of frozen, snow-deep woods. The major countered that his mission demanded speed now more than ever. At length, Gist gave in, and Washington left Jacob van Braam "in Charge of our Baggage." He entrusted to the Dutchman some money "to provide Necessaries from Place to Place" once the frostbite sufferers were sufficiently recovered to move again, and he instructed him to set out for Frazier's with "the most convenient Dispatch." As for Washington, taking the French commandant's reply and other "necessary Papers," he "tied [himself] up in a Match Coat"—a heavy garment made of very coarse "match cloth"—and watched as Gist showed him how to prepare his pack so that it could be carried most efficiently. Then, "my Pack at my back, with my Papers & Provisions in it, & a Gun," he "set out with Mr. Gist, fitted in the same Manner, on Wednesday the 26th."[7]

It was Gist who set the pace—moving so fast that, according to Washington, it was "scarcely supportable." Thirsting from the journey, the men had difficulty chipping through the thick ice that locked up every stream and spring. The pair made eighteen miles that first day, stopping only when a conveniently vacant Indian cabin offered itself. Gist recorded in his diary that "The Major was much fatigued," but he did not give him much time to rest. Washington had impressed upon Gist the urgency of the mission, and Gist took him seriously. Accordingly, at two o'clock in the morning of December 27, the pair roused themselves and continued to walk. The moonlight was sufficiently amplified by the snow on the ground that they had no trouble seeing their way.[8]

Washington recorded what happened when later that day they arrived at "a Place call'd the Murdering Town." He narrated: "We fell in with a Party of French Indians, which had laid in wait for us, one of them fired at Mr. Gist or me, not 15 Steps [away], but fortunately missed."[9]

The whole story was, of course, rather more complex than Washington's customarily laconic account. At Murthering Town, they saw several Indians, one of whom stepped forward and, in English, announced that he knew Christopher Gist, whom he called by his Indian name. Gist did not recall ever having met the Indian, but he did think there was something strangely familiar about him. He could not be sure, but he seemed to remember him as one of the hangers-on at Joncaire's strong house. Washington did not remember him at all, and when the Indian asked why the pair were traveling on foot, he brightened with an idea. Perhaps this Indian could show them the absolutely shortest shortcut through the woods and to the Allegheny River. When he asked the Indian if he could do this, the man enthusiastically replied in the affirmative.

We do not know how Gist felt about this arrangement—was he bothered by the nagging feeling that he had seen this Indian with the Frenchman Joncaire?—but he acquiesced. Moreover, the Indian obligingly shouldered Washington's pack, which did not prevent him from also carrying his own rifle. If Gist harbored any suspicions (clearly, Washington did not), they may well have been allayed as the miles piled up without incident. After about ten miles, Washington announced that he was sufficiently tired to make camp for the night. The Indian responded with a kind offer to relieve the major of his rifle so that they could continue to push on.

Washington had been quite happy to relinquish his pack, but he demurred when it came to his weapon. At this, the Indian made a great display of being offended, and his benign manner suddenly changed. He now demanded that everyone keep moving, delivering a dire warning that Ottawas were out and about. If the party stopped to make camp here, they would all surely be scalped. The only safe thing to do, he insisted, was to keep walking until they reached his cabin. No harm would come to them there.

At this juncture, Gist became frankly suspicious. First, the Indian wanted to get Washington's rifle. Second, he was suddenly very anxious that they all go to his cabin. Third, he had instantly become quite surly. But most of all, it seemed to Gist that the Indian was leading them too far northeast to soon reach the nearest ford across the Allegheny.

Gist asked him pointblank: How far was the cabin? The reply was more than slightly ominous: As far as a gunshot can be heard.

Biding his time, Gist invited the Indian to lead in that direction. It seemed to Gist that he was now turning even more sharply away from the Allegheny. Nevertheless, they continued to follow him. But Washington was also growing uneasy.

Gist asked again: How far from the cabin now? "Two whoops," the Indian replied, meaning the distance at which the cry of a warrior could be heard. This must have struck both white men as yet another veiled threat.

Two full miles passed.

We are near, the Indian said.

Washington, persuaded at last that he and Gist were being led astray, told him that they would halt at the very next water. At this, the Indian, "15 Steps" ahead of Gist and Washington, led the two into a meadow. Once all were in this clearing, he wheeled suddenly about, raised his rifle, and fired at them.

George shouted to Gist: "Are you shot?"

Gist had not seen the Indian fire, but he had heard the shot.

"No," he answered.[10]

Stunned, the two white men watched as the Indian broke into a run, then dashed behind a white oak to reload. Shaking off the shock, Washington and Gist sprinted after him. Washington later wrote no more than, "We took this Fellow into Custody." The fact was that Gist was all for killing him, but the major restrained him even as the Indian calmly continued to load his rifle. Before he could load the ball, however, Gist and Washington laid hold of him. Presumably at Washington's insistence, they resumed their journey, this time making the now unarmed Indian walk ahead by no more than a few paces. When they reached a small creek, Washington called a halt and told the Indian to build a fire. As the Indian busied himself in that task, Gist quietly said to Washington: "As you will not have him killed, we must get him away and then we must travel all night."[11]

Surely the weary major was now running on pure adrenalin. He agreed without hesitation. Then Gist set about giving the appearance that he was preparing to make camp.

"I suppose," he remarked to the Indian, "you were lost and fired your gun."

It was a crafty thing to say. If the Indian replied yes, then that would give the lie to his tale about being near his cabin. If he answered no, then he would be virtually admitting to attempted murder. In the end, he said only that he knew the way to his cabin, which was very close.

"Well, do you go home," Gist continued, "and as we are much tired, we will follow your track in the morning; and here is a cake of bread for you, and you must give us meat in the morning."[12]

In later life, Washington expressed admiration for Gist and gratitude for all that he had taught him about the wilderness. We can only wonder if Washington fully appreciated the skill with which Gist handled this would-be assassin. Undeniably, Gist would have preferred to kill the Indian but, yielding to his commander, he did the next best thing: he intimidated him into making an escape. The Indian had to assume that he was marked for death; therefore, when Gist gave him an opportunity to leave, he did so without causing further trouble. Not that Gist left anything to chance. He stealthily followed the Indian to ensure that he was in fact leaving the campsite and was not lying somewhere in ambush. After Gist had assured himself of the man's departure, he returned to Washington shortly after 9 p.m. and told him that they had to get moving right away. His assumption was that this Indian would rouse his brothers to pursue and hunt them down. The major's profound weariness is evident even in his lean diary account: we "walked all the remaining Part of the Night without making any Stop; that we might get the start, so far as to be out of the reach of their Pursuit the next Day, as [we] were well assur'd they wou'd follow upon our Tract as soon as it was Light."[13]

The pair tramped all that night and, with brief periods of rest, "continued traveling 'till it was quite Dark."[14] Snow was an enemy. It not only made the going rough, forcing knees to be raised high to lift reluctant feet through the heavy white packed powder; it also made tracking a very easy matter. With each weary step, the men traced out a line, deep and unmistakable, pointing directly to their whereabouts. The knowledge that each step betrayed them doubtless gave the two men all the energy they needed to maintain their pace.

At about the time that it became "quite Dark," Gist discovered Indian tracks in the snow. He assumed that they had been made by hunters, who meant no harm or were even friendly. Then again, they might be intent on murder. Neither Gist nor Washington wanted to chance finding out. Concerned that the hunters might return the way they had come, Gist advised that he and Washington split up, then rendezvous at a point closer to the shore of the Allegheny. They did this and, agreeing that they had come far enough to be out of immediate danger, they spent what remained of the night of December 28 in sleep.

On the twenty-ninth, they reached the Allegheny, some two miles above a place called Shannopin's Town—a location within the city limits of modern Pittsburgh. Washington noted in his diary: "We expected to have found the River Froze, but it was not." The solid ice extended "only about 50 Yards from each Shoar." In between was an icy torrent: "the Ice I suppose had broke up above [upriver], for it was driving in vast Quantities," Washington observed. This was a cruel disappointment for the all-but-spent travelers. They had expected to stroll across a solidly frozen river, and now "There was no way for us to get over but upon a Raft." Of course, that raft did not exist. So they "set about [making one] with but one poor Hatchet, & got finish'd just after Sunsetting, after a whole days Work."[15]

They had trudged day and night in fear for their lives. They spent an entire day building a long raft using nothing but a single hatchet. Now that it was finished, they did not delay another moment. "We got it launch'd, & on board of it, & sett off." What happened next obviously made a vivid impression on Washington, because he narrated the events with a degree of detail that seems lavish compared with his usually sparse diary prose:

> *Before we got half over, we were jamed in the Ice in such a Manner, that we expected every Moment our Raft wou'd sink, & we Perish; I put out my seting Pole, to try to stop the Raft, that the Ice might pass by, when the Rapidity of the Stream through [threw] [the raft] with so much Violence against the Pole, that it jirk'd me into 10 Feet Water, but I fortunately saved my Self by catching hold of one of the Raft Logs. Notwithstanding all our Efforts we cou'd not get the Raft to either Shoar, but were oblig'd, as we were pretty near an Island, to quit our Raft & wade to it. The Cold was so extream severe, that Mr. Gist got all his Fingers, & some of his Toes Froze . . .*[16]

Nearly drowned in the swift and icy current, Washington had the strength to lift himself back onto the raft, despite what must have been the added weight of his rough match coat, which, soaking, would have almost instantly frozen solid around him. The two men then struggled to "get the Raft to either Shoar," but in the rushing, ice-loaded current, they could not. Fortunately, a mid-river island loomed ahead; they abandoned the raft on which they had expended a full day's work, and waded into the icy stream.

That little island was a lifesaver, but it must have been a most bleak and barren wintry place. The two men were cold, unspeakably cold, Washington encased in ice, Gist suffering from frostbite. But they still had their lives—as well as the packs on their backs, their guns, their hatchet, and the French commandant's reply to Governor Dinwiddie. These blessings notwithstanding, they must also have been painfully aware of their unenviable position. They were two freezing men on a little wilderness island in the middle of a bitterly cold rushing torrent. Washington had written that he fell into ten feet of water. Assuming that the depth of the Allegheny in this area was consistent, both men were also aware that it was probably too deep for them to wade from the island to the opposite shore. Were these thoughts sufficient to keep them awake through the night they spent on that little piece of land? Or did their exhaustion overwhelm their anxiety and let them sleep as they shivered?

Dawn brought fresh hope. Expecting to see the same roiling water they had struggled with the night before, they beheld instead that the river had frozen solid overnight and that "the Water was shut up so hard that We found no Difficulty in getting off the Island on the Ice." They walked to the opposite bank and hiked ten miles to John Frazier's trading post. There they found a party of "20 Warriors that had been going to the Southward to War, but coming to a Place upon the Head of the Great Cunnaway [Great Kanawha River], . . . they found [seven] People kill'd & Scalpt"—that is, all scalped, "but one Woman with very Light Hair." The Indians instantly "turn'd about; & ran back, for fear of the Inhabitants [of the town] rising & takeing them as the Authors of the Murder." To Washington, the Indians related the scene in gory detail, reporting "that the People were lying about the House, & some of them much torn & eat by Hogs; by the Marks that were left, they say they were French Indians of the Ottaway Nation, &ca. that did it."[17]

From early boyhood, Washington must have heard many tales of Indian massacres, but as far as we know, this was the first time he came so close to the scene of one—perpetrated, apparently, by members of the very tribe his would-be assassin had mentioned. Historians believe that the massacre the Indians had stumbled across was that of Robert Foyles, his wife, and five children—seven victims who were killed on the

Monongahela River rather than the Great Kanawha. In March 1754, Governor Dinwiddie himself alluded to the massacre in a letter to his superior, the royal governor James Hamilton, mentioning it as an example of what could be "constantly" expected if the "Incursions of these People [i.e., the French] with their Ind[ians]" were permitted to continue unchecked. He elaborated on how, "last Year . . . some of their Ind's Came to our Frontiers, Murder'd a Man, his Wife and five Children, Robbed them of all they had, and left their Bodies to be tore in Pieces by the wild Beasts."[18] For Washington, as for Dinwiddie, Indian depredations were inextricably linked to the French invasion of the Ohio country. The French, he believed, put the Indians up to these crimes. As he listened to the bloody account, Washington must have felt a fresh sense of the importance of his mission.

The major now ordered horses at Frazier's trading post, and because "it requir'd some time to hunt them," he decided to walk "about 3 Miles . . . to visit Queen Aliquippa, who had express'd great Concern that we [had] pass'd her [without paying a visit] in going to the [French commandant's] Fort." Alliquippa—or Allaquippa—was often described as a Delaware female chief, but she may really have been a Seneca. In either case, she was a highly influential figure in the region, and Washington took advantage of the time required to "hunt" his horses to redress the slight committed on the outward journey, when he had failed to call on her. To augment his amends, Washington "made her a Present of a Match Coat; & a Bottle of rum, which was thought much the best Present of the two."[19]

Washington and Gist left Frazier's on New Year's Day 1754 "& arriv'd at Mr. Gists [new settlement] at Monongahela [on] the 2d." Here Washington "bought Horse Saddle &ca.," leaving Frazier's horses to be sent back to their owner. On January 6, he noted an encounter with "17 Horses loaded with Materials & Stores for a Fort at the Forks." He must have been gratified to see that Governor Dinwiddie was already starting to fortify the Forks of the Ohio—a measure that, he now well knew, was urgently necessary. On the next day, Washington met "a Family or two going out to settle" in country that the French were about to invade. On this same day, January 7, Washington at last arrived at Wills Creek, gateway to the comforts of the Tidewater. He took a moment to write his reflections on the journey now all but completed. It was, he noted, "as fatiguing . . . as it is possible to conceive, rendered so by excessive bad weather: From the first Day of December 'till the 15th. there was but one Day, but what it rain'd or snow'd incessantly." He continued his plaint: "Throughout the whole Journey we met with nothing but one continued Series of cold wet Weather; which occasioned very uncumfortable Lodgings, especially after we had left our Tent . . ."[20]

Washington reached Belvoir on January 11, "where I stop'd one Day [with the Fairfaxes] to take necessary rest; & then set out for, & arrived at Williamsburg, the 16th. & waited upon His Honour the Governor with the Letter I had brought from the French Commandant, & to give an Account of the Procedures of my Journey."[21]

One month to the day after Washington had set off from Fort Le Boeuf he stood before Lieutenant Governor Robert Dinwiddie and put into that man's hands the letter from Legardeur de St. Pierre. The governor read it, then listened to Washington's report. He asked the young major to put his report into writing so that he, Dinwiddie, could present it to the Virginia Council. Washington rushed to put down on paper some seven thousand words, closing modestly with a compliment to the man who had trusted him with this most important mission: "I hope what has been said will be sufficient to make your Honour satisfied with my conduct; for that was my aim in undertaking, and [my] chief study throughout the prosecution of it."[22]

As Washington later noted, "There intervened but one Day between my Arrival in Williamsburg, and the Time for the Council's Meeting, for me to prepare and transcribe, from the rough Minutes I had taken in my Travels, this Journal."[23] Nor was Dinwiddie content merely to have the Council privy to the report. No sooner did Washington hand it in than

Dinwiddie ordered its publication as *The Journal of Major George Washington, Sent by the Hon. Robert Dinwiddie, Esq; His Majesty's Lieutenant-Governor, and Commander in Chief of Virginia, to the Commandant of the French Forces on Ohio. To Which Are Added, the Governor's Letter, and a Translation of the French Officer's Answer.* Printed as a pamphlet by William Hunter of Williamsburg, it was also widely copied and reprinted in newspapers throughout Virginia and the other colonies. Almost overnight, George Washington was at least moderately famous—and the colonies were duly alerted to the French menace on the western frontier.

On February 15, 1754, the journal was officially presented to the Virginia House of Burgesses, which responded by voting the parsimonious sum of £10,000 to fund the military protection of the entire frontier. To Washington personally, the Burgesses were rather more generous, voting him £50 "to testify our Approbation of his Proceedings on his Journey to the *Ohio*."[24]

6

A NEW MISSION

Unity of purpose was hardly to be taken for granted in mid-eighteenth-century colonial America. The English colonists thought of themselves first and foremost as citizens of their particular colony—they were Virginians or New Yorkers—and then, after this, they counted themselves as English men and women. Most certainly they did not think of themselves as *Americans,* people who shared not only a continent but also a common fate. Even within a particular colony, there was much self-interest and dissension. Having returned from his errand into the wilderness, George Washington had the gratitude of the Virginia House of Burgesses and the governor. Also, those people who liked the governor and agreed with his policies applauded young Washington's mission accomplished. But there were plenty of politically powerful folk in Williamsburg who did not care for Governor Dinwiddie. These especially included people who had an interest in land speculation schemes that competed with the Ohio Company. They tended to see Washington's mission as a propaganda stunt intended to dramatize and exaggerate the French threat in order to curry favor with the crown and get government assistance in settling the vast territory granted to the company. Washington thus found himself in the uncomfortable position of being criticized, in some quarters, for his very success.

Of course, Governor Robert Dinwiddie had it much worse. He had long been acutely frustrated by the House of Burgesses, which did not share his sense of urgency concerning the French threat. The Burgesses had adjourned on December 19, 1753, without voting to authorize the defense funds Dinwiddie had requested. Perhaps even worse, the Burgesses did not even address what Dinwiddie had presented as another pressing issue: developing more positive relationships and military alliances with the Indians. All the legislative body could be stirred to do was extend a law, about to expire, authorizing the use of militia to repel invasion.

Dinwiddie did not give up. Independently of the Burgesses, he called for a council with the Indians, to be held in May 1754 at Winchester, Virginia, in the hope of hammering out some durable alliances. He also moved up the next session of the Burgesses from April 18, 1754, to February 14, and, as we saw in chapter 5, officially presented the Burgesses with a printed copy of Washington's journal the day after that new session began. In addition to the general French threat, the journal more specifically demonstrated the French intention to build a fort at Logstown—that vital interface between the worlds of the white colonists and the Indians—during the spring. Surely, Dinwiddie reasoned, this revelation would stun the House of Burgesses into action, bringing "them into a proper way of thinking when they meet."[1]

Regardless of what some others might think, the urgency was not the product of Ohio Company propaganda, but a hard fact. Dinwiddie understood the importance of raising a body of troops quickly and then rushing them to the Ohio so that they could block the French advance. If the English waited until the French had established themselves—had built a fort and recruited Indian allies—it might be downright impossible to extirpate them.

To his credit, Governor Dinwiddie did not wait for the Burgesses to wake from their deliberative stupor. Well before Washington's return, he had sent men to build a fort at the Forks of the Ohio, and even before the Burgesses' new session began in February, he decided to send a force to assist and guard those men. His first thought was simply to enlist a regiment of volunteers, but he was stymied by his discovery that the Virginia militia law did not authorize him to pay soldiers raised in this way. His only recourse, therefore, was to round up two hundred men—for that is the size of the force he had decided was required—from some combination of frontier traders and frontier militia, send them out, then hope that the Burgesses would indeed vote to fund them. As he thought the matter over, he decided that, after the contingent of two hundred had been dispatched, he would ask the Burgesses to authorize an additional four hundred. At the same time, he would appeal to the governors of the other colonies to provide even more men and supplies. Given the highly fractured and competitive nature of the colonies, he could by no means depend on getting the aid he sought from outside of Virginia. But it was worth a try.

On January 21, 1754, just five days after Washington returned from the expedition to the French commandant, Dinwiddie directed him, in his capacity as adjutant of the Northern Neck, to enlist into active militia service a hundred men from Augusta and Frederick counties. At the same time, Dinwiddie asked Captain William Trent to raise an additional hundred men. A native of Lancaster, Pennsylvania, Trent was the partner of the prosperous trader George Croghan. He had worked for the Pennsylvania Assembly as a dispatch rider and as a conveyor of official gifts to the Indians, and he functioned as an agent for the Ohio Company. Other traders consistently looked to him for leadership, and Dinwiddie had shown considerable acumen in choosing him to recruit men from among the trading community. Both he and Trent well knew that the traders would be highly motivated, since their present and future livelihoods were at stake. After all, they could hardly afford to lose their Indian trading partners to the French. Yet Dinwiddie showed less savvy when it came to defining the chain of command for this expedition of reinforcement. The Council of Virginia recommended that Washington be given overall command of the militiamen and any other men Trent might be able to raise. Dinwiddie decided, however, to divide the force fifty-fifty between Washington and Trent and left the question of overall command unaddressed. It is never a good idea to commit a military force to the field without unambiguously nominating its commander. At that, Dinwiddie also failed to address who would take command when the four hundred additional men he intended to request from the Burgesses arrived.

As if the seeds of discontent were not sown thickly enough with regard to command, there were thorny problems inherent in the very structure of the force. According to the governor's instructions, Washington was to secure fifty men from Frederick County, to be raised by the county lieutenant, Lord Fairfax. The other fifty were to come from Augusta County, where James Patton was county lieutenant. Both detachments were to be in Alexandria by February 20 so that Washington could train them. The governor anticipated that the quota of one hundred militiamen could easily be found in volunteers at the rate of the legally prescribed fifteen pounds of tobacco per day. In the unlikely event that the requisite number could not be raised exclusively from volunteers, the shortfall would be made up with a draft—the names to be drawn by lottery. Thus there was a fair chance that Washington's force would be a mixture of volunteers and conscripts. In contrast, Trent would lead volunteers, only motivated by the knowledge that they were fighting for their professional survival.

On paper, the task of raising a hundred militiamen seemed simple enough. The militia law was clear: every free white male resident of Virginia twenty-one years of age or older was obliged to answer the call to military service, either in person or by supplying (at his own expense) a substitute. Moreover, each militiaman was required to furnish his own rifle and ammunition. While no Burgess dared to believe that every eligible Virginian would comply with the law, they assumed that there would be no problem in raising an adequate number.

As it turned out, there was a very serious problem. Despite the law on the books, the militia was virtually without infrastructure. Almost no one was prepared to answer the call. And even if they had been, the colony of Virginia had never put into place a logistical plan to supply horses, wagons, provisions, and other equipment. The fact was that Virginia had a militia law, but no militia.

Much as Dinwiddie had forged ahead in the absence of the Burgesses' authorization, so Washington was not about to let the absence of a militia stop him from raising one. After securing a nod from Dinwiddie, he sent the trusty Jacob van Braam to Augusta County to help the county lieutenant recruit the necessary men. Washington himself went to Frederick County to assist Lord Fairfax. When he arrived, he found a nasty surprise. Dinwiddie had warned him that the militia was in "very bad order,"[2] but, Washington now discovered, that turned out to be an overly optimistic assessment. Not only had Lord Fairfax been unable to raise a single volunteer; he could not even produce a roll of adult males liable to service. There was never any registration and, therefore, no records. This left the draft as Fairfax's only other option, but he proved unable to implement it. Just why he could not has never been adequately explained, but Washington's most thorough biographer, Douglas Southall Freeman, speculated that the county lieutenant feared a demonstration of resistance if he tried. Records reveal that on September 4, 1754, ten men were fined ten shillings each or imprisoned for twenty days because they had refused to guard French prisoners when ordered to do so. Freeman believed that this instance of near-mutiny was evidence of just how resistant the men of Frederick County were to military service. In this climate, Lord Fairfax did not dare attempt to draft anyone.

After waiting hopefully until February 11, Washington secured a letter from Fairfax reporting to the governor that the militia draft had failed. With the letter in hand, he started back to Williamsburg. When he arrived, he discovered that van Braam had had no better luck in Augusta

County, which failed to furnish any militiamen even though the area had
been devastated by an Indian raid during the summer and therefore
should have been motivated by the simple instinct of self-defense.

In what we can only imagine was righteous rage, Dinwiddie convened
the Council and announced his intention to throw the book at anyone
who defied the militia act. To motivate militia officers, he vowed to
relieve any who failed to perform their duties, chief among which was
producing the required men. The Council listened, then took the wind
out of the governor's sails by bringing up a serious problem with the existing law. Yes, it authorized the immediate raising of the militia in the event
of invasion, but the law also seemed to restrict the militia thus raised from
acting beyond the bounds of Virginia.

Yes, the governor must have testily conceded. *So what?*

As the councilors pointed out, there was by no means universal agreement on whether the Forks of the Ohio lay within Virginia. The junction
of the Monongahela, Allegheny, and Ohio Rivers was, according to many,
within Pennsylvania. Governor Dinwiddie might raise his militia here,
and he might march it westward, but once it reached the Forks it might
simply refuse to go any farther, let alone fight.

It was hard enough to fight the French; Dinwiddie and Washington
were also expected to tangle with recalcitrant citizens, intercolonial com-
petition, and the vagaries of the law.

Even as his efforts to raise a mere two hundred men floundered,
Dinwiddie addressed the House of Burgesses when it reconvened on
February 14, summarizing Washington's report on his mission to
Fort Le Boeuf. Dinwiddie reported as fact that 1,500 Frenchmen,
together with an unspecified number of Indians, were preparing an
imminent advance to Logstown, where they would build a fort and,
indeed, construct many more forts along the Ohio River. Dinwiddie
predicted a horrific frontier war, replete with Indian massacres and
other depredations. On February 15, he underscored his message by
delivering Washington's journal, together with the French

commandant's letter, into the hands of the Burgesses.

Dutifully, the Burgesses convened a Committee of the Whole to discuss the governor's request for defense funds. At best, the drift of the discussion was unenthusiastic. At worst—well, it was much worse. A number of Burgesses declared their opinion that Washington's report was a fantasy intended only to promote the Ohio Company. One Burgess even declared that the Ohio country really *did* belong to the French after all! Only after much anguished effort was Dinwiddie able to cajole the Burgesses into voting £10,000 for the defense of the entire frontier. Grossly inadequate as this sum was, the Burgesses attached to the appropriation a rider that hobbled the governor even further. They stipulated that fourteen leading men of Virginia (or any nine of that number), with the consent of the governor, were to be tasked with deciding how the money should be spent. In this stipulation, it is quite possible to see an early premonition of the American Revolution. The governor was an appointee of the crown, whereas the Burgesses (who were chief among the "leading men") were elected by the colonists. In effect, the Burgesses were giving themselves a strong voice in the allocation of money appropriated for military purposes. The governor raged that the provision was "very much in a republican way of thinking" and was strongly tempted simply to dissolve the Burgesses right then and there.[3] Satisfying as that would have been, Dinwiddie knew that he needed the money, and he needed it now, strings and all. So he accepted the appropriation as passed.

With the £10,000 in hand—more or less—Dinwiddie decided to bypass the dysfunctional militia system and start from scratch by raising six companies of fifty volunteers each. As an incentive, he was prepared to offer much more than the fifteen pounds of tobacco paid to militiamen. He announced that 100,000 acres were being reserved adjacent to the proposed fort and another 100,000 were reserved elsewhere along the Ohio. After the volunteers successfully concluded their service, the entire 200,000 acres was to be divided among them. And, to be on the safe side, Dinwiddie also threw in the customary fifteen pounds of tobacco.

George Washington was a major of militia. The new force, however, was not a militia force, and Dinwiddie had to appoint new officers to command the volunteers. Washington did not expect to be given command of all three hundred men, but he hoped that Colonel William Fairfax would be selected and that Fairfax would appoint him his second. When Fairfax protested frail health, however, Washington appealed directly to the governor. He worked on all the connections he possessed, one of whom, Virginia Council member Richard Corbin, told Washington that he might be in line for a commission at a level higher than that of major. Emboldened by this intelligence, Washington inquired of Dinwiddie point-blank: What would a lieutenant colonel of volunteers be paid?

The answer was no munificent sum. Dinwiddie told him it would be fifteen shillings a day, which prompted Washington to respond—doubtless in spite of himself—that it was too little. Washington knew that British regular officers made more. Dinwiddie countered that the colonial officers would also receive provisions in addition to their salary, which, he claimed, more than redressed the inequity of the provincial and regular salaries. The governor's explanation must have mollified—if not satisfied—Washington, because he wrote to Corbin, asking him to put in a good word for his promotion. He began, however, with what seems a sincere flush of modesty: "The command of the whole force is what I neither look for, expect, nor desire; for I must be impartial enough to confess, it is a charge too great for my youth and inexperience to be intrusted with." Surely, the expedition to Fort Le Boeuf had built Washington's confidence, but it seems simultaneously to have dosed him with sobering reality. Still, he continued to Corbin: "Knowing this [the limitations of "my youth and inexperience"], I have too sincere a love for my country, to undertake that which may tend to the prejudice of it. But if I could entertain hopes that you thought me worthy of the post of Lieutenant-colonel, and would favour me so far as to mention it at the appointment of officers, I could not but entertain a true sense of kindness." That Washington was not merely couching his appeal for a recommendation in conventional protestations of modesty but revealing a mature understanding of the current level of his professional development is suggested by the conclusion of the letter: "I flatter myself that under a skilful commander, or man of sense, (which I most sincerely wish to serve under) with my own application and diligent study of my duty, I shall be able to conduct my steps without censure, and in time, render myself worthy of the promotion that I shall be favoured with now."[4] In effect, Washington deemed military promotion a payment-in-advance for the commander he would become—"in time"—after learning all he could from a skilled superior.

In the meantime, Washington set about recruiting volunteers, a task for which he managed to secure compensation based on his active-duty rank as major and not just on his annual district adjutant's stipend. He set up a headquarters in Alexandria and, after a week of hard work, managed to recruit twenty-five "loose, Idle Persons that are quite destitute of House, and Home, and I may truly say many of them of Cloaths." The frontier was the realm of remarkable men like Christopher Gist, but also belonged to the feckless dregs of colonial society. Washington's first twenty-five volunteers were all but naked. They were barefooted and shirtless. "The generality of those Men, who have enlisted for this Expedition are much in want of, and press greatly for Cloathings," Washington wrote to Dinwiddie on March 7. Moreover, they really wanted to *look* like soldiers: "to be put into a Uniform dress" and "would gladly do it at their own Expence to be deducted out of their Pay." In fact, Washington, the frustrated recruiter, complained that the failure to furnish a uniform "was the greatest objection to enlisting and many refus'd solely on that account after coming purposely to do it with the Expectation of getting a Regimental Sute." Washington explained to the governor that uniforms would not only be a strong inducement to enlist, but would confer a significant tactical advantage: "It is the Nature of Indians to be struck with, and taken by show and this will give them a much higher Conception of our Power and greatness and I verily believe

fix in our Interest many that are now wavering and undetermin'd whose
Cause to Espouse—If it was only a Coat of the Coursest red which may
be had in these parts it would answer the Intention—red with them is
compared to Blood and is look'd upon as the distinguishing marks of
Warriours and great Men—The shabby and ragged appearance the French
common Soldiers make affords great matter of ridicule amongst the
Indians and I really believe is the chief motive why they hate and despise
them as they do."[5]

Although Washington had admitted his inexperience to Corbin, he
wrote to Dinwiddie as if from a wealth of tactical insight. The apparent
contradiction is important. Reviewing the military record Washington
compiled during the American Revolution, most historians have judged
him to be at best a mediocre tactician but a great leader of men.
Evidently, this dichotomy was present from the very inception of his military career. Despite his sense of inadequacy to all the demands of high
military office—he had led seven men into the wilderness; now he might
lead two or three hundred—Washington possessed a native insight into
what motivated the individual warrior. This insight would never desert
him through a long military career.

Yet, in the present instance, finances were inadequate to fund insight.
The money was not forthcoming. Anxious to preempt a call to advance
the cash himself, Washington bewailed his financial inability in another
letter to Dinwiddie on March 9, although he implied that this was not so
much a case of insufficient means as it was an unwillingness to risk never
being reimbursed. That risk, he wrote to the governor, "is . . . too great
for me to run, thô it would be nothing to the Country." It was an early
statement of what became, little more than twenty years later, the refrain
Washington would often repeat to the Continental Congress in its perpet-
ual struggle to fund the Continental Army during the American
Revolution. Immediately after he wrote this complaint, Washington
thought the better of it: "But I must here in time put a kirb to my
requests, and remember that I ought not to be too importunate; other-

wise, I shall be as troublesome to your Honour, as the Soldiers are to me."[6]

❦

Despite a handful of additional recruits who wandered into Alexandria, Washington was altogether shown up by William Trent, who was reportedly already near his hundred-man quota of Ohio country recruits. Even so, Trent wrote to Washington that this force was too weak on its own to assist in the construction and guarding of the fort. A friendly Indian had informed him that Commissary La Force was being very free with threats. Another Indian reported the imminent approach to the Ohio River of four hundred Frenchmen, a fact that greatly alarmed many of the local Indians. Christopher Gist, who had rendezvoused with Trent, reported knowledge of even larger movements of French forces along the Ohio. Trent urged Washington to get under way as soon as possible. Gist, he wrote, had assured him that George Washington would not let them down.[7]

Washington left no record of how this communication made him feel. We can only imagine. Several hundred Frenchmen were invading. The advance guard of the English—a hundred frontiersmen—urgently needed reinforcement, but all Washington had to offer was an "army" of somewhat more than twenty-five loose, idle, homeless, and practically naked vagabonds.

As for Dinwiddie, we have a better idea of how he felt at this juncture. He seemed almost blithely unconcerned by the near non-existence of an army. Stymied by the militia law, through which he might have been able to recruit two or three times the number of volunteers he called for, Dinwiddie declared his opinion that three hundred volunteers were better than eight hundred militiamen. This assertion would have been unrealistic even if Dinwiddie actually had three hundred volunteers. Given the fact that Washington had just told him that all he had was a ragtag twenty-five, the governor's judgment was downright fantastic. With greater justification, Governor Dinwiddie took comfort in assurances that a thousand Cherokee and Catawba warriors would rush to the aid of Virginia, and he learned that an "independent company" of British regulars was being sent from South Carolina, as were two independent companies from New York. Nor did he rely entirely on these assurances. Dinwiddie was vigorous in his correspondence with the governors of other colonies, appealing to them for funds to help defend the Ohio frontier. That he was getting caught up personally in the martial spirit is suggested by his quietly obtaining an officer's uniform for himself.

Dinwiddie also occupied himself with the question of who should be overall commander of the projected three hundred Virginia volunteers. He had distressingly few candidates from which to choose. Other than the Cartagena expedition in which Lawrence Washington had participated, Virginia had never engaged in any major military operation. For that reason, the colony had almost no veteran officers. At length, Dinwiddie decided to confer overall command on Joshua Fry. While it was true that he had never served in an army, Fry was nevertheless a remarkable man who commanded ample respect. He had been born in Somerset, England, and was educated at Oxford before he immigrated to Virginia sometime before 1720. He had been master of the grammar school at the College of William and Mary and also a professor of mathematics and natural philosophy. He served in a number of civic offices and in the House of Burgesses. Like Washington, he was a county surveyor, but his surveying skills surpassed those of the major, and he earned considerable renown as the coauthor of a justly famous and quite ambitious 1751 "Map of the Inhabited Parts of Virginia."

After conferring a colonelcy on Fry, Dinwiddie set about commissioning other officers, beginning with the promotion of militia captain

George Muse to major. English-born Muse had served in the Cartagena campaign and was adjutant of Virginia's Middle Neck. One Adam Stephen was commissioned a captain. Scottish born, he offered two valuable assets: experience in the Royal Navy and credentials as a practicing physician in Virginia. John Augustine Washington applied for a lieutenant's commission, but was offered nothing higher than ensign. He did not join.

On March 1, 1754, having chosen his officers, Dinwiddie wrote to Maryland governor Horatio Sharpe: "We are in much distress for proper officers, but have taken all possible care of choosing the best we have, but not so well acquainted with the arts of war as I could wish, but as our cause is just, I hope for the protection of Heaven." Not very encouraging, especially coming from an optimist. Two weeks later, he sent Washington a letter of instructions, together with a commission as lieutenant colonel. The actual commission is lost, but a note from Richard Corbin survives: "I enclose your commission. God prosper you with it."[8]

Dinwiddie had made Washington second in command under Fry, and his letter of instruction authorized him to purchase uniforms for his men, provided that "Care shd be taken of buying the Cloth at the cheapest rate." (As it turned out, there would be no time to buy the uniforms.) His pay, as lieutenant colonel, would be 12s. 6p. a day. "I have sent to the Treasurer for Money," Dinwiddie wrote, then continued: "if he disappoints me, I shall nevertheless send You some immediately . . ."[9]

The pay, Washington took note, was 2s. 6p. less than the 15s. the governor had promised earlier and that Washington had pronounced insufficient. This bothered him deeply. He calculated that, at the prevailing rate of exchange, the pay was about 10s. a day less than that of a British regular of the same rank. To compound this disparity in pay, Washington and his volunteer officers would be serving alongside officers of independent companies, who would be paid at the rate of British regulars. Finally, adding insult to injury, despite the governor's earlier assurance that the officers would be supplied with provisions in addition to their pay, those provisions, it now turned out, would not be officer's fare, but the rations of a common soldier. Washington was torn between, on the one hand, his eagerness to serve and gratitude to the governor for entrusting to him an important command and, on the other, his anger over broken promises and the morale-eroding discrimination shown between British regulars and colonial volunteers. He rationalized by fixing blame on the Council of Virginia rather than on Governor Dinwiddie, but he nevertheless announced to Colonel Fairfax his intention of resigning his commission in protest. Fairfax did his best to dissuade Washington from this step, and he promised to intercede with Dinwiddie in an attempt to raise the compensation of the colonials.

In truth, it may have been that, angry though he was, Washington did not require a great deal of dissuading. He was excited not only to be a high-ranking officer in an important expedition, but also to be leading the expedition's vanguard. Dinwiddie, anxious to get soldiers on the march as quickly as possible, directed Washington in a letter to depart immediately with "what soldiers you have." Colonel Fry would follow later with the rest of the troops as soon as they were assembled. Dinwiddie made it clear that Washington was to "act on the defensive," unless "any attempts are made to obstruct the works [the building of the fort] or interrupt our settlements." In that case, the governor authorized the new colonel to "make prisoners of or kill and destroy" all "offenders."[10]

As of March 20, the day Washington received Dinwiddie's instructions and commission—both of which had been drawn up on the fifteenth— Washington had recruited fifty men and received from other recruiters another twenty-five. He wrote to Dinwiddie on the twentieth that very few officers had arrived, "which has occasioned a very fatiguing time to me, to manage a number of selfwill'd, ungovernable People." Nevertheless, "I shall implicitly obey your Honour's Commands, and March out with an Expedition." He was in the process of securing "Waggons for the conveyance of Provisions &ca which till now could not travel for heavy roads"; in other words, the roads had been too muddy for baggage transportation.[11] As it was, even now, the ten heavy cannon Dinwiddie had sent the expedition would have to await warmer, sunnier, and drier weather before they could be pulled over the soggy ruts that passed for highways in colonial Virginia.

As always, speed was the key. Washington decided that he could march with the wagons as far as Wills Creek. Once there, he would resort to pack animals to carry provisions for the rest of the march to the Ohio. He sent a message to Captain William Trent, ordering the packhorses.

Volunteers continued to trickle in, and Washington did his best to instill in them some semblance of discipline. He also worked feverishly with John Carlyle to obtain sufficient supplies for the expedition. Born in Dumfrieshire, Scotland, Carlyle was a prominent Alexandria merchant and an investor in the Ohio Company. He was well connected, having married Sarah Fairfax, the daughter of Colonel William Fairfax and sister-in-law of Lawrence Washington. Dinwiddie had commissioned Carlyle on January 26, and the next day sent him an order to "procure a sufficient Qu[anti]ty of Flower, Bread, Beef & Pork, for 500 Men for six or eight Months." The post of commissary was potentially quite prof-itable—"I am in hopes it may turn out 500£ per ann[um].," Carlyle wrote—but it was also "attended with great trouble & fatigue & care."[12] In fact, even with Carlyle's expert efforts, it proved so difficult to collect all that was needed that Washington finally decided to begin the march with sufficient supplies to get what was now a 120-man force only as far as Winchester, which was about forty miles short of Wills Creek. At Winchester, he would collect the additional provisions required for the rest of the journey.

For his part, Dinwiddie also had to accept less and less. North Carolina responded to his call by voting funds and recruiting a force of volunteers expected to number 750. That was good, but Maryland had decided not to send any troops at all, and Pennsylvania's intentions remained a mystery. These setbacks served only to persuade Dinwiddie all the more of the pressing urgency of the expedition. The quicker the troops reached the Ohio, the fewer French and Indians there would be to deal with.

Washington divided his 120 men into two companies, assigning one to the Dutch interpreter, Jacob van Braam, and the other to one Peter Hog (pronounced *Hoag*), a fifty-year-old Scot rumored to have fought in the Jacobite Rising of 1745, the ill-fated attempt to restore the Stuarts to the thrones of Scotland and England. Under these officers were five subalterns, two sergeants, and six corporals—almost certainly none of them veterans.

Barely trained, inadequately supplied, without the much-desired uniforms, and led by inexperienced officers, 120 men followed Lieutenant Colonel Washington out of Alexandria on April 2, 1754. They were bound for the Blue Ridge town of Winchester, ninety-seven miles away, accompanied by just two wagons. Washington's plan was to obtain more wagons and supplies at Winchester for the march to Wills Creek. From Wills Creek to the Ohio, the men would subsist on what the pack animals carried until the road west could be sufficiently cleared for the wagons to be brought up. In any case, it was believed that men and horses could to some degree live off the land. It was far from an ideal arrangement, but it traded the security of plenty for the virtue of speed.

The first day's march ended six miles outside of Alexandria—not bad progress for a column of 120 men, even with light supplies. On the morning of the second day, the expedition turned to the northwest and trundled across a road paralleling the Potomac. After a total of five days, they were fifty-seven miles from Alexandria, having picked up the pace sufficiently to achieve an average of better than eleven miles a day. Now, however, the going would be harder. They had to crest the Blue Ridge at Vestal's Gap, then descend to the Shenandoah River, which would be crossed by ferry. These seventeen miles consumed two full days, but, considering the long uphill climb to Vestal's Gap, Washington approved of the progress.

Once across the Shenandoah, the expedition was on the road to Winchester. It was familiar country to Washington, who had surveyed here in 1748. He led his men to the small town, which they reached—as far as can be determined—by the afternoon of April 10. Waiting there for him was the company recruited by Captain Adam Stephen. This brought the total strength of Washington's command to 159. The number would have been 155, had the lieutenant colonel not learned of a scheme by four of his men to desert. We know that Washington issued a handsome reward of £1 4s. to the soldier who reported the scheme—the award worked out to 6s. per would-be deserter—but we don't know how he punished the deserters or if he made any effort to ascertain the reason for their discontent. The typical punishment was flogging, and Washington was by no means too softhearted to employ it; however, it is doubtful that he wanted to drag four injured men on a march through the wilderness.

Washington was pleased that Adam Stephen and his men had arrived, but he was distressed that absolutely nothing had been done to assemble the required wagons. The lieutenant colonel personally set about "impressing"—drafting into government service—some sixty wagons by roaming the town and indicating which ones he wanted. Of these, no more than eight or nine were actually delivered, so he wearily made the rounds to impress more. It was like carrying water in a sieve. Each day, he would impress a quantity of wagons, and each day only a small fraction would be delivered. "Out of seventy-four wagons impressed at Winchester," he wrote to Governor Dinwiddie, "we got but ten after waiting a week." And there was worse: "some of those [were] so badly provided with teams [of horses] that the soldiers were obliged to assist them up the hills." Washington added that "it was known [the people of Winchester] had better teams at home." Not that Washington was self-righteous. He observed in a letter to the governor that he had fudged some legal niceties in his exercise of the impressment law, since, in Frederick County, he did not have any official authority. "I doubt not that in some points I may have strained the law," he wrote, "but I hope, as my sole motive was to expedite the march, I shall be supported in it, should my authority be questioned, which at present I do not apprehend, unless some busybody intermeddles."[13]

With far fewer wagons than he wanted—just a dozen—Washington left Winchester bound for Wills Creek on April 18. Winchester was ninety-seven miles from Alexandria, and Wills Creek another forty or so miles from Winchester. As for the Forks of the Ohio, it lay about 160 miles beyond Wills Creek.

Time was wasting. Washington had lost a whole week in Winchester engrossed in the frustrating attempt to impress a sufficient quantity of wagons. To make up for the delay, he decided to ride ahead of the column to select campsites and survey fords and crossings. As he crossed the Cacapon River, he was intercepted by an express rider with messages from Captain Trent. They all said essentially the same thing: eight hundred French soldiers were closing in on the Forks of the Ohio. Trent and his hundred men were expecting to be attacked at any hour. Reinforcements were needed—*now!*

Washington understood. But he also understood the ineluctable fact that the French were eight hundred strong, and he had just 159 men. Assuming he even reached the Ohio in time to reinforce Trent, who would reinforce *him?*

Washington found another messenger and forwarded Trent's communiqués to Colonel Fry, who was still gathering troops in Alexandria. Then he rode to the cabin of Job Pearsall on the South Branch of the Potomac, where he awaited the arrival of his command, which now seemed quite meager. After they reached him on April 20, he rode ahead again, calling at the trading post of Colonel Thomas Cresap in Old Town, Maryland. Just before he reached Cresap's he heard a report that the English fort at the Forks of the Ohio, as yet unfinished, had been captured by the French. He did not want to believe it. But he admitted to himself that it might well be true.

7

BATTLE IN A BOWER

An older, more experienced commander, possessed either of a philosophical turn of mind or simply the stock of common sense that accumulates with age and a knowledge of a half-century of North American warfare, would have conceded that the wilderness of western Pennsylvania was no place for an army. Open meadowlands, few and far between, were enclaves, rare oases in a vast desert of virgin forest that was beautiful to contemplate but impassable by supply wagons and wheeled artillery. The easiest means of transport was on the rivers, but these did not necessarily go where the army wanted to go, and they were fiendishly fickle, rising to flood in the rains—rains that turned solid earth to soup—and falling below a navigable level in drought. And then there was the matter of fighting. Armies were meant to fight on fields, arrayed in ranks and columns, as free to maneuver as the pieces on a chessboard. There were no military manuals for mud, mountains, and forest, uncongenial elements to the soldiers of the mid-eighteenth century.

These facts should have been discouraging enough, but there was worse: first, a rumor that the French had captured the English fort on the Ohio, the very objective Washington was supposed to reinforce. Then,

Washington noted in his diary on April 20 the rumor "was confirmed by Mr. *Wart* [Edward Ward], the Ensign of Captain *Trent,* who had been obliged to surrender to a Body of One Thousand *French* and upwards, under the Command of Captain [Claude Pierre Pécaudy, sieur de] *Contrecoeur,* who was come from *Venango* . . . with Sixty Battoes [*bateaux*], and Three Hundred Canoes, and who having planted eighteen Pieces of Cannon against the Fort, afterwards had sent him a Summons to depart." That was the bad news, but there was also a little good. According to Ensign Ward, "the *Indians* kept steadfastly attached to our Interest."[1]

After delivering his news, Ward pulled from his sodden coat two documents that had been placed in his charge and presented these to the lieutenant colonel. One was a formal summons from the French commander, charging that the Ohio Company's trespass into French domains betrayed a greater and greedier concern for trade than for maintaining "the union and harmony existing between the Crowns of Great Britain and France." The other was the transcription of a speech by the Half-King, who, of course, had been counting on the military presence of the fort at the Forks of the Ohio to keep at bay the numerous French-allied tribes that were longtime enemies of the Iroquois. Now that the fort had surrendered, the Half-King sent a speech of exhortation tempered by pleading. He called on the governors of Pennsylvania and Virginia to be of "good courage and come as soon as possible." He promised, "you will find us ready to fight as you are yourselves." But then he concluded on a note of high pathos: "If you do not come to our assistance now, we are entirely undone, and I think we shall never meet together again. I speak with a heart full of grief."[2]

On April 23, Washington held a "Council of War . . . in order to consult upon what must be done on Account of the News brought by Mr. *Wart.*" The facts, Washington noted, were these: Trent's garrison "consisted only of Thirty-three effective Men." Washington had 159. The French had more than a thousand, in addition to artillery. "It was thought a Thing impracticable to march towards the Fort without sufficient Strength"; nevertheless, the Indians—especially the Half-King—were asking for help, so it was decided "proper to advance as far as *Red-Stone-Creek,* on *Monaungahela,* about Thirty-seven Miles on this Side of the Fort, and their to raise a Fortification, clearing a Road broad enough to pass with all our Artillery and our Baggage, and there to wait for Fresh Orders."[3]

Awash in news of new disaster, Washington next wrote almost blithely to Maryland governor Horatio Sharpe on April 24 of the "glowing zeal I owe my country." Far from despairing at the loss of the fort, he expressed confidence that it would "rouse from the lethargy we have fallen into, the heroick spirit of every free-born Englishman to assert the rights and privileges of our king . . . and resque [rescue] from the invasions of a usurping enemy, our majesty's property, his dignity, and lands." As if suddenly cognizant of his youth and not wanting to seem to lecture the governor, Washington closed his letter with the hope that Sharpe would "excuse the freeness of my expressions" as the "pure sentiments of the breast" of a "most ob't and Very humble serv't."[4]

Even stopping short of the fort, there were many forest miles to cover, miles that had not merely to be traversed, but carved through, sometimes yard by yard, with the edge of an axe. At the end of the trail were the French, who outnumbered Washington nine to one. Yet the lieutenant colonel saw only reasons to advance. There were the interests of the Ohio Company, which, bound up with his future prospects for prosperity, were likewise *his* interests; there was his "glowing zeal" to serve king and country; and there was the even more pressing urgency of the Half-King's call for help.

For his part, the Half-King was truly anxious for British aid. As steward of the Iroquois frontier, he was highly vulnerable. Yet the Iroquois were always sophisticated and canny diplomats, and even though the French were allied with the Hurons, whose enmity with the Iroquois had been forged in the so-called Beaver Wars that spanned the seventeenth through early eighteenth centuries, the Half-King could probably have come to a comfortable understanding with the French, had he chosen to. Like Washington, however, he was moved by more than a single cause, including a personal agenda. On the frontier, diplomacy was important, but it went only so far. If he was ever inclined to negotiate with the French, the Half-King had only to remind himself that they had killed, boiled, and eaten his father. No explanation survives of how this unhappy event had come to pass, but the Half-King mentioned the outrage frequently and always pinned his hatred of the French on it.

Of course, there was also the more recent insult, of which Washington had learned back in November during the outward leg of his expedition to the French commandant. The Sieur de Marin had insulted the Half-King, dismissing him as a "child" who talked foolishly of possessing the land claimed by the French. Marin had sneered: "You say this land belongs to you, but there is not the black of my nails yours . . . If people will be ruled by me, they may expect kindness, but not else!"[5]

A father killed, boiled, and eaten was one thing. To be spurned, scolded, threatened, and dismissed as "child" was another altogether. Marin's affront had put the Half-King beyond compromise, and he was therefore more eager than ever to join forces with the English. Washington, woefully undermanned, was grateful for this, to be sure. He was glad that during that November 1753 meeting, he had proclaimed to the Half-King the great difference between English purposes and French, assuring him that the "only motive of our conduct is to put you again in possession of your lands, and to take care of your wives and children, to dispossess the French, to maintain your rights and to secure the whole country for you."[6]

Had the Half-King swallowed whole this self-effacing speech from a land-hungry stockholder in the Ohio Company? Washington was confident that he had, for now he wrote to Governor Dinwiddie that the sachem was firmly under his control. More than twice Washington's age, the Half-King doubtless had seen things differently in November and surely saw them differently now. He was pleased that *he* had succeeded in persuading the Virginian to help *him* fight the French. He later remarked to the colonial Indian agent and interpreter Conrad Weiser that Washington was "a good-natured man but had no experience."[7]

In short, the two allies simultaneously overestimated and underestimated one another. Washington assumed he held the Half-King in the palm of his hand, that he fully understood the Indian's motives and, not least of all, that the Half-King could muster the substantial Indian force Virginia and the Ohio Company needed to evict a thousand Frenchmen from their land. For his part, the Half-King assumed he could use the callow commander as a means of raising and manipulating the large English force *he* needed to evict the French. Neither man fully understood the other, and both hoped to gain more than either had to offer.

Washington's inexperience may have contributed to his optimistic zeal, but he was both more savvy and more prudent than the sachem gave him credit for. Washington believed that, in the Half-King and his warriors, he had a valuable weapon that he must use. He also understood that loyalty demanded action and that the failure to act would not only disappoint the Indians, but would permanently forfeit their support. Governor Dinwiddie had promised reinforcements, hundreds of men in all. At this moment, however, only a handful were reported—and that vaguely—within marching distance. To press an attack against perhaps a thousand French and Indians with the 159 men he presently commanded would be suicide. To do nothing, however, would lose what chance of Indian support he had. Therefore, Washington resolved to demonstrate boldness by advancing to Red Stone Creek, a position sufficiently forward to put him within striking distance of Fort Duquesne, yet far enough away from the fort to safely await the arrival of sufficient reinforcements to make an attack feasible. It was a reasonable plan, and Washington applied to it a competence far in excess of the Half-King's dismissive estimate of him. Trained and experienced as a surveyor, he had made meticulous observations of the rugged country lying between Wills Creek and the Forks of

the Ohio during his earlier treks between these points. He decided
that the place where the Red Stone Creek joined the Monongahela
River, thirty-seven miles above the Forks and Fort Duquesne (the name
the French gave to the captured English fort), was the best place to take
his small band and await the arrival of the others. True, Washington had
never seen this spot for himself, but he thought it all out. He knew that
the Ohio Company had built storehouses there, which could shelter
both ammunition and men. Because it was on the Monongahela, the
Red Stone Creek site could be used as a staging area from which to send
heavy supplies and artillery swiftly to positions prime for attacking
Fort Duquesne.

Washington immediately set about tackling the formidable problems
of getting the Red Stone Creek expedition under way. He had to prepare
his little band for a hard trip across the Chestnut Ridge, a formidable fold
of the Allegheny Mountains, steep, treacherous, and nearly three thousand feet high, lying directly across the proposed route. Through
Chestnut Ridge, his men would have to hack out a road passable by supply wagons and artillery. Had Washington sought advice from traders and
others personally familiar with the Ridge, he would have been told from
the start that the project was impossible. But Washington consulted no
one, not even Colonel Joshua Fry, who was still back east with his men at
Alexandria. Instead, Washington summarily dispatched riders with letters
to the governors of Virginia, Maryland, and Pennsylvania, telling them
where to send more troops and asking Governor Dinwiddie in particular
for a sufficient number of boats to ply the Monongahela. Washington also
persuaded an Indian youth who had accompanied Ensign Ward to return
to the Half-King with a speech he had written out: "This young man will
inform you where he found a small part of our army, making towards
you, clearing the roads for a great number of our warriors, who are ready
to follow us, with our great guns, our ammunition and provisions."
Washington requested that the Half-King meet the advancing force "on
the road . . . to assist us in council." With a flourish, he signed the speech

"Caunotaucarius," the Mingo name that the Half-King himself had bestowed on him the winter before, the name than meant Taker of Towns.[8]

The speech was carefully calculated to encourage and embolden. In it, Washington's small detachment became "part of our army," soldiers were promised in "great number," and guns were likewise characterized as "great." The picture was one of massive forces on the move. It is quite possible, even probable, that Washington himself believed all of this to be true, that massive reinforcements *would* be sent. After all, at twenty-two, he had the ear of no fewer than three governors, as well as the cooperation of the great Half-King. But it is also possible that Washington wrote the sachem neither more nor less than precisely what he knew the man wanted to hear. In either case, as Washington prepared to march, he could only hope for the best.

Almost immediately, however, that hope began to appear forlorn. The first of "our army" to report to Washington was a handful of men, perhaps forty, whom Captain Trent had enlisted, cavalierly promising them pay of 2 *s.* a day. The trouble was that Governor Dinwiddie had allocated to Washington a daily troop allowance of only 8 *p.* per soldier. Washington explained this to the new arrivals, who made no complaint at first, but who also refused to do any work. Announcing that he would not feed idlers, Washington ordered the volunteers to get to work alongside his own detachment to clear the road to Red Stone Creek. They agreed, provided they were paid what Trent had promised them. Washington was in a bind. If he consented to pay them 2 *s.* on the assumption that the governor would make good on the funds, then the rest of his troops, 8 *p.* men all, would be demoralized at best and angered to mutiny at worst. Nor, it seems, did Washington have the authority to make his work order stick. Trent had enlisted them as volunteers, and, therefore, they were not subject to the stricter provisions of the militia law. Washington could neither compel nor punish them. Worse, they were hardly gentlemen, but the roughest of wilderness sorts—odd jobbers, trader's helpers, freelance adventurers—restless denizens of the geographical frontier as well as the moral frontier that separates law from lawlessness.

Washington temporized, telling the men that he would settle the question of payment pending instructions from the governor, which Ensign Ward would bring back from Williamsburg. In the meantime, he ordered Trent to look after *his* men and to keep them separated from the other troops. Trent proved to have no more authority over this rabble than Washington, and the forty men soon scattered. While relieved to be rid of them, Washington also realized that he now had forty fewer hands to build his road, work on which began about April 25 and proceeded at a glacial pace. The man-narrow trail not only had to be widened to accommodate wagons and artillery, but cleared of trees and then of stumps, which were innumerable. At best, the column advanced four miles a day, but on many days the men were lucky to push two miles, and that, more often than not, through torrential, incessant rain. On May 7, having progressed about twenty miles from Wills Creek, the column was confronted by the upper stretch of Casselman's River. Normally a tame and shallow stream, the river had been transformed by the rains into a raging torrent, and Washington, anxious though he was to move forward, dared not attempt to ford it. For the next two days, he set his men to building a bridge strong enough to support heavy wagons and "great guns."

Once they had crossed Casselman's River, the expedition encountered a series of English traders, haggard and threadbare, trudging eastward from the Ohio. They spoke of fleeing from the French, and addressing Washington directly, advised him to turn around and do the same. More than one trader reported the arrival of some eight hundred French reinforcements in the vicinity of the Forks of the Ohio. Hearing the anxious murmurs of his own men in response, Washington assured them that, yes, he meant to lead them to meet the enemy, but that the traders told traders' tales, wildly exaggerating the numbers. He put more stock in the word of Robert Callender, a frontier entrepreneur who owned and operated at least three prosperous trading houses in these parts and who

encountered Washington's party on May 9. Callender reported that he
had seen just five Frenchmen at a trading settlement established by
Christopher Gist. That, Washington knew, was only a few miles distant.
And Callender had more news: the party he saw was led by Commissary
La Force.

Michel Pépin, the man called La Force, whom Washington had met at
Fort Le Boeuf, held the French colonial office of commissary of stores on
the upper Ohio. This made him a man of great influence and power,
especially among the Indians and frontiersmen who relied on the supplies
he alone regulated. When Callender spoke with one of the French party,
he was told that they were on the hunt for deserters. But both Callender
and Washington knew that a man as important as La Force, renowned as
an interpreter and frontier diplomat, would not be leading a routine
police patrol. Clearly, this was much more: an advance party reconnoitering for a general advance—an invasion.

Mired in mud, drenched with rain, laboring over every stump, and
assailed by the gloomy narratives of retreating English traders,
Washington's blood suddenly warmed at the prospect of closing with La
Force. He was cheered even more by the news that the Half-King had not
only received his speech, but had greeted it with great pleasure. Callender
reported that the sachem was marching with fifty warriors to meet
Washington, but the lieutenant colonel did not let this welcome news lull
him into complacency. He knew from firsthand experience that whenever
the French encountered Indians, they would instantly lavish gifts, liquor,
and a wealth of promises to wrest them from the camp of the English.
Washington decided to detach twenty-five of his precious small number
to intercept the Half-King and his warriors before the French found
them. In addition, this detachment, under Captain Adam Stephen, was to
look for any possible way to move supplies to Red Stone Creek via water
and, lastly, to keep eyes wide open for La Force. Intriguingly, Stephen
recorded in his diary that Washington had ordered him to *apprehend* La
Force and his party, whereas Washington himself recorded having ordered

Stephen to *withdraw* if he encountered the party and merely to report its whereabouts. Twenty-five to five were good enough odds for any army, and it doubtless would have been very hard for Captain Stephen to withdraw from such an encounter empty-handed. Washington must have known this, and we can only assume that if La Force were to be captured, the young lieutenant colonel wanted to make sure he could claim personal credit for it.

While awaiting the return of Captain Stephen, Washington pressed the rest of his men to push the road ahead. Although the mud remained unforgiving and the rain unceasing, dispatch riders now brought Washington encouraging news almost daily. Colonel Fry had finally arrived at Winchester, Virginia, with a hundred men and would presently begin the march to join Washington. North Carolina's governor sent a message with a pledge of 350 men, and Maryland's chief executive reluctantly agreed to dispatch two hundred. Pennsylvania could send no troops, but the governor promised £10,000 cash. Most gratifying to Dinwiddie, even the distant New England colonies now volunteered assistance. Massachusetts governor William Shirley resolved personally to lead six hundred troops into Canada, which would tie down many French soldiers who might otherwise be shipped to Fort Duquesne. "I hope," Washington confided to his journal, "that will give [the French] some work to do . . ."9 Unfortunately, Washington was insufficiently experienced to appreciate the gulf that separated the promises of politicians from their fulfillment. Few of the forces pledged would ever materialize.

If Washington lacked the political seasoning to look skeptically on the good news he received, he had no shortage of intimate acquaintance with wilderness travel and a keen appreciation for its daunting hardships. Or so he thought. On May 16, he encountered two more eastward-bound traders, who registered their shock that Washington would even think of trying to clear a road across Chestnut Ridge. They knew the ridge well, they said, and they assured him that it could never be crossed by wagons, let alone artillery. These were not the first to deliver a discouraging word, but they were the first, apparently, whose words resonated with the lieutenant colonel. He questioned the traders about the feasibility of a water route, and when he did not receive an absolutely negative reply, he resolved to order some canoes built so that he could personally explore the Youghiogheny River, which ran through Chestnut Ridge all the way to the Monongahela at Turtle Creek. Usually, this body of water was too shallow for canoes laden with heavy cargo, but the rains that had bedeviled the expedition had also swollen the unassuming Youghiogheny, making it deep enough, Washington hoped, for navigation.

With optimism rekindled, Washington was about to start work on the canoes when, on May 17, the indefatigable Ensign Ward returned from his errand to Williamsburg with a letter from Governor Dinwiddie. It reported the arrival in Virginia of an "independent company" from South Carolina and the anticipated arrival of two more such companies from New York. Washington needed the manpower, but he knew that these companies were commanded by regular British officers, who had nothing but contempt for "provincials" such as he. He remembered Lawrence's tales from Cartagena, where his British commanding officer would not even allow the Virginia troops to disembark from their ships. The prospect of the imminent arrival of the independent companies must have curdled whatever satisfaction Washington took in Dinwiddie's news that he had "laid Yr Letters before the Council, & We approv'd of the Caution You have taken in halting at red Stone Creek, 'till you have assembled a sufficient Body to secure Yr-Selves & Cannon &ca & then to proceed to Monongahela."[10] This now seemed unmistakably to mean that Dinwiddie was relieved that his youthful protégé planned to await the arrival of troops under the command of British regulars—mere captains, lieutenants, and ensigns—to whom Washington, a colonial lieutenant colonel no less, would be humiliatingly subordinate in any action against the French.

This was a blow harder than any stump, colder than any torrent of rain, and more discouraging than the gloom of frightened traders. And that wasn't the half of it. Dinwiddie did not mention it in his letter, but Ward gave Washington the news that the legislative committee regulating the pay of Washington and his officers and men had set a cap on regular compensation—12s. 6p. it would be—and had voted not to supply an allowance to officers to supplement their rations. As Washington had feared, the Burgesses intended that he and his officers should eat no more and no better than the lowliest private soldier. Washington also well knew that the officers and men of the independent companies would be receiving substantially higher pay, including a ration allowance.

These were the very issues over which Washington had earlier threatened to resign his commission. We can only assume that, as a good commander, he made some effort to keep this distressing news from leaking to his command, but either he did not try very hard or his efforts to prune the grapevine were miserably unsuccessful. Officers caught wind of the impending outrage, quit working on the road, and instead drafted a protest to Governor Dinwiddie, in which they threatened to resign *their* commissions upon the arrival of the higher-paid independent company officers.

Plagued by the elements, told that his chosen route was impassable, and anticipating an invasion, Washington now faced a crisis of command. His disaffected officers made no attempt to circumvent their commander, but properly observed the chain of command by presenting him with their letter for transmission to the governor. Washington could have condemned it as insubordinate and refused to accept it, but, he reasoned, his officers had the right to protest through channels. Moreover, he concurred in their grievances and, if anything, felt they had not gone far enough. The legislative committee in Williamsburg had imposed a tight limit on the number of noncommissioned officers, the cadre of managers most essential to the operation of any military force. Washington observed that the officers' protest made no mention of this.

To many men, the prospect of resigning might have looked most inviting at this point. But not to George Washington, and he was not long deciding how to handle the letter of protest. His later career would give full play to his genius for not merely surviving disaster, but for turning defeat into victory at best or, at the very least, enduring defeat while simultaneously denying outright victory to his adversary. A glimmer of this genius was evident now. He resolved to send the letter of protest, accompanied by a letter of his own, which would drive home his officers' grievances even as it asserted his own right to command, regardless of the regular army status of the approaching independent companies and their officers.

He began the letter of May 18 forthrightly: "I am heartily concerned, that the officers have such real cause to complain of the Committee's resolves; and still more to find my inclinations prone to second their just grievances." He continued, "nothing prevents their throwing down their commissions . . . but the approaching danger, which has too far engaged their honor to recede till other officers are sent in their room, or an alteration made regarding their pay." Thus Washington did what he would always do: maintain loyalty to his command, even against higher authority. Yet he did not place that loyalty above quite everything else. The next paragraph he devoted to himself:

> *Giving up my commission is quite contrary to my intention. Nay, I ask it as a greater favor, than any amongst the many I have received from your Honor, to confirm it to me. But let me serve voluntarily; then I will, with the greatest pleasure in life, devote my services to the expedition without any other reward, than the satisfaction of serving my country; but to be slaving dangerously for the shadow of pay, through woods, rocks, mountains,—I would rather prefer the great toil of a daily laborer . . . than serve upon such ignoble terms . . .*

After asking for the governor's reconfirmation of his rank and authority, he proposed to put his service on a voluntary footing rather than suffer the dishonor of accepting the "shadow of pay." He concluded the paragraph by elevating the situation beyond the merely personal: "for I really do not see why the lives of his Majesty's subjects in Virginia should be of less value, than of those in other parts of his American dominions; especially when it is well known, that we must undergo double their hardship." Before closing, he reiterated: "I find so many clogs upon the expedition, that I quite despair of success; nevertheless, I humbly beg it, as a particular favor, that your Honor will continue me in the post I now enjoy, the duty whereof I will most cheerfully execute as a volunteer, but by no means upon the present pay."[11]

Writing the letter to Governor Dinwiddie seems to have renewed Washington's energies. He was determined now to speed events along. He was willing to await reinforcement by the independent companies before beginning an all-out assault on Fort Duquesne, but he was clearly anxious to capture La Force and his party before the regulars could horn in. To ensure success, he decided to secure the immediate assistance of the Half-King and his party. To hasten their arrival, Washington sent an Indian messenger to meet them, but he deliberately withheld a message Dinwiddie had enclosed for delivery to the sachem. Never scrupling in the manipulation of his Indian allies, Washington reasoned that curiosity would spur the Half-King's progress, so he told the messenger to inform his chief that he had at headquarters a speech the governor intended for his ears. With the messenger en route, Washington boarded a canoe on May 20 with a lieutenant, three soldiers, and an Indian guide to explore the Youghiogheny River. In the meantime, since the rains had subsided, he ordered his main body to continue clearing an overland road toward Red Stone Creek. No longer willing to trust to his optimistic impulses, Washington did not want his men to wait idly in the hope that the Youghiogheny would indeed prove navigable.

Less than half a mile downstream, Washington's group encountered a trader who engaged them in conversation. He told Washington that he knew the Youghiogheny well and that there was no point in going farther. It was by no means consistently navigable. Less heedless than he had been when he first received his commission, Washington decided to suspend the canoe-building project for now, but to continue downriver nevertheless. Perhaps the river could not be navigated all the way, but it still might prove an easier route than hacking a road through an even more doubtful wilderness. The little party pressed on, and when the water became too shallow, they built a raft to carry themselves and the canoe, and when it became too shallow even for a raft, they waded.

By alternating among canoe, raft, and wading, they traveled about ten miles before encountering a fresh problem. The Indian guide suddenly rose to announce that he would go no farther. Washington responded not with anger, but with an offer of presents, which he knew to be the sovereign lubricant in white-Indian relations. After much dickering, the guide agreed to continue in return for a fancy ruffled shirt and, incongruously enough, a homely match coat. With the bargain struck, the party made camp for the night, Washington concluding hopefully that, as long as the river became no shallower, it would provide canoe passage at least most of the way to the wide and deep Monongahela. Come morning, therefore, they launched the canoe with fresh enthusiasm. Along the way, Washington noticed that the water began to run more swiftly and yet more swiftly, until, as he recorded, "we came to a fall, which continued rough, rocky and scarcely passable, for two miles, and then fell, within the space of fifty yards, nearly forty feet perpendicular."[12] With that ended the notion of using the Youghiogheny to reach the Monongahela. Artillery was not meant to shoot the rapids or survive the falls.

Yet another failure and disappointment. It was time to rest and then return. By May 23, Washington and his party were where they had started, at the Great Crossing of the Youghiogheny. Waiting for them there were Captain Adam Stephen and the detachment of twenty-five men who had been on the scout for the past two weeks. Washington brightened. Perhaps Stephen had news of La Force.

The captain reported that they had reached the Monongahela near Red Stone Creek. There they had encountered a group of Indian traders, who told them that "some" French troops commanded by an officer calling himself Jumonville had been afoot along the Monongahela, but that the miserable weather had driven them back to Fort Duquesne. Doubtless, the vagueness of this intelligence dismayed Washington, but Stephen had more. He promised one of the traders the very substantial sum of £5 if he would trek back down to the Monongahela and spend a few days spying on the French in their fort. Less than a week later, the man returned chock-full of information, which came in a flood, according to Captain Stephen, including an "account of everything at Fort Duquesne, the number of French at that post, the number employed daily on the works [fortifications], the number sick in the hospital and what accidents had happened since their arrival at that place, the dimensions of the fort, the breadth and depth of the ditch [the moat surrounding the fort], the thickness of the ramparts, in what places it was stockaded with only the length of the stockades."[13]

A bargain at £5, the intelligence seemed too good to be true, so remarkable was its detail. In fact, both Stephen and Washington decided it was rather *too* remarkable. The only way to secure such intelligence would have been for the trader to tell the French exactly what he was about. The two officers concluded that they had a double agent on their hands, and if that indeed were the case, the hunters had become the hunted. The spy would have alerted the French to the location and number of the reconnoitering party, and that is why the captain had led his men back to the Great Crossing and what he thought would be the safety of greater numbers. So there it was, the sum total of Washington's efforts at a grand reconnaissance: he had found no quick way to a field from which Fort Duquesne could be attacked, and the only intelligence he had secured bore the strong suspicion of treachery from a double agent. With Captain Stephen and his command in tow, Washington and his small party left Great Crossing, marched over Laurel Hill, and on May 24 located the main body of troops, who, the road being as bad as it was, had made little progress toward Red Stone Creek.

The troops did have one piece of tantalizing, if obscure, information for their commander. It was a message from the Half-King, transcribed by Washington's Indian interpreter, John Davison. Much as Washington was forced to labor through the broken English of his interpreter of French, the Dutchman van Braam, so he had to plow through the semi-literate writing of his interpreter of Indian tongues:

> *To the forist, His Majesties Commander Offiverses to hom*
> *this meay concern:*
> *On acc't of a freench armey to meat Miger Georg*
> *Wassiontton therefore my Bortheres I deesir you to be awar*
> *of them for deisin'd to strik ye forist English they see ten days*
> *since they marchd I cannot tell what nomber the half-King*
> *and the rest of the Chiefs will be with you in five days to*
> *consel, no more at present but give my serves to my Brothers*
> *the English.*[14]

Washington interpreted this to mean that the French were advancing in unspecified number ("I cannot tell what nomber") and that the Half-King was on his way to council. Pressing an Indian messenger further, Washington was told that about half the French garrison had departed Fort Duquesne on a secret mission of some sort. Later on the twenty-fourth, an Indian trader fresh from Christopher Gist's settlement reported having seen two Frenchmen there the day before. Based on this sighting, the trader concluded that a strong French force was on the march.

An attack now seemed imminent. No reinforcements had arrived, and it appeared certain that Washington would be greatly outnumbered. And yet, after toiling through rain, mud, and the vagaries of colonial government, the prospect of even a desperate one-sided battle was intensely exciting to Washington. Immediately, he looked for ground on Great Meadows, their present location, favorable to a strong defensive position. He soon identified a pair of gullies that ran parallel to one another. Though shallow, they seemed to the inexperienced commander a kind of minor miracle: natural trenches, ready-made. He ordered his men to deploy within the gullies, and he positioned his wagons between them, forming a defensive square. In this way, Washington and his men passed the night of May 24.

When the morning of the twenty-fifth brought no attack, Washington grew impatient. Commandeering the wagon horses, he sent men riding bareback in search of the French. He also detached smaller foot parties to probe the woods. Apparently, Washington did not think it necessary to improve upon the "trenches" nature had provided, because he put the rest of his troops to work not digging deeper ditches, but clearing away brush and undergrowth around his camp. It did not occur to him that this would expose his position to enemy fire; on the contrary, he believed that he was clearing unobstructed fields of fire, the better to cut down any attackers. In a letter to Governor Dinwiddie, he crowed that he was now in possession of a "charming field for an encounter."[15]

But the encounter never came. One by one, Washington's scouting parties returned to report absolutely nothing at all. Thus the twenty-fifth passed without event, as did the twenty-sixth. At two o'clock on the morning of the twenty-seventh, a sentry woke the camp with a shot. Washington mustered all his men, only to discover that a half-dozen had gone missing and were presumed to have deserted. Still, Washington posted a strong guard until well after sunrise, when Christopher Gist rode into camp.

He had a story to tell.

At noon the day before, fifty French soldiers had entered his settlement while he was out. The two Indians charged with looking after things in his absence reported that Commissary La Force was at the head of this band and, in a most surly manner, had threatened to kill Gist's cow and destroy his property. When the Indians begged him not to do so, La Force relented, and angrily rode on. As soon as Gist learned what had happened, he rode off to warn Washington. He told the lieutenant colonel that, while riding to his camp, he picked up the tracks of many white men. Presumably these had been made by La Force and his party, and they were just five miles outside Washington's present position. There was more: Gist had learned that the French canoes were at Red Stone Creek. The significance of this was wonderfully clear to Washington. La Force and fifty men were far from their landing place, but very close to him. Isolated, they were ripe for attack.

Washington summoned Captain Peter Hog and ordered him to take a detachment of seventy-five men to locate the French force. In his later career as commanding general of the Continental Army, George Washington would more than once reveal himself to be less than a master of tactics. He did so now, committing the cardinal sin of dividing his army in the face of the enemy. Perhaps he assumed that Gist's estimate of the size of the French party, fifty men, was exaggerated. Perhaps he was fearful of leaving undefended and thereby losing a makeshift headquarters so conveniently furnished by nature with parallel trenches. Perhaps he figured that Hog, encountering the French, would drive them back upon his position and that he and Hog could thereby trap them in the jaws of a pincer. Perhaps, reasoning that seventy-five men could move more swiftly through the woods than twice that number, he was fearful of losing his chance to overtake and engage La Force. We don't know. Washington left no record of the rationale behind his tactical decision. Nor did he explain why he had sent Hog to apprehend La Force rather than going after him personally. We do know that Washington sat down almost immediately to dash off a letter to Dinwiddie, who was now at Winchester, giving him an account of the past few days and nights, informing him that Captain Hog was in pursuit of La Force and his detachment, and then devoting most of the rest of the letter to a request for goods to be distributed in payment to the Indians. On the verge of his maiden battle, when one would assume the commander's thoughts would be focused on combat, Washington plaintively wrote: "I have been oblig'd to pay Shirts for what they [the Indians] have already done which I cannot continue to do." Adding a brief closing paragraph and a postscript hoping "your Honr will excuse the Haste with which I was oblig'd to use in writing this," Washington gave the letter to Gist to carry to Winchester.[16]

After Gist rode off, the rain returned and dense clouds made a moonless night even darker. About nine that night, an Indian runner known to history only as Silverheels arrived with a message from the Half-King. That worthy announced himself to be six miles from Washington's camp and, at this location, reported having seen the footprints of two Frenchmen.

The message was thrilling in its effect on Washington. Of the eighty or so men remaining in camp, he chose forty to set off with him through the rainy night for the camp of his comrade the sachem. He was determined not to let La Force elude him. It was, however, no easy matter to move through a forest on a moonless night with sheets of rain descending like curtains. The men felt their way over a trail that, even in daylight, was barely distinguishable from the mud and brush all round. The going was slow, as the party frequently lost the trail and had to double back to regain it. Dawn was breaking by the time Washington sighted the makeshift shelter of the Half-King.

We don't know what the Half-King looked like. By modern standards, he must have appeared much older than his years. Perhaps he already showed signs of the illness that would kill him before the onset of winter. Washington's tall, youthful vigor surely made a striking contrast. Nevertheless, the young man respected the old chief as a figure of dignity and importance, although he must have been dismayed that only Monacatoocha (the Oneida chief he had met earlier), a pair of armed warriors, and two boys carrying muskets accompanied the old sachem, along with six or seven other Indians, all unarmed. Washington had been told to expect a fully equipped force of fifty. However, if he was disappointed, he concealed it. Despite having marched all night, he entered into an immediate council of war with the chief and his seconds. This time, the customary long speeches were abridged. Washington straightforwardly proposed that the Half-King and his warriors join him and his men in attacking La Force and his party, and with neither preamble nor hesitation, the Half-King agreed, leading Washington and others to the spot where he had seen the footprints. From here, the Half-King sent two Indians to follow the trail, locate the French camp, and report back. The others, soundless, without passing a word of conversation, waited in the woods.

The two scouts returned more quickly than anyone had anticipated. They reported a secluded bower nestled among rocks just a half-mile off the trail. In and around this the Frenchmen were camped.

On the moist black earth, the Half-King and Washington scratched out a plan of attack. The bower was well concealed, but concealment was not cover. Listening to the scouts, both men understood that they could surround the French position and attack from all sides.

Based on the scouts' report, the situation seemed ideal, but even in the simplest of battles, reality is rarely as clean as the plan that precedes it. As he neared the bower, Washington saw that the approach of his left flank would be amply sheltered, but that the right would be exposed before the left and right could complete the encirclement of their objective. Washington ordered Captain Stephen to assume command of the left flank while he took the more dangerous right. To Stephen's left were the Indians. With the deployment settled, the attackers crept closer to the bower. Between seven and eight a.m., the disposition of troops, with infinite stealth, was completed. In formation now, the attackers advanced, still in a creeping crouch.

At about a hundred yards from the French bower, they stopped. This distance was not selected arbitrarily. For one thing, to move closer would bring the right flank clearly into the open. Even more important, one hundred yards was the maximum effective range of the "Brown Bess" muskets most soldiers carried in the mid-eighteenth century. At the time of the French and Indian War, these were very long weapons, the barrel alone measuring nearly four feet (those used two decades later in the Revolution were several inches shorter), and heavy: about fourteen pounds without a bayonet. Washington appreciated that, having lugged this awkward weapon through rugged, rain-soaked forest miles, his men would be understandably anxious to start shooting. Now came the test of an officer's nerve. Ideally, the command to fire should not be given at greater than fifty yards from the objective. The idea was actually to take, not to give, the first fire. A well-disciplined infantry unit stood its initial losses in order to put its own volley at such close range that most shots found their mark. For it was crucial that each shot be made to count, especially when fairly small numbers of men were engaged. As previously mentioned, in a classic European-style battle of the period, three parallel ranks of soldiers would be deployed against the enemy. The front rank would fire a simultaneous volley and either kneel to reload or, in a precisely drilled maneuver, break right and left and march to the rear, becoming the new third rank, where they would reload while what had been the second rank, and was now the first, let fly. These troops would then kneel or move to reload while the third rank fired, by which time the original first rank would be ready to fire again. And so it would go, the idea being to maintain a constant series of volleys, at least one volley every fifteen seconds. Since in this kind of battle, both sides consisted of close formations of troops, accuracy of fire was far less important than speed. Shoot anywhere into a mass of people, and you were likely to hit someone. However, in the backwoods of Pennsylvania and with no more than forty men, Washington was not mounting a great formal attack, but a surprise pounce. Accuracy of aim *did* count, which meant getting close and exposing oneself to enemy fire. Yet speed couldn't be sacrificed, either. A

soldier was most vulnerable while reloading, and reloading a muzzle
loader like the Brown Bess was a complicated, time-consuming procedure. To reload after firing, the shooter had to draw the musket's hammer,
or cock, halfway back, withdraw a paper cartridge from the pouch he carried, bite off the top of the cartridge, shake some of the powder into the
priming pan of the musket, shut the pan, position the musket barrel up,
put the cartridge into the muzzle, shake out the rest of the powder into
the barrel, take a ball from his bullet pouch, insert the ball into the muzzle, withdraw the iron ramrod from its holder under the barrel, insert it
into the barrel, tamp down the ball and powder, return the rammer to its
holder, fully cock the weapon, aim, and, at long last, fire—then immediately repeat the entire procedure so that he could fire again. In all, twelve
distinct motions were prescribed in the manual of arms Washington used,
which meant that a good soldier could fire five rounds in the time it took
a mediocre shooter to get off two. It was in every man's interest to be—or
to become—a good soldier.

Washington looked to his right and then to his left. When he was certain that all weapons were ready and everyone was in position to continue
the advance, he rose to his full height, drew his sword, stepped into the
clearing, and gave the command clearly. If he followed the European cus-
tom to which he would adhere years later during the Revolution, it was
this: *The army will advance!* Then, at about fifty yards: *Fire at will!*

Those Frenchmen who loitered outside their bower now ran back to
fetch their muskets. Firing commenced, but later, no one remembered
which side fired first. A few men fell, including, among the Virginians,
Lieutenant Thomas Waggener, wounded at Washington's side. The caliber
of a musket of the period was 0.75, three-quarters of an inch. A lead ball
of this size weighed a bit more than an ounce. The ball was capable of
inflicting a wound at three hundred yards, although the weapons were so
inaccurate that no responsible commander would allow his soldiers to
shoot from such a distance. At fifty yards, the ideal range, a three-quarter
inch, one-ounce ball had more than sufficient muzzle velocity to tear a

large hole in a man. At this range, there was often an entrance wound as well as an exit wound. The entrance injury was little larger than the diameter of the ball. The site of the exit might be three or four inches across. When a modern bullet enters its target, the impact causes it to expand. A lead ball does not expand, but the tissue, shattered bone, and even the densely packed air the ball pushes before it create a jagged, irregular exit wound that is particularly hard to dress and especially prone to infection.

Presently another Virginian, unnamed, fell dead, and two or three more sustained wounds. All of the Virginia casualties were on the exposed right wing. Of the French, several went down; ten would die instantly, and the wounded, save one, would soon join them. Washington drank it all in with mounting exhilaration. It was not blood lust, but something else, which he tried to describe to his brother, John Augustine, in a letter dispatched from Great Meadows on May 31: "I fortunately escaped without a wound, tho' the right Wing where I stood was exposed to & received all the Enemy's fire and was the part where the man was killed & the rest wounded. I can with truth assure you, I heard Bulletts whistle and believe me there was something charming in the sound."[17]

Washington and Captain Stephen pressed the attack, Stephen approaching close enough to capture an officer. Now the French began to give ground. Some broke and ran, only to be summoned back by their commander. They returned meekly, hands in the air. A casual observer might have marveled at their obedience. Washington, however, understood that the men had seen the Indians. On the extreme left of the attack, the Indians had completed the encirclement and closed on the enemy from the rear. It was a fate far preferable to surrender to the Virginians than to run into the arms of the Half-King's warriors. As for the French wounded, who could neither run nor raise their hands in surrender, half a dozen Indians descended upon them, hatchets or clubs upraised, hatchets or clubs coming down, splitting bone, crushing skulls, bringing death. This was followed by a grasp of the dead man's forelock, a sharp upward tug, the flash of a freshly honed scalping knife drawn back in a single deep gash across the broad front of the head, and another, more forceful tug to pop out a bloody scalp lock, still rooted in the flesh of the severed crown.

Washington let the Half-King's warriors have their way with the wounded. For one thing, he understood that this was how Indians fought and, he believed, the way they had to be allowed to fight. For another, far from medical aid and in an age innocent of antisepsis and therefore powerless against infection, wounds generally brought death, more or less agonizing, sooner or later. Finally, Washington had no desire to be burdened with the care of the enemy's wounded, not out here, with miles between him and his Great Meadows camp and even more miles between that camp and Winchester, the nearest sizable town. He could not afford to sacrifice mobility.

After disposing of the wounded, the Half-King demanded the same bloody vengeance on the unhurt prisoners, all twenty-one of them, including none other than Commissary La Force. To this, Washington said no and, at length, the sachem sullenly yielded to his ally. Of the thirty-three French engaged at the battle in the bower, twenty-one survived unwounded to be taken prisoner; one wounded man, somehow overlooked, escaped death at the hands of the Indians, and one soldier, a man named Mouceau, escaped altogether and returned to Fort Duquesne, there to tell the tale.

George Washington's maiden battle had consumed no more than a quarter hour. Among the Virginians losses had been minimal: one killed, two or three wounded. For the French, defeat was total. The commander of the force, Joseph Coulon, Sieur de Jumonville, had been killed—the Half-King claimed credit—and the wily La Force had been captured. For Washington it was, on the face of it, a complete triumph.

On the face of it.

As Washington started his prisoners on the march back to his camp at Great Meadows, the officers among them began to protest. They were, they said, attendants upon the slain Jumonville, an ambassador of the

French crown, who was in this Ohio country to serve notice on the
English interlopers that they were trespassers on the domain of Louis XV.
By the laws of civilized nations, they demanded to be treated not as prisoners of war but as ambassadors and thus returned, under suitable escort,
to French control at Fort Duquesne.

It is not known what reply, if any, Washington made at this time, but
it is likely that he told them what he later told Dinwiddie and others.
Ambassadors do not travel with large armed contingents, nor do they
skulk secretly through the wilderness, holing up in isolated bowers.
Ambassadors travel openly and with few attendants. Had Jumonville
passed through English country in this manner, he would have been
granted safe passage. This, or words to this effect, expressed Washington's
position from the end of the battle through the French accusations of
murder that were to follow. But if the lieutenant colonel hoped to bolster
his case with incriminating evidence found among the documents recovered from the person of Jumonville, he should have been sorely
disappointed. Chief among these was an official summons, or *sommation*,
signed by Contrecoeur, commandant of Fort Duquesne, dated May 23,
1754, and addressed to the "commandant of the English troops on the
lands of the King of France." It was an order to withdraw from the Ohio
country or suffer eviction by force of arms, despite the desire of France to
preserve peace between the crowns of the two nations. This was fully consistent with the captured officers' assertion that they were an embassy, as
was a second document belonging to Jumonville. It was a set of orders,
also signed by Contrecoeur, specifying the names of officers, twenty-eight
men, and one English interpreter to constitute an expedition charged
with locating the road that connected with the road newly opened by the
English. The expedition was directed to traverse this road in order to
investigate an Indian claim that the English were making preparations to
attack the French, despite the state of peace that existed between the kings
of France and England. The orders stipulated that, should Jumonville discover hostile intentions, he was to serve the English commander with the

sommation, await a reply, and return with it to Fort Duquesne.[18]

Objectively viewed, the sommation and the orders that accompanied it do suggest that both Contrecoeur and Jumonville thought of the expedition as an embassy. Looking at these papers, however, Washington asserted that they were neither more nor less than a ruse, cover for a mission of espionage. "In strict justice," Washington wrote to Dinwiddie on May 29, "they ought to be hanged as spies of the worst sort." Their objective, he said, had been to pose as an embassy, gain admission to English headquarters, ascertain the disposition of troops, then return to Fort Duquesne with the information.[19]

George Washington was anxious that no taint of dishonor attach to this, his first battle and his first victory. Historians would identify the skirmish as the first battle of the French and Indian War, itself the overture to and New World theater of the titanic and ruinous Seven Years' War, which consumed Europe as well as the Asian and oceanic colonies of Europe. Washington had no intention of starting a war. He believed the French had struck the first blow by taking the fort at the Forks of the Ohio and that, therefore, a war was already under way. His conscience was in all probability clear. But another thought surely now loomed, perhaps for the first time. Up to the moment of victory, glorious battle had wholly occupied Washington, single-mindedly shaping his will to overcome the myriad problems of weather, terrain, discontented soldiers, and the opacities of colonial government. Now there was another awareness dawning. This victory against thirty-three Frenchmen huddled in a bower would not go unanswered. What George Washington had no way of knowing was just how personal that answer was to be.

"A CHARMING FIELD FOR AN ENCOUNTER"

After the battle in the bower, Washington withdrew to Great Meadows, to the spot he had called on May 25 "a charming field for an encounter." On that day—it must have seemed long ago, although it was just the day before yesterday—he had seen no need for digging trenches or otherwise improving on what he had judged perfectly adequate terrain for defense. Now, however, the parallel gullies that had struck Washington as natural trenches—cover and concealment ready-made—did not seem quite so deep or nearly as secure.

Now, Jumonville was dead, killed by the Half-King in an ambush led by George Washington. The two documents recovered from his corpse supported—certainly did not contradict—the protests of the Frenchmen that they were ambassadors of Louis XV, on an embassy to warn the English to vacate the Ohio country and ascertain English intentions. One of the documents specified that if the English remained east of the "Great Mountain," they were not to be disturbed. The document went on to instruct Jumonville to treat all Indians encountered as friends.

Washington was not disturbed by the documents. As far as he was concerned Jumonville and his men were spies. To bolster this interpretation, Washington pointed out that an expedition of forty men constituted too large an entourage for an embassy and that, if they really were on a diplomatic mission, why would they take pains to skulk in a secluded bower? Moreover, Washington believed that the French party had actually been two miles closer to his camp than when they were discovered. This, he was sure, meant that they had seen him and his men and had purposely withdrawn, but probably not before sending two runners back to Contrecoeur to report on Washington's location and strength. The lieutenant colonel had no proof of this, but he believed it to be true, and he reported it to Dinwiddie.

With the objectivity that historical distance provides, Washington's interpretation not only seems highly questionable, but also smacks of pure rationalization. The official French view of the skirmish paints a much uglier picture. Captain Contrecoeur reported to Governor Duquesne on June 2, 1754, that the English under Washington surprised the Jumonville party and opened fire on it. Jumonville signaled that he had a message to deliver, whereupon the English ceased fire and closed in on Jumonville. He read the *sommation* through once, aloud then began reading it a second time when he was summarily shot—dead. Yet we must also recognize that the presumed objectivity of historical distance is itself illusory. Whatever Washington did—or permitted the Half-King to do— was done in the context of what both Washington and Dinwiddie viewed as a French act of war: the seizure of an English fort at the Forks of the Ohio. The Half-King certainly believed he and his English allies were already at war with the French. As Washington wrote to Dinwiddie on May 29, "The Sense of the Half King . . . is . . . that [the French] have bad Hearts, and that this [claim of being ambassadors] is a mere pretence, they never designed to have come to us but in a hostile manner." More important, Washington noted to Dinwiddie, had he failed to attack, had "we [been] so foolish to let them go," the Half-King, by his own vow, "never would assist us in taking another of them." And in all of this,

Washington assured his patron, there was a genuine prize: the wily Commissary La Force. To have lost him, "I really think wd tend more to our disservice than 50 other Men, as he is a person whose active Spirit, leads him into all parlys [parleys—diplomatic councils with Indians], and brought him acquainted with all parts, add to this a perfect use of the Indian Tongue, and g[rea]t influence with the Indian."

On the morning of May 29, Washington was told that the French wanted to speak with him. He agreed. They asked "me in what Manner I looked upon them, whether as the Attendants of an Embassador, or as Prisoners of War: I answered them it was in Quality of the Latter."[1] On the next day, Washington sent his prisoners, under a guard of two officers and twenty men, to Winchester, to which Governor Dinwiddie had already repaired. "Monsiur La-Force, and Monsieur Druillong [Ensign Pierre Jacques Drouillon (Druillon), Sieur de Macé] beg to be recommended to your Honour's Notice," Washington wrote in one of three letters of May, "and I have promis'd they will meet with all the favour that's due to Imprison'd Officer's: I have shew'd all the respect I cou'd to them here, and have given some necessary cloathing by which I have disfurnish'd myself, for having brought no more than two or three Shirts from Wills C[ree]k that we might be light I was ill provided to furnish them."[2] One need look no further for proof that Washington's attack had possessed the perfect element of surprise than the fact that it caught the French officers wearing very little clothing.

Later this very day, he wrote another letter to Governor Dinwiddie to "recommend to your Honour's particular Notice" the officers he "had the Honour of taking." He repeated essentially what he had already written earlier in the day: "I have assur'd them they will meet with all the Respect and favour due to their Charactr and Personal merit: and I hope they will do me the justice to acquaint your Honour that I neglected no mean's that was in my power to render their confinement here easy." Clearly, the lieutenant colonel was at pains to ensure that he could not be accused of mistreating his captives, even if he regarded them as prisoners of war and not as ambassadors. Yet, after he wrote and sealed this second letter to Dinwiddie, he penned a third—again on May 29—in which he explained that

> *Since writing the other [letter], I have still stronger presumptions, indeed almost confirmation that they were sent as Spyes, and were order'd to wait near us till they were truly informd of our Intention's, situation, strength, &ca and were to have acquainted the Commander therewith and laid lurking near for Reinforcements before they served the Summon's . . . . I doubt not but they will endeavour to amuse your Honour with many smooth Story's as they did me but were confuted in them all and by circumstances too plain to be denied almost made asham'd of their assertions—I dare say your Honour will treat them with respect which is due to all unfortunate Person in their Condition But I hope give no Ear to What they will have an opportunity of displaying to the best advantage having none by to contradict their reports.*[3]

Having sent Dinwiddie a letter asking him to receive the prisoners as honorable officers, Washington sent another, calling them lowdown spies, who would surely attempt to besmirch his honor with "smooth Story's" about the battle in the bower. Washington tried to preempt these by furnishing the most damaging of them to the governor: "I have heard since they went away that they shd say they calld to us not to Fire, but that I know to be False for I was the first Man that approach'd them & the first whom they saw, and imediately upon it ran to their Arms and Fir'd briskly till they were defeated." He ended this letter by assuring Dinwiddie that these men who ask "the Priviledges due to an Embassy" should "in strict Justice . . . be hang'd for Spyes of the worst sort being authorizd by their Comr at the expence of a Character which shd be Sacred to all Nations and trifled with or used in an Equivocal way."[4]

In this rapid-fire series of three letters we may read something of Washington's growing anxiety. In the first flush of a first victory, his pride had been unalloyed. Then, increasingly, the honor of that triumph appeared in danger of being stained. Perhaps Washington's anxiety was nothing more or less than fear of false accusation. Yet, in reading this series of letters, it is difficult to avoid seeing the thought process of a man trying to persuade *himself*—not just his governor and patron—that he had acted honorably. A commander must act with absolute decisiveness, and yet the business of command, in all its consequences, is often rife with an ambiguity that spawns indecision. Young Lieutenant Colonel Washington wanted to learn the military art, but this lesson in military leadership's gray area, a region of disturbing moral compromise, was entirely unanticipated.

Whatever ambivalence he felt in the course of the day, Washington's first letter of May 29 had reported to the governor the particulars of the battle in the bower with considerable pride, pointing out that "we had only one Man killd, and two or three wounded." He assured Dinwiddie that the Half-King, heartened by combat, was now a firm ally and that he "has declar'd to send" the scalps of the Frenchmen just slain in battle, along with a hatchet, "to all the Nations of Indian's in union with" the Iroquois as a call to arms. He "promis'd me to send down the River for all the Mingo's & Shawnesse to our camp, where I expect him to Morrow with 30 or 40 Men."[5]

All of this seemed quite hopeful. Indian warriors and Indian sachems, Washington knew, liked to talk—and talk and talk—but what they most respected was bold action that achieved tangible results. The battle in the bower had been just that, and after all the talk it was the action that would pay off by once and for all cementing the elusive alliance between the influential Half-King—with all the warriors from several tribes willing to follow him—and the English.

Yet Washington continued to Dinwiddie: "I shall expect every hour to be attackd and by unequal number's, which I must withstand if there is 5 to 1 or else I fear the Consequence will be we shall lose the Indians if we suffer ourselves to be drove Back."[6]

Outnumbered five-to-one and still expecting victory? This could not have been very reassuring to the governor. Perhaps anticipating this, Washington noted that he had "dispatchd an express immediately to Colo. Fry . . . desiring him to send me Reinforcements with all imaginable dispatch." And he added a further assurance: "Your Honour may depend I will not be surprizd, let them come what hour they will," only to step back from it with "and this is as much as I can promise—but my best endeavour's shall not be wanting to deserve more." Finally, yet another backward step: "I doubt not but if you hear I am beaten, but you will at the same hear that we have done our duty fighting as long [as] there was a possibility of hope."[7]

In the course of a few paragraphs and sentences, George Washington had journeyed from pride in victory, to doubt, to the probability of defeat tempered by "a possibility of hope." It was a trek far more harrowing than the physical journey from Williamsburg to the Ohio frontier. Yet the young commander did not let it paralyze him. The express he sent to Colonel Joshua Fry was admirably clear and calm but appropriately urgent: "If there does not come a sufficient Reinforcement we must either quit our g[roun]d & retn to you or fight very unequal Number's which I will do before I will give up one Inch of what we have gaind—The great haste I am in to dispatch the bearer prevents me from being particular at this time . . ."[8]

He also set his men to work digging entrenchments and what he described in a letter to John Augustine Washington, written on May 31, as "a Pallisado'd Fort."[9] On one level, building a fort was a good way for Washington to hold his little band together—which, at the moment, consisted of just over a hundred men, since he had sent thirty off as an escort for the Half-King and another twenty-two as a prisoner-of-war guard. Washington had sufficient common sense as a leader to know that idle men are subject to all manner of disorderly conduct, ranging from apathy to melancholy to panic. Building a fort would give them something to do. More importantly, however, for a vastly outnumbered body of men desperately awaiting reinforcement, a fort was a necessity, and that is precisely what Washington called it: Fort Necessity.

The description "Pallisado'd Fort" makes Fort Necessity sound a lot grander than it was. Reading further in his letter to John Augustine Washington, we discover that the fort was under construction as of May 31 and that the lieutenant colonel hoped it would "be finished today." Considering that construction probably was not begun before May 29, the result of a three-day building project could hardly have been very impressive. In fact, Fort Necessity was not completed until June 3, but those three extra days did not yield a marvel of military architecture. The Half-King almost certainly delivered an adequate assessment when he dismissed the fort as "that little thing upon the Meadow."[10]

But Fort Necessity would be the scene of the second battle of the French and Indian War, the site of George Washington's first gallant—if ill-advised—stand, and the site of his first defeat. Here, in the space of a single battle, he gained lessons in leadership and military reality that would serve him a lifetime. For these reasons, the site of Fort Necessity is preserved today as a National Battlefield, and the fort itself has been reconstructed in the twentieth century—not once, but twice.[11]

It is one thing to unearth and restore a great stone monument from the past—a pyramid, a sphinx, a stately Greek temple, a stout Roman fortress—for these were built to endure through the ages. In contrast, what Washington and his men hacked out of the forest and scratched into the moist soil of Great Meadows was intended to last just long enough for help to arrive. Most structures tossed up along the American eighteenth-century frontier were ephemeral, and Fort Necessity was more ephemeral than most. Its location, about eleven miles east of Uniontown, Pennsylvania, on U.S. Highway 40, has long been known, marked by low ridges and shallow depressions—the depressions believed to mark the perimeter of the "pallisado," or stockade wall. The ridges that remained did not form a complete enclosure, so it was assumed that some of the ridges had washed away in floods over the years. Throughout much of the nineteenth century, experts and amateurs alike debated whether Fort Necessity had been a triangle or a diamond in shape. An archaeological investigation undertaken in 1901 determined that the ridges formed a diamond, and when the site was established in 1931 as a National Battlefield, archaeologists accepted the diamond as the basic shape of the fort and began digging. They unearthed fragments of stockade posts, the location of which in relation to the depressions and ridges seemed to lend credence to the theory that the fort had been diamond shaped. In 1932, therefore, the fort was reconstructed on the excavation site as a large, albeit irregular, diamond. A high wooden stockade enclosed a space approximately 130 by 100 by 90 by 100 feet in circumference. A "firing step" ran along the inside perimeter of the wall. This was a conventional feature of stockade forts, consisting of mounded, hard-packed earth on which soldiers could step in order to elevate head and shoulders just above the level of the stockade, so that they could get a shot over it. The shot fired, they would step down off the firing step to reload under the complete cover of the stockade wall. Behind the firing step, the 1932 reconstruction workers placed a walk. Within the fort, about seventy-five feet from its southeast corner, they placed a square log cabin storehouse that was about eighteen feet on each side.

It was hardly a grand structure, but it didn't deserve to be derided as a "little thing upon the Meadow." However, the 1932 reconstruction, as it turned out, bore little resemblance to the original.

By 1952, the reconstruction was falling apart, and the National Park Service decided to rebuild it. The old debate about whether the fort had been a triangle or a diamond resurfaced, so archaeologists began reexamining the evidence. Not only did they do some new digging, they also reviewed all the documentary records they could find. A new one came to light in this year, a deposition by one John B. W. Shaw, who had been a member of the Virginia Regiment at the fort under Washington. He wrote: "There was at this Place a Small Stocado Fort made in a Circular form round a Small House that Stood in the Middle of it to keep our Provisions and Ammunition in, And was cover'd with Bark and some Skins, and might be about fourteen feet Square, and the Walls of the Fort might be eight feet Distance from the said House all Round." This description—of a fort neither diamond shaped nor triangular, but round—was supported by the new excavations and by another document written by a Colonel James Burd in 1759. Burd commanded a force of two hundred men who were clearing a road from Chestnut Ridge to Red Stone Creek. He noted in his diary on September 10 that he "Saw Col. Washington's fort, which was called Fort Necessity. It is a small circular stockade, with a small house in the center; on the outside is a small ditch goes around it about 8 yards from the stockade. It is situate in a narrow part of the meadows commanded by three points woods. There is a small run of water just by it."[12]

For a reason that will be apparent in the next chapter, the Burd document presents something of a puzzle, but based on both the Shaw and Burd accounts and on further excavations in 1952 and 1953, the archaeologists determined that the original stockade was indeed circular—and remarkably small: just fifty-three feet in diameter, with an overall perimeter circumference of 168 feet. The entrance, located on the southwest sector of the circle, was three-and-a-half feet wide. The archaeologists dug exploratory trenches out from the location of the stockade and were able to locate the "small ditch" Burd described. It was, in fact, not a trench, but two sets of mounded earthworks bracketing the fort—rather like angle brackets, with rounded points—on its east and west sides. These mounds would provide cover for men shooting from a kneeling position. The reconstruction that still exists today, built in 1953, reflects these discoveries. Although no archaeological evidence of the storehouse could be found, a fourteen-foot-square log structure was included in the reconstruction, based on Shaw and Burd. This building looks like a miniature log cabin with a gable roof, but Shaw described a roof covered with bark and skins, and common sense suggests that a gable roof was too elaborate for a structure hurriedly built out of "necessity." More likely, the storehouse was nothing more than a low log shed, with a simple slanted roof made of bark and skins.

Crude as it was, Fort Necessity was a highly unusual structure. Frontier stockades were, in fact, typically triangular or diamond shaped in plan. They were simplifications of the pentagonal layout of forts that had, by the mid-eighteenth century, been in vogue for some seventy-five years, since the French military engineer Sébastien le Prestre de Vauban (1633-1707) first created the design. The most elaborate frontier forts, including the French Fort Duquesne at the Forks of the Ohio, actually employed the pentagon design. The projecting corners of the pentagon structure allowed defenders to create a crossfire, which made the field of fire outside the fort far more lethal. At virtually any point from which an attacker might strike a pentagonal fort, he would potentially be exposed to defensive fire from at least two different angles and positions. Of course, under urgent and primitive circumstances, Washington could not have been expected to build the equivalent of Fort Duquesne, let alone a more elaborate version of the Vauban plan; however, the simpler triangle or diamond would have been within the capabilities of his men, materials, and time, and would have provided at least some opportunity for effective crossfire. By instead choosing the circular design, Washington made it difficult for his men to concentrate their fire in any particular direction.

As a teenager in Barbados, where he saw a fine example of a European-style bastion fort, Washington seemed to take naturally to fortification, as if he possessed a native understanding of this military art. Had this experience and instinct deserted him in the exigencies of the wilderness?

Perhaps not, or, in any case, not entirely. The circular design was easier to build than either the square or the diamond, and it required less material. To make up for the tactical shortcomings of the design, Washington built the two angle-bracket-shaped earthwork mounds outside the fort. These provided the acute angle that allowed for concentrated defensive crossfire. These mounds were probably intended as the first line of defense, with the stockade as a fallback position and a means of protecting ammunition and provisions as well as withstanding a prolonged siege. This would also explain why the Fort Necessity stockade was so small. At fifty-three feet in diameter—with a log storehouse in the middle—it provided very little room for fighting. Washington probably did not see this as a problem, since he intended to do most of his fighting outside of the stockade.

None of this excuses another weakness implicit in Burd's description of the fort, however. "It is," he wrote, "situate in a narrow part of the meadows commanded by three points woods."[13] The keyword is *commanded*. The wooded points were hills—including one just sixty yards from the stockade, well within accurate and effective musket range—from which an attacker could fire down into the fort and its defenders. Even a commander only marginally more experienced than Washington would have avoided placing camp or a fort adjacent to high ground he did not control. Yielding the high ground to a potential attacker is by any measure a fatally flawed tactic.

❦

The three letters Washington wrote to Dinwiddie on May 29 provide ample evidence that the young commander had become keenly aware of the precarious position in which he had placed himself and his command. Attack from a force five times his present size was imminent. Yet in the

midst of this crisis there arrived Governor Dinwiddie's reply to the letter
Washington had forwarded from his officers in which they threatened to
resign their commissions because their pay was lower than that of officers
of the independent companies. On the eighteenth, Washington had written to Dinwiddie that his "inclinations [were] prone to second their just
grievances," and he warned that "nothing prevents their throwing down
their commissions . . . but the approaching danger. Which has too far
engaged their honor to recede till other officers are sent in their room, or
an alternation [alteration] made regarding their pay, during which time
they will assist with their best endeavours voluntarily, that is, without
receiving the gratuity allowed by the resolves of the Committee."[14] On
May 25, the governor replied sharply: "Sir," he began:

> *I can assure You I am concerned & no less surpirz'd to find*
> *by Yr Letr of the 18ᵗʰ of this Mo. such ill timed Complaints*
> *& and I conceive not altogether founded in such real Cause*
> *as I am sorry to find You think they are—You certainly judge*
> *very rightly of the Importance of the Service & that Yr Honrs*
> *are engag'd too far to recede from it, which I hope an atten-*
> *tive reflection on w[ha]t I am going to observe will satsfie*
> *You & the other Gent. there is not so great Provocation to*
> *withdraw Yrselves from as You seem to think at present—The*
> *first Objectn to the Pay if made at all shd have been made*
> *before engaging in the Service. The Gent. very well knew the*
> *Terms on which they were to serve & were satisfied then with*
> *it . . .*[15]

Dinwiddie continued his chastisement in this vein, disputing various particulars in the officers' complaint. He then turned on Washington himself:

*Now Colo. W: I shall more particularly answer wt relates to
YrSelf, & I must begin with expressing both Concern &
Surprize, to find a Gent. whom I so particularly consider'd,
& from whom I had so great Expectats. & Hopes, appear so
differently from himself, & give me leave to say mistakenly
as I think, concurring with Complaints in general so ill
founded. I am sensible of Yr Difficulties & You may believe
I shall not let Your Merit pass Unnotic'd. I believe You sincerely attach'd to Yr Countrie's Welfare & Prosperity, which
You know very much depends on the Success of Your present
Ecpeditn & this I perswade myself will sweeten the Toils,
that You will hereafter reflect on with Pleasure & engage
You to think of nothing less than resigning Yr Comd or
countenancing in any sort the Discontent that cd never be
more unseasonable or pernicious than at present.*[16]

Washington was clearly disturbed by Dinwiddie's reprimand, and he
responded to it at length in the first of the three letters he wrote on May
29. After assuring the governor "that nothing was farther from my intention than to recede, thô I then pressd and still desire that my Services may
be voluntary rather than on the present Pay" and even chiding Dinwiddie
for charging him "with ingratitude," Washington persisted in standing his
ground: "I cou'd not object to the Pay before I knew it," he wrote. Then
he reminded Governor Dinwiddie that "the first Estimation allowd a
Lieutt Colo. 15/ and Majr 12/6 which I then complaind very much off
[of]; till your Honour assurd me that we were to be furnish'd with proper
necessary's and offerd that as a reason why the pay was Less than British:
after this when you were so kind to prefer me to the Comn I now have,
and at the same time acquainted me that I was to have but 12/6 [as a lieutenant colonel]."[17]

At first glance, we tend to share Governor Dinwiddie's somewhat self-righteous opinion that disputes about pay at this juncture were at best, "unseasonable"; yet, if we think it through, what emerges is not a selfish or petulant George Washington disputing shillings and pence when absolute patriotism is called for. Instead, we see an officer so thoroughly principled that he was unwilling to allow even a crisis of the greatest urgency and danger trump what is right and honorable. He sided with his subordinates in a just complaint, and by making common cause with the other officers he eschewed false altruism. Yet he also reaffirmed his patriotic commitment. Washington's point here was that even on the frontier, faced with overwhelming danger, right is right, and doing right should never require compromising with what is wrong. It makes for a far more powerful fable of the character of the future Father of His Country than Parson Weems's celebrated cherry tree tale—and unlike the Weems confection, it is a *true* story.

But there was more here than principle. Washington was not an absolute idealist. He adhered to principle when principle was right and not merely for the sake of adhering to principle. In the end, after defending his protests and those of his officers, and after repeating that he would rather serve gratis than accept unequal pay, he declared that his "circumstances" did not "correspond with my Inclination," and, therefore, he would accept 12s. 6p. after all.[18] George Washington was a pragmatist, a principled pragmatist.

❧

Fort Necessity took longer than expected to complete—it was not finished until June 3—but the French, although expected at any day, failed to approach as one day succeeded another. Late on June 2, the thirty-man escort Washington had sent with the Half-King to collect Indian allies returned with some eighty Indians—what Washington described as "25 Familys"—which included numerous women and children in addition to warriors. In reporting this to Governor Dinwiddie on June 3, Washington put it in an optimistic light by relaying the Half-King's assurances that Big Kettle, a Seneca chief to whom he had spoken, pledged the "good Intentions" of most of the Indians in the Ohio country to assist "the 6 Nations [the Iroquois confederacy] and their Brother's the English agt the French." They were waiting, the Half-King explained, "only . . . to see us begin."[19]

Washington also reported that the Half-King had dispatched Monacatoocha to Logstown "with 4 French Scalps two of which was to be sent to the Wyandotts &ca and the other two to the 6 Nations telling them that the French had trickd them out of their Lands for which their Brother's the English . . . joyn'd hand in hand . . . for that they int[en]d with their Brothers to drive the French beyond the Lakes." Monacatoocha, Washington wrote, "has order's to draw all the Indians from Ohio and then repair to our Camp."[20]

This promise of many warriors sounded most impressive—in theory—but for the present Washington "proposed to the Half King sending [the Indian] Women and Children into the Inhabitants [the inhabited regions, away from the frontier], for as they must be supported by us it may be done at a less expence there than here . . . we find it very difficult procureing Provisions for them."[21]

Then Washington returned to the subject of his battle with the Jumonville party. He related that three French deserters had revealed to an Englishman, "a Man of Veracity" named Crawford (probably the licensed Pennsylvania trader Hugh Crawford), that the French were holding two English traders "confind in Irons at . . . Fort [Duquesne]" and that "Jumonvilles Party was all chosen Men fixd upn" to "kill or take Prisoner's all the English they'd meet with." Insofar as it vindicated Washington's attack on the party, this was the good news. But the deserters also brought bad: "that 1100 Men were now in the Fort and Reinforcts expected." Nevertheless, with a bravado as game as it was unwarranted, Washington declared: "If the whole Detacht of the French behave with no more Risolution than this chosen Party did I flatter myself we shall have no g[rea]t trouble in driving them to the D_____ Montreal." With that, he once again rehearsed the battle in the bower: "So that we had but 40 Men with which we killd and took 32 or 3 Men besides those who may have escap'd." Now he made that great exploit seem a mere cakewalk—and, besides, "We have just finish'd a small palisadod Fort in which with my small Number's I shall not fear the attack of 500 Men."[22] We cannot help wondering whether Washington wrote all this to kindle confidence in Dinwiddie—or in himself.

Washington was eager for reinforcements, but the warriors—especially encumbered as they were with women and children—were also so many more mouths to feed. By June 10, Washington wrote to Dinwiddie that "We have been extreamly ill used by Major Carlyle's Deputys." The trader and merchant John Carlyle was the expedition's commissary and had six deputies under contract to supply provisions. For the acute shortages he was now experiencing, Washington blamed them rather than Carlyle himself because "he is a Gentleman." Washington wrote: "He, I believe has been decivd, and we have suffer'd by those under him." As of the tenth, the men (and women and children) at Great Meadows had been without flour for six days "and none upon the Road to our relief that we know of. . . We have not Provision's of any sort in the Camp to serve us 2 Days thô I have sent time after time acquainting therewith."[23]

Hungry, bracing daily for the onslaught of the French, Washington received on June 10 a welcome visitor, Christopher Gist, who brought shocking news. Colonel Joshua Fry, Washington's commanding officer, was dead. He had fallen from his horse some days earlier, had failed to recover from his injuries, and succumbed on May 31.

George Washington, aged twenty-two, was now commander in charge of the expedition to save the Ohio frontier. It was a command he had earlier confessed himself unequal to because of his youth and lack of military experience. But there was no backing down now. On June 9, the first of the promised reinforcements had arrived at Great Meadows: three companies of the Virginia Regiment under the command of Major George Muse, 181 soldiers in all. They were welcome, as were the nine swivel guns—small, trainable cannon—they brought, but they had come with little in the way of provisions (save for some rum), and the specter of hunger loomed that much larger.

Major Muse's Indian interpreter, Andrew Montour, also arrived. Dinwiddie had commissioned Montour to recruit and command a force of 200 Indians. The son of the Oneida sachem Carondawana—Big Tree—whose wife was the daughter of a French trader (named Montour) by a Huron woman, Andrew Montour lived among the Iroquois and worked as an interpreter and agent for the colony of Pennsylvania. He was also a most prosperous trader himself. He spoke French, English, and several Indian languages, but because his mother, known as "Madame Montour," had been a loyal friend of the English, his own allegiance lay resolutely in that direction as well. He looked European, except that he painted his face in the manner of an Indian. His clothing was a hybrid of Euro-American and Native American garb. The Moravian mission leader, Count Nicholas Ludwig von Zinzendorf, founder of the Pennsylvania town of Bethlehem, once met Montour and described him as wearing "a brown broadcloth coat, a scarlet damaskin lapel waistcoat, breeches over which his shirt hung, a black cordovan neckerchief decked with silver bugles, shoes and stockings and a hat. His ears were hung with pendants of brass and other wires plaited together like the handle of a basket."[24] Montour was by no means universally admired; some thought him an able and honest trader, while others believed that he consistently delivered less than he promised when it came to exerting influence on the Indians. As for Washington, he was grateful for another interpreter and an adviser on dealing with Indians.

Muse presented Washington with two things: a medal from the governor, intended to convey his confidence in the young commander and to lend a little added weight to his new authority, which was conveyed in the second item Muse handed over—a packet of letters from Dinwiddie. These included various instructions along with a commission as full colonel, enabling Washington officially to replace Fry as commander of the Virginia Regiment. Dinwiddie named his own friend, Colonel James Innes, to overall command of all the forces. Adam Stephen was promoted from captain to major, and George Muse from major to lieutenant colonel.

Washington had no objection to answering to Innes and may well have been relieved to have an older, more experienced officer above him; however, he was put off by Dinwiddie's instructions with regard to the officers of the independent companies, who, the governor explained, "having their Commos. [commissions] sign'd by His M[ajest]y imagine they claim a distinguish'd rank & being long trained in Arms expect suitable regards. You will therefore consult & agree with Yr Officers to shew them particular marks of Esteem, which will avoid such Causes of Uneasiness as otherwise might obstruct His Majesty's Service wherein All are alike engag'd . . ." What this came down to, Washington feared, was that he, a Virginia *colonel,* would be effectively subordinate to James Mackay, *captain* of an independent company. "Your Honour may depend," Washington replied to Dinwiddie on June 10, "I shall myself, and will endeavour to make my Officer's shew Captn McKay all the respect due to his Rank & merit." Then he added: "but should have been particularly oblig'd if your Honour had declar'd whether he was under my Command, or Independent of it." Despite the vagueness of Dinwiddie's instructions on this point, Washington pledged to "inculcate harmony, and unanimity"—at least "as far as I am able."[25]

Sometime after he wrote this reply to the governor, word finally came of the approach of the French. Washington dispatched Indian scouts and deployed his men to their battle stations. Around dusk, there was an alarm: *The French were coming.* Now Washington would have to fight a night battle—a rare occurrence in eighteenth-century warfare.

But no Frenchmen materialized, not through the long night.

On June 11, Washington dispatched another small detachment to re-connoiter. On the twelfth, two of these scouts returned, reporting that they had seen some French troops in the woods—but only a few. Some of his Indians, however, reported the presence of about ninety Frenchmen nearby. Ordering Muse to man the swivel guns, Washington rode out with 130 white troops and thirty Indians on a mission to capture the French detachment. His blood ran high. But just as he was about to leave, he discovered that the message of the Indian scouts had been misinter-preted. There were not *ninety* French soldiers, just *nine* French deserters, who were straggling toward Great Meadows. Washington sent a detach-ment of Indians to bring them in.

Now there was nothing to do but return to camp and brood on the fact that all food would be exhausted in just two more days. He had taken the initiative in this crisis, bombarding Carlyle with messages demanding provisions and hiring fifty or sixty horses to transport provisions from Wills Creek, assuming food had reached that place. If it had not, the horses would not go to waste. Washington gave instructions that they were to be returned to Great Meadows loaded with ammunition. For at this point, both commodities were equally necessary to survival.

THE BATTLE ON
THE MEADOW

We know that Washington and his men were both hungry and frustrated.
We do not know if they were also scared. They certainly had a right to be,
but Washington's diary and letters give no hint of such an emotion.
Indeed, we cannot even guess whether he personally felt relief or disappointment to learn that only nine deserters—not, as he was first told,
ninety French soldiers—were on the march. Regardless of what he might
have felt, Washington sent the trader-interpreter Andrew Montour and a
few Indians to escort the deserters to Fort Necessity for questioning. After
they arrived, Washington wrote, "I caused them to be drest"[1] —remarkably, he must have found spare clothes in the fort's meager stock of
supplies—then began the interrogation.

"They confirmed us in our Opinion, of the Intention of M. *de
Jumonville's* Party," Washington carefully—perhaps defensively—noted,
meaning that the so-called "ambassador" was really what Washington had
thought he was, a spy, the advance guard of a French invasion force. The
deserters reported that "more than One Hundred Soldiers were only waiting for a favourable Opportunity to come and join [battle against] us;

that M. *de Contrecour* expected a Reinforcement of Four Hundred Men; that the Fort [Duquesne] was completed; and its Artillery a shelter to its Front and Gates; that there was a double Pallisadoe next to the Water; that they have only eight small Pieces of Cannon; and know what Number of Men we are." Five hundred men were ready to attack from a very well furnished fort. That was not good news to the commander of no more than four hundred men with little ammunition and less food. It was news so unpleasant, in fact, that Washington recorded the French possession of eight artillery pieces as if that were *good* news: "*only* eight small Pieces of Cannon." Against these, Washington had nine much smaller guns—the swivels Muse had brought with him.[2]

Still, it was not likely that the French would bring all of their artillery against Fort Necessity, and while five hundred versus four hundred (including the hundred British regulars due to arrive any day under James Mackay) gave a distinct advantage to the French, this was not necessarily an overwhelming superiority of numbers. But then the deserters continued: "They also informed us that the *Delaware* and *Shawnese* had taken up the Hatchet against us."[3]

That darkened the situation considerably. Washington well knew how Indians fought and, more to the point, how they treated a beaten enemy. He had seen that firsthand, in what his own Indian allies did to the wounded of the Jumonville party. His response to this news was hardly panic, but it was nevertheless naïve: "resolved to invite those two Nations [the Delawares and the Shawnees] to come to a Council at Mr. *Gist's*. Sent for that Purpose Messengers and Wampum." He believed that he could talk them out of turning against the English. On June 13, he also "Perswaded the Deserters to write [a] Letter, to those of their Companions who had an Inclination to Desert."[4] Perhaps some of the French could be talked out of fighting, too. It would be most interesting to know how Washington attempted to persuade them, but his letter does not survive.

Probably on June 14, Captain Mackay arrived with the "independent company" of British regulars from South Carolina. Washington had dreaded this arrival even more, it seems, than that of the French. The regulars were better paid and better fed than the colonials, and in the absence of unambiguous instructions from Governor Dinwiddie, it was quite possible that *Captain* Mackay, a British officer, effectively outranked *Colonel* Washington, a mere provincial. Yet if there was to be trouble with Mackay, clearly Washington was determined that it would not start with a provocation on his part. He made it a point to greet the captain and his men warmly, and, biting his tongue, he refrained completely from giving any orders.

For his part, Mackay had good reason to feel better qualified for command than twenty-two-year-old Washington. Born and raised in Scotland—he was the son of a military officer, Hugh Mackay, laird of Scoury—James Mackay immigrated to Georgia with no less a personage than Governor James Ogelthorpe. He was a military veteran of some fifteen years, mostly fighting Indians on the Georgia frontier. If he resented even a hint of subordinating himself or his men to a provincial colonel, he did not immediately show it—and, indeed, responded cordially to Washington's welcome—but he also chose a campsite apart from that of Washington and his men. For his part, Washington refrained from inspecting either the camp or the company, but then he sent to Mackay the parole and countersign—the secret password and acknowledgment used by Washington's command to prevent infiltration—only to have Mackay politely reject them. He did not believe it proper, he said, to receive these from a colonial colonel because the independent company was a separate force. His commission came from the king, Mackay explained, and Washington's from the governor; clearly, the governor could not issue a commission superior to that of the king. Mackay did not insist that Washington be subordinate to him, but that the colonial and the regular forces be separate nevertheless.

The rejection of the parole and countersign was very provocative, and Washington wrote to Dinwiddie about it on June 15:

*For want of proper Instructions from your Honour I am
much at a loss to know how to act, or proceed in regard to
[Mckay's] company: I made it my particular study to receive
him (as it was your Honour's desire) with all the Respect
and politeness that was due to his Rank, or that I was capable of shewing: and don't doubt from his appearance and
behavr but a strict intimacy will ensue, when matter's are
put in a clearer light. but at present I assure your Honour
they [the independent company] will rather impede the
Service than forward it, for having Commissions from the
King they look upon themselves as a distinct Body, and will
not incorporate and do duty as our Men—but keep separate
Guards, Incamp separate &ca.*

Washington went on to explain that he had "not offer'd to controul
[Mackay] in anything, or shewd that I claimd a superior Command, but
in giving the Parrole & Countersign which must be the same in an Army
consisting of 10 Different Nation's, to distinguish Friends from Foes—He
knows the necessity of this, yet does not think he is to receive it from
me." At this point, Washington started a new paragraph and, with it, took
a new tone. What had begun as a hopeful prediction of "strict intimacy"
developing between Mackay and himself, now gave way to exasperation:
"Then who is to give it [the countersign and parole]? am I to Issue these
order's to a Company? or is an Independent Captn to prescribe Rules to
the Virginia Regiment? this is the Question, but how absurd is obvious."
Washington now appealed to Dinwiddie to exercise his authority unambiguously: "It now behooves Honble Sir that you lay your absolute
commands on one or tother to obey—this is indispensably necessary for
nothing clashes more with reason than to conceive our small bodys, can
act distinctly [separately] . . ." Washington assured the governor that

"Captn McKay and I have liv'd in most perfect harmony since his arrival and have Reason'd on this calmly, and don't doubt but if we shd have occasion to exert our whole force but we shall do as well as divided authority can. We have not had the least warm dispute," but then sought to show how Mackay challenged not just his authority, but the governor's as well: "He thinks your Honour has not a power to give commissions that will command him." Finally, Washington defined the crux of the issue: "It must be known who is to Command before order's will be observ'd, and I am very confident your Honour will see the absurdity & consider the Effects of Captn McKays having the direction of the [Virginia] Regiment, for it would certainly be the hardest thing in Life if we are to do double & trible duty, and neither be entitled to the Pay or Rank of [regular British] Soldiers."[5]

We do not know if there was fear in Washington's camp. Washington makes no mention of it. There were hunger and frustration, without a doubt. And the growing frustration almost certainly moved Washington to decide to march out of the confines of Fort Necessity in order to resume a project begun on the outward march from Alexandria: clearing a road to Red Stone Creek, which would allow for the passage of wagons and artillery to Great Meadows and other points approaching the forks of the Ohio so that an advance fort could be constructed there to challenge Fort Duquesne.

No doubt, cutting a road to Red Stone and building a fort there were important projects in the long term; however, in the face of intelligence that warned of the approach of five hundred Frenchmen, leaving Fort Necessity virtually undefended seems at the very least an instance of grossly misplaced priorities. To be sure, the work would give the men something to do—always important in an army—and it would give Washington the feeling that he was doing something. It might also serve to impress the wavering Indians, persuading them that a much larger English force was preparing to venture into the frontier. Although Mackay had brought with him "5 Days allowance of flower, and 60 Beeves," which surely helped to relieve the immediate crisis in provisions, Washington continued to press Governor Dinwiddie on the urgent need for food—"I am much grieved to find our Stores so slow advancing"[6]—so it is likely that he also intended to obtain some interim provisions at Christopher Gist's settlement en route to Red Stone. Finally, as we are about to see, Washington had a diplomatic motive for leaving just now.

Nevertheless, could anything justify his leaving Fort Necessity at this potentially critical moment? The few modern historians who take note of this episode chalk it up as another tactical error due to Washington's inexperience. Perhaps it was. Yet while the young colonel was not a great tactician—and, as his record in the American Revolution attests, never would be—he was an extraordinary leader of men. Idle waiting is nearly as destructive to an army as bullets and disease. Washington may well have sensed that his men needed to be moving and working—*now* more than ever.

It would be convenient for the portrayal of Washington's early leadership genius also to suggest that he now wanted to separate his Virginians from the privileged and overpaid members of the independent company. But the facts of the matter do not support this stroke of biography. For Washington expected the men of the independent company to work on the Red Stone road alongside his Virginians, and he asked Mackay to order them to do so. Mackay declined—unless (he said) the colonel would authorize regular British army daily pay of one shilling for this work. This, Washington knew, would provoke outrage—perhaps even mutiny—among the Virginians, who were paid a mere 8p. per day. He explained how the disparity in pay would affect morale. Mackay apparently did not disagree, but protested that he lacked the authority to order his men to work for less. It was not, he said, that his company was special, but that it was subject to the martial law that applied to the entire Royal Army.

Further exasperated, Washington returned to his letter to Dinwiddie, adding to it on June 15: "We shall part tomorrow—I shall continue my March to red Stone while the [Independent] Company remains here but this Sir I found absolutely necessary for the Publick Interest . . . I . . . shall continue to compleat the work we have began with my poor fellows—we shall have the whole credit as none other's have assisted."[7]

On June 16, Washington led three hundred Virginians out of Fort Necessity to work on the Red Stone Creek road. Doubtless, he was intent on impressing the regulars, at their leisure in camp, with the martial prowess of this regiment of "provincials." Instead, as he wearily noted in his diary, we "were extremely perplexed, our Waggons breaking very often." (Another source transcribes "perplexed" more pointedly as "embarrassed."[8]) The way was rough on wagons, to be sure, but it is also likely that Washington and his men were the victims of sharp practices by local Virginia planters, who sold the regiment (at premium prices!) inferior wagons hurriedly cobbled together of "green" (uncured) wood, which contracted as it dried, weakening each structural joint. Not only did the shoddy vehicles embarrass the regiment and its commander, they greatly impeded progress, and—since Washington saw fit to carry his nine swivel guns with him—might have resulted in damage to what little artillery he had. (Mackay was supposed to have brought along some badly needed cannon, but, deciding that the condition of wilderness roads made this impractical, left them behind.)

On June 17, presumably while en route to Red Stone, Washington "dispatched an Express to the *Half-King,* in order to perswade him to send a Message to the *Loups* [the Delawares]; which he did." By the eighteenth, Washington had reached Christopher Gist's settlement, and on that same day "eight *Mingoes* [a small tribe associated with Iroquois and sometimes called the Ohio Senecas]" arrived from Logstown. They told Washington that a "Council must be held" and at this meeting declared that they wanted to ally themselves with the English, even though they themselves "were amongst the *French*" and "complied with some of their Customs." Think nothing of this, the Mingoes said, explaining that they were actually "naturally inclined to fall upon [the French], and other Words to that Purport." They told Washington that they "had brought a Speech with them; and desired to deliver it with Speed," but the colonel suspected "that their Intentions towards us were evil; wherefore I delayed giving them Audience until the Arrival of the *Half-King*."[9] Clearly, Washington believed that regardless of what they said, the Mingoes were spies in the service of the French.

The Half-King arrived later in the day, and Washington convened the council, which included "several of the *Six Nations* [Iroquois], *Loups and Shawnese,* to the Number of Forty."[10] Washington took comfort in the presence of the Half-King, whom he trusted more than any other Indian, and the traders/Indian interpreters Andrew Montour and George Croghan.

The council began on June 18 and did not conclude until June 21: a stately, doubtless tedious, progression of formal speeches, delivered, translated, then responded to with speeches of similar stateliness, requiring both careful composition and translation. In sum, Washington declared that he and the other English had come to fight in league with the Iroquois and the Delawares. He invited the Indian men to send their women and children to the English settlements, where they would be protected in the coming combat. He then advised that the time had come for the Indians of the Ohio country to choose and declare sides—the English or the French—and to accept the consequences of their choice.

In the end, after three exhausting days of talk and translation, the result was everything Washington could have wished. Neither the Iroquois nor the Delawares would take up the hatchet against the English; on the contrary, they renewed their pledge of allegiance. Moreover, he had

been able to obtain from Gist some badly needed provisions and would
soon receive from Dinwiddie as well as John Carlyle (the principal vict-
valler, or commissary, to the Virginia regiment) assurances that food and
other supplies were on the way. All of this was most reassuring; however,
Washington still had to deal with the matter of those eight Mingoes. They
"had told me there were Sixteen Hundred *French*, and Seven Hundred
Indians on their March, to reinforce those at the Garrison" of Fort
Duquesne. Washington believed this "News to be only Soldiers
Discourse"—exaggerated rumor—or perhaps it was a deliberate fabrication on the part of the Mingoes. To make sure, "I perswaded the *Half
King* to send three of his Men to inquire into the Truth of it." They were
"sent in a secret Manner, before the Council broke up, and had Orders to
go to the Fort, and get what Information they could from all the *Indians*
they should meet, and if there was any News worth while, one of them
should return, and the other two continue their Rout as far as [the French
trading settlement of] *Venango* . . . in order to obtain a perfect Knowledge
of every Thing."[11]

It is apparent that Washington had become reasonably sophisticated in
the employment of Indians in war between the colonial powers. Like the
French, he began using them as agents of reconnaissance, for they could
travel more or less freely between the French and English forts, camps,
and settlements. Concluding that the Mingoes were indeed "treacherous
Devils, who had been sent by the *French* as Spies," Washington made no
accusations, but instead sent them on their way after the council had broken up, "though not without some Tale ready prepared to amuse the
French, which may be of Service to make our own Design succeed." In
modern terms, he had planted "disinformation," responding to the
Mingoes' "many Questions [concerning] by what Way we proposed to go
to the [as yet unbuilt English] Fort [at Red Stone], and what Time we
expected to arrive there" by deliberately calling a halt to work on the road,
then telling the Mingoes that "we intended to keep on across the Woods
as far as the Fort, falling the Trees, *&c.* [but that] we were waiting here for

the Reinforcement which was coming to us, our Artillery, and our Waggons to accompany us there." So the Mingoes left, armed with a grossly inflated picture of English strength. No sooner did they leave than Washington resumed "marking out and clearing a Road towards *Red-Stone.*"[12]

Whatever pleasure Washington may have derived from the promises made at the conclusion of the council and from his deception of the Mingo spies was short lived. Shingas, a Delaware chief second in influence only to the Half-King himself, informed Washington that the Delawares would not camp at Great Meadows, near Fort Necessity—although he did vaguely allow the possibility that warriors might be persuaded to align themselves with the English. As for the Shawnees, who had declared their allegiance at the council, they simply vanished. There was still the Half-King, of course, whose loyalty Washington had come to expect. He had assumed that the Half-King and his warriors would accompany the Virginia regiment as it hacked out the Red Stone road. To the colonel's dismay, however, they retreated to their camp at Great Meadows as soon as the council ended. He was told that the Half-King *might* come back if he were sent wampum and a speech inviting him to join in welcoming Monacatoocha, the pro-English Oneida chief who was believed to be on the move and about to arrive to join the English.

On the evening of June 25, three—just three—of the Half-King's warriors came to Washington, bearing a note from Croghan "informing me what Pains he was at to perswade any *Indians* to come to us."[13] As for the Half-King, he wanted to come, Croghan reported, but had been injured and was unable to make the trip.

The council, which had seemed a triumph at its conclusion, now appeared a total failure. Most immediately, the defection of the Indians meant that Washington would not have the services of experienced scouts to give him advance warning of any French approach as he labored on the Red Stone road. More significant, however, was the unmistakable intimation of the ultimate failure of the entire Indian-English alliance. With this came an erosion of Washington's faith in Montour and Croghan, who talked much about the influence they wielded among the Indians but consistently failed to deliver.

Beyond his disappointment, Washington had a realistic understanding of the problem with the alliance. It was his first experience with a difficulty he would repeatedly face years later while struggling to hold together the Continental Army in the American Revolution. It was a problem of resources and supply—or, more accurately, the lack of them.

All military and political agreements between whites and Indians were accompanied by the offer of presents to the Indians. This was more than symbolic. The gifts were typically not mere trinkets but items of genuine need, including rifles, ammunition, powder, and clothing. Ill supplied, Washington had been able to offer only the most meager of presents. He was expecting more and better gifts to come with the long-tardy shipment of food and other provisions due him, but they had not arrived by the time of the council. The Indians clearly interpreted the poverty of presents as indicative of the general poverty of Washington and the other English. By June 23, all of the flour and bacon Washington had with him was gone. There remained a handful of stringy steers and cows. Croghan had signed a contract pledging delivery of ten thousand pounds of flour and two hundred horses. By the time of the council, he had delivered no flour and no more than twenty-five horses. Reportedly, an Indian sarcastically asked the colonel if he intended to starve them as well as the English.[14] Finally, precisely because the Indians moved freely between the camps of the French and the English, it must have been apparent to them that the French enjoyed superior numbers of men fit for combat.

Learning firsthand what it meant to wage war on less than a shoestring was one bitter lesson that would prepare the commander for the great struggle that was yet some two decades in the future. Yet more vivid must have been the sensation of facing a superior enemy even as all anticipated support collapsed beneath him. The Delawares, the Shawnees—gone. Some of the Half-King's Iroquois were camped at Great Meadows, but they no longer showed much inclination to join the English in a fight against the French. Few were even willing to serve as scouts. As for the Half-King himself, Washington must have doubted that he had really been injured. It may have been his way of avoiding a frank refusal.

This feeling—of facing an enemy alone, of being left hung out to dry, to twist in the winds of war and destiny—could not have been comfortable to George Washington. Yet he did not waiver. There was a glimmer of hope in the news that Monacatoocha was on his way, but Washington did not wait for him. Instead, he put his men on a ration of parched corn and apportioned to them the fresh meat of what few cattle he had. Then he made a new plan. He wanted to push through the road to Red Stone so that he could set about building there a fort bigger than Fort Necessity, one that would allow him to hold out until sufficient reinforcements arrived. Once reinforced, he would advance to Fort Duquesne and take it.

Finishing the road would take time, and Washington knew that the French might attack at any moment. He believed that the French had two options for moving against him. One was to come up the Red Stone. The other was to march out from Fort Duquesne along the trail that led to Gist's settlement. If his troops were fully supplied and well fed, he could have counted on them to cut the road rapidly, so that he could quickly transport all of his men to Red Stone and swiftly build a new fort. But, Washington well knew that his men were subsisting on near-starvation rations. Therefore, he decided to concentrate his forces at the two places the French might attack. He sent Captain Andrew Lewis with a detachment of officers and sixty men to work on the road. He and the rest of the troops would remain at Gist's.

Lewis and his detachment set off on June 27. Either that night or on the morning of June 28, Washington received a message from Chief Monacatoocha. He had personally seen the arrival of reinforcements at Fort Duquesne and had heard the French say they were going to attack Washington and his command with a mixed force of eight hundred white soldiers and four hundred Indians.

These were not the words of Mingo spies, but of a longtime friend of the English. Moreover, this information was corroborated by the report of the French deserters, who had said that reinforcements were on their way. One other piece of information bothered Washington. Recently, two English soldiers had vanished. Perhaps they had deserted and defected to the French, revealing Washington's whereabouts, his strength, and maybe even the critical state of his supplies.

It all added up. The French would attack—and very soon. Washington hurriedly convened his officers in a council of war. All agreed that the force, small as it was, needed to be consolidated immediately. Lewis's Red Stone road detail, Mackay's independent company, and Washington's main command—all should be brought together in order to mount a credible defense against the onslaught that now seemed imminent. The best place to assemble would be Gist's settlement, which was about midway between Lewis and Mackay, and which was also the current location of the swivel guns. Immediately, Washington sent dispatches to Lewis and Mackay, then ordered his men to dismantle all of the fences they could find at Gist's and use them to set up a stockade-like palisade. Washington was improvising yet another fort.

To Washington's satisfaction and great relief, Mackay and his independent company rode up that very night. There was no dispute. They were willing to fight. Lewis arrived a bit later, on the afternoon of June 29. Washington felt heartened by these developments—but then was confronted by another disappointment. Those Indians who still lingered around Gist's settlement were panicky. They had picked up inflated reports of the French reinforcements—numbers exaggerated by a combination of rumor and, doubtless, French design. Individually and collectively, the warriors warned the colonel that they would leave the English unless the force withdrew to Fort Necessity on Great Meadows, where the Half-King and his warriors were camped.

Suddenly, the decision of the first council of war seemed less viable. Washington therefore convened another. This time, he and his officers reasoned that supplies at Gist's had become even more scarce than at Fort Necessity. Four hundred men were now consolidated at the Gist settlement and had between them neither bread nor bacon and just twenty-four cattle, mostly cows. Nor could the meat supply represented by the cattle be extended by preservation. The settlement was down to a single quart of salt. The French might make a direct attack, but they also had the option of a siege. It would be easy for them to interdict supply convoys and thereby force the small starving army into surrender. If the French were in the least imaginative, they could hasten that surrender by closing in so tightly that those twenty-four cattle would have no place to graze. In this way, while strangling the English resupply route, they could also starve the cows, reducing what little food supply was on hand.

The best-case scenario, as Washington and his officers now saw it, would be a direct attack by the French. Even if they were outnumbered, Washington felt he had a fighting chance. But suppose the English did manage to eke out a victory and avoid annihilation at Gist's. The best that could be hoped for was breathing space to effect a withdrawal from Gist's settlement. Such a withdrawal would expose the retreating column to Indian attack.

No. There was now little room for doubt. What the Indians clamored for was indeed the best of a limited variety of bad courses of action. Withdraw now to Great Meadows—*before* a French attack—and the English would be closer to promised supplies (even as the French would be forced to extend their lines of communication). Moreover, the two routes along which the French would have to advance from Fort

Duquesne converged at Great Meadows. This meant that no matter how the French approached, they would be detected. At Gist's, a surprise attack was a greater danger. Finally, the Indians left no real choice at all. Unless Washington returned to Fort Necessity, they would desert him.

The soldiers had been hungry when Washington led them out of Fort Necessity and put them to work on the road to Red Stone. Now, according to his own minutes of the council of war, they were in a "Starving Condition," having "wanted meat & Bread for Six days already."[15] And now—having recalled Lewis and summoned Mackay—he ordered them all to turn around and make the difficult trek back to the little fort on Great Meadows. Only this time, it would be even harder. Hoping to transport up to Gist's the provisions he believed had arrived at Fort Necessity, Washington had already sent back the teams and wagons that had hauled the swivel guns and other baggage. Now, therefore, he had just two teams and a handful of other horses to take everything back to the fort. It fell to the hungry troops to pull the swivels themselves. All the ammunition was to be loaded onto the two wagons. Whatever space remained would be packed with other cargo. Private baggage would be left behind.

That was the plan. But when the loading began, it soon became apparent that the two available wagons could not even hold all the ammunition, let alone other supplies. Washington loaded what he could on the available pack horses, then ordered his own mount to be loaded with powder, shot, and whatever else needed to be transported. He would walk the thirteen rugged miles back to Fort Necessity. The other officers followed their leader, relinquishing their horses so that they could be loaded with precious cargo. Everyone, officers and men, would walk. Although he was uncomplaining in self-sacrifice, Washington remained a pragmatic man. He offered some soldiers four pistoles each—a fair amount of money—to retrieve his personal baggage and carry it on their backs.

Had they been well fed and amply stocked with teams and pack animals, the regiment and independent company would have found the thirteen miles separating Gist's settlement form Fort Necessity difficult enough; the so-called "road" was, according to Adam Stephen, "the roughest and most hilly of any on the Allegheny Mountains."[16] Subsisting on parched corn and being obliged to transform themselves into beasts of burden, the men found that road a veritable agony.

Driven by fear of horrific death at the hands and hatchets of French-allied Indians, they should, in the best of circumstances, have also been buoyed by the brotherhood of shared hardship. But these were hardly the best circumstances. The men of the independent company, who had shown soldierly conduct in marching out to Gist's settlement when summoned, now returned to their former attitude of assumed privilege. They did not assist the Virginians in loading the ammunition and other supplies for the return to Great Meadows, and now, on the march, they refused to help draw the swivels, nor would they so much as assist in clearing obstacles from the path. All such, they protested, was work for porters and laborers, not soldiers of the king. As Washington had feared, the recalcitrance of the independent company was a contagion that soon infected his own men, many of whom grumbled under the weight of their burdens. Adam Stephen recalled that they "became as backward as the regulars,"[17] and Washington and the other officers continually had to order, exhort, and cajole the men to continue the journey.

Perhaps Washington conjured for them visions of the food and other supplies that must by now be waiting for them at Fort Necessity. If he did, all must have been heartbroken to find, as they entered the fort on July 1, that its storehouse was as empty as ever. Late that day, their spirits were lifted by the arrival of a convoy—only to be dashed again when it was discovered that it carried nothing but a few sacks of flour.

In the fullness of time, George Washington would became famous for leading armies in the extremity of want—most notably through the winter of 1776 at Valley Forge, but also through every winter of the long war for independence. Here was his very first experience of commanding hungry, tired men, men he had marched to an advance post, had put to hard labor—first in clearing a road and then in erecting palisades at Gist's settlement—then had marched back, requiring them to take on burdens customarily left to animals and obliging them to do so on a diet of nothing better than parched corn. Expecting relief at Great Meadows, they found almost none. Privation and the presumed proximity of the enemy stirred a fog of terror. For many, the only answer seemed a further retreat, a renewed march designed to put more miles between themselves and the French before an attack made that impossible.

As hungry as anyone else, Washington carefully considered the advisability—perhaps the necessity—of withdrawing yet closer to the English settlements. The decision to return to Fort Necessity had been predicated on the assumption (according to Washington's minutes) that they would be "Supply'd with a Stock of provisions Sufficient to serve us for some months."[18] Without these—without enough to support his soldiers and the Half-King's Indians—how could he hope to hold Fort Necessity?

But then he thought the desperate situation through. His men were surely too weak to haul the swivel guns any farther, yet how could he abandon those guns to the French? Moreover, the teamsters who had driven the disappointing convoy told him that two Independent Companies from New York had reached Alexandria some three weeks earlier. Presumably, these men would soon be sent to him. Besides, Governor Dinwiddie had promised even more reinforcements.

Washington made his decision. He would hold Fort Necessity.

He sent a dispatch to Wills Creek reporting his situation and requesting that reinforcements and provisions be sent to him immediately. This done, he put his much-wasted army to work improving the fort. For, suddenly, there seemed much to be done. Washington had left Fort Necessity well pleased with it. Having returned, however, he now saw it as grossly inadequate. He ordered soldiers to fell trees in order to strengthen the stockade, and he directed that the trenches outside the fort's wall be extended past the small branch that ran nearby. This would ensure that under fire and even under siege, his men would still be able to fetch water, protected by a mound of earthworks.

Walking about the fort, Washington recognized that the marshy ground probably limited the French options for attack to a single direction, the south. He therefore concentrated on strengthening that approach to the fort. If, however, he was inclined to congratulate himself on having chosen to place his fort in a place that limited an attacker's possible approaches, further reflection should have given him pause. He had built his fort on bottomland—hence the marshy quality of the ground—meaning that it was surrounded by high ground, which gave any attacker an advantage. Moreover, Fort Necessity was within musket range of the surrounding woods. An attacker could fire from concealment as well as cover. Perhaps Washington recognized all this now. Most likely, however, he did not. For he ordered his men to clear more of the ground around the fort in order to provide a field of fire the better to repulse an attack. This work, of course, was as beneficial to the enemy as to his men, clearing for them a field of fire as well as a field for advance. Washington may have learned something about the tactics of fortification during the few days he had spent away from Fort Necessity, but he had not learned enough.

❧

Not nearly enough. And clearly, the Indians concluded as much. By July 2, those who had been camped at Great Meadows melted away, including the Half-King himself. He later explained to Conrad Weiser—a Pennsylvanian who was one of the few truly effective diplomats in white-Indian relations—that he regarded Washington as "a good-natured man but had no experience." The Half-King elaborated, complaining that Washington "would by no means take Advice from the Indians." In particular, "he lay at [Great Meadows] from one full Moon to the other and made no Fortifications at all, but that little thing upon the Meadow"—Fort Necessity, of which the colonel was so proud. The Half-King continued his tactical critique, pointing out that Washington had placed Fort Necessity "where he thought the French would come up to him in open Field," whereas, had he "made such Fortifications as the Half King advised him to make he would certainly have beat the French off." Either the Half-King failed to detail or Weiser failed to record just how he had advised Washington to place and build his fortifications, but the chief judged that, in the Battle of Great Meadows, "the French had acted as great Cowards, and the English as Fools." As for himself, he "had carried off his Wife and Children, so did other Indians before the Battle begun, because Col. Washington would never listen to them, but was always driving them on to fight by his Directions."[19]

Young Colonel Washington was better than many other English military leaders in dealing with Indians, but he shared the white perception that failed to appreciate the political sophistication of Indian diplomacy. What Washington saw as a breach of loyalty, a desertion, the Half-King regarded as prudence. After all, you do not attach your life and fortunes to a leader who relies on a little fort, ill-sited at that, for protection against attack by superior numbers. Washington had earlier assured the Half-King and his followers that "The only motive of our conduct" in acting against the French was "to put you again in possession of your lands, and to take care of your wives and children, to dispossess the French, to maintain your rights and to secure the whole country for you; for these very ends are the English arms now employed."[20] Reading this today, it is difficult to believe that the Half-King, long experienced in dealing with white settlers, took this at face value. Indeed, it is difficult to imagine that Washington himself believed the Indians had accepted this tale of unconditional altruism. Yet he was shocked nevertheless when the Half-King and his people decamped. Despite all that Washington had managed to learn in a short period of time about white-Indian relations, to have expected unthinking allegiance from the chief seems the height of naiveté or, at the very least, wishful thinking.

In fact, the "desertion" of the Half-King was nothing more than the culmination of the failure of Anglo-Indian diplomacy. It was not Washington's fault, but it was his problem. He had inherited the general English failure to deal with the Indians as politically, socially, and economically sophisticated individuals. In the long term, this would greatly weaken the British position in the French and Indian War. In the short term, it left George Washington without the level of reconnaissance he had become accustomed to. On the night of July 2/3, he sent some soldiers to reconnoiter, knowing full well that they did not possess the Indians' skill in tracking men through the woods. Washington realized that he was as good as blind. He therefore dispatched pickets to every point at which they might hear or see the approach of the French. This meant thinning his already thin ranks that much more. And if four hundred men were few to begin with, Washington had also to contend with exhaustion, privation, and sickness. As of nightfall on July 2, he counted just 284 men fit for duty—of which a number had been sent out as sentinels.

✾

As it turned out, the first sign of the approach of the French was not at all subtle. At daybreak on July 3, everyone heard a single musket shot. One of Washington's sentinels called for the guard. He had been shot in the heel. Washington ordered his men to arms. The attack, he believed, would come at any moment.

What came, however, was rain. By sunup, it was a drizzle, but it was soon hard and steady. Fort Necessity, the lowest point in a surrounding marsh, became a basin, the defensive trenches quickly filling with water in which the men had no choice but to crouch, awaiting the onslaught.

They waited, and they waited. At nine o'clock—about five soaked hours after Washington had issued his order to arms—his sentinels began sending reports. One, breathless, described the French and Indians as on the march, all of them naked, and now just four miles distant. A second report—more sober, but not less terrifying—estimated that nine hundred French soldiers were approaching from the Monongahela.

With water rising and mud churning, there was only one useful command Washington could give: *Keep your powder dry.*

A small circular stockade fifty-three feet in diameter with waterlogged trenches just beyond it. Four hundred men, a third of them too hungry or too sick to fight. The rest huddled in the stockade, or crouching in the muddy water of a trench, or kneeling or lying at a distance behind whatever clump of cover Washington himself had failed to clear. They were men who had been living for well over a week on nothing but parched corn and, before that, a little stringy beef. Their commander was twenty-two years old. The captain of the independent company did not pay him much heed, and the Indians—there never were very many of them to begin with—had all drifted away.

Keep your powder dry. It was, at least, something to focus on as the insistent drumming of the rain marked each minute.

❦

Recalling events a year or two after they happened, George Washington said that a sentinel fired his musket at about ten. Others who were present put it at eleven—the hour Washington himself reported in a July 19 account to Governor Dinwiddie. Whatever the precise time, the sentinel had caught sight of troops and used his musket to alert Fort Necessity. Washington subsequently reported to Dinwiddie that this sentinel managed to kill three Frenchmen, but his gunfire also provoked the French to make their move.

As Washington reported it, they began "to fire upon us, at about 600 Yards Distance." Such fire was premature, of course—six hundred yards being at least six times the effective range of eighteenth-century muskets. Either Washington's sentinel had the French spooked or, as Washington suspected, "this distant Fire of the Enemy [was] only an Artifice to intimidate, or draw our Fire from us."[21]

To *intimidate?* Washington and his men believed that the attacking force consisted of nine hundred men, more than three times the number defending Fort Necessity. Doubtless, this was intimidation enough. Yet Washington was not intimidated. He ordered his men not to return the French "Salute" until they were nearer.[22]

It is important to read the report Washington and Captain Mackay jointly prepared for Dinwiddie in the context of other accounts of the battle. As Washington tells it, the French advanced "in a very irregular manner"—although later he described the advance as coming in three columns. The later recollection suggests the good order of a menacing advance, while the first, more immediate report, suggests disorder, as if something were amiss with the French tactics.

Captain Louis Coullon de Villiers, the French commander, later admitted in a report to his own superiors that something *had been* amiss. Coullon de Villiers was the older brother of Jumonville, the "ambassador" who had been killed in the Battle of the Bower. Understandably, he was hungry for a measure of revenge, and perhaps it was an over-eagerness that drove him to act rashly at the first report of an English musket. The lowliest leader of a patrol or a platoon knows that, when moving in proximity to an enemy's front, it can be quickly fatal to expose your flank. To fight the enemy effectively, you must *face* him, not present to him the side of your moving column—especially when that enemy can shoot massed

volleys from fortified cover. It was precisely this blunder that Coullon de
Villiers committed.

From the July 19 report to Dinwiddie, it is apparent that Washington
had deployed some of his men in the open field in advance of his
trenches. This should have enabled him to open fire on the exposed
French flank. Yet, except for noting the irregularity of the French advance,
Washington must have failed to appreciate the significance of Coullon de
Villiers's tactical error. Certainly he did not attempt to exploit it. Instead,
he wrote to Dinwiddie that the French advanced to "another Point of
Woods, about 60 Yards off, and from thence made a second Discharge."
This led him to conclude that they "had no Intention of attacking us in
the open Field, we retired to our Trenches, and still reserved our Fire; as
we expected from their great Superiority of Numbers, that they would
endeavour to force our Trenches."[23]

A more experienced commander—or one who had a more instinctive
grasp of tactics—would have exploited his enemy's error. Instead,
Washington and Mackay took pains to portray themselves as
commanders whose cool heads allowed them to proceed strictly by the
book: always let the enemy fire the first volley, and do not fire until you
are at optimum range.

No sooner did Washington order his troops to withdraw to their
trenches than he concluded that the French were not preparing to storm
them. Accordingly, he "gave Orders to fire, which was done with great
Alacrity and Undauntedness."[24]

The "Undauntedness" was apparently not as complete as the report to
Dinwiddie suggests. Landon Carter, a wealthy planter who served in the
Virginia Regiment and kept a remarkable diary spanning from 1752 to
1778, recorded that Washington's second in command, the newly promoted lieutenant colonel George Muse, was quite daunted indeed. Carter
recorded that, "instead of bringing up the 2d division to make the Attack
with the first, he marched them or rather frightened them back to the
trenches, so that the Colo. at the head of the Carolina independent com-

pany was greatly exposed to the French Fire and were forced to retire to the same trenches, where they were galled on All sides by 1,100 French and Indians who never came to an Open ground but fired from behind trees."[25] Carter wrote "Colo." as an abbreviation for "Colonel," but doubtless he was referring to *Captain* Mackay.

The difference between Washington and Mackay's account and Carter's diary entry is striking and suggestive. Whereas the two commanders portrayed the withdrawal to the trenches as a purposeful tactical response to defend the trenches after the French had failed to advance to do battle across the open field, Carter reveals it instead as a retreat compelled by the cowardice of a key Virginia officer. Charitably, we may conclude that Washington and Mackay thought it unseemly to report to the governor the cowardice of a brother officer. Less generously, we may see the suppression of Muse's cowardice in this report as a refusal to concede (or, at any rate, to report) a failure of tactics. Whatever the reason for leaving Muse out of the report, his action must not have remained a secret, for his was the only name omitted from a list of officers the House of Burgesses officially thanked for their participation in the Battle of Great Meadows.

Cowardice. That is also what the Half-King—although he was not, of course, present at the battle—accused the French of. Perhaps he had heard how they fought: not by advancing across the open field and storming Fort Necessity, but, as Washington put it in a later recollection, by keeping "up a constant, galling fire upon us" from "every little rising, tree, stump, stone and bush."[26]

Yet was this cowardice? Or was it the tactic of a commander more pragmatic than the Half-King and more experienced than Washington? Consider Washington and Mackay's July 19 report to Dinwiddie: "We continued this unequal Fight, with an Enemy sheltered behind the Trees, ourselves without Shelter, in Trenches full of Water, in a settled Rain, and the Enemy galling us on all Sides incessantly from the Woods . . ."[27] Washington complains that the enemy is sheltered, but his men are not.

What, then, was the point of building Fort Necessity, if not to provide shelter from which to defend against an *exposed* enemy? To any objective reader, this sentence stands as a ringing condemnation of Washington's tactics at the Battle of Great Meadows. His fort provided only wet misery, no real shelter. Worse, because it was situated in a clearing surrounded by woods, it actually provided the *enemy* with ample shelter. We cannot help but wonder if both authors of this report—Washington and Mackay—were equally aware of the import of this description. It is a complaint about being trapped. What goes unspoken is the plain fact that Fort Necessity was a trap of Colonel Washington's own making—as, doubtless, the Half-King had tried to warn him.

With Washington and his men trapped in a little stockade surrounded by woods and now practically under water, why would Coullon de Villiers have exposed his men to a charge? He enjoyed far superior numbers, which meant that he had far more firepower. He could keep picking away at his enemy, who, after all, wasn't going anywhere.

The French did not fire on Washington's men alone. "The Enemy . . . deprived us of all our Creatures; by killing, in the Beginning of the Engagement, our Horses, Cattle, and every living Thing they could, even to the very Dogs."[28] The last of the meat shot away, together with the remaining means of non-pedestrian transportation, the jaws of the trap tightened inexorably, and, as long as the French kept pouring on the fire, there was no way for Washington to hold out, let alone prevail. Nevertheless, for the entire day and then as day eased into evening, against overwhelming numbers and a hail of lead that vied with the rain, Washington kept his men in the fight. He went from soldier to soldier, speaking to each, from time to time taking up a position beside each and fighting along with them. When he saw panic sweep over the trench, when he saw how his men in the fog of war had begun to shoot at one another, he wasted no words, but leaped into the flooded entrenchment to interpose his own tall figure between the muskets of his troops. This turned their fire back upon the enemy.

As fierce as the firefight was, the rain was an enemy to both defender and attacker, nearly drowning men and surely drenching powder and cartridges. There was, finally, no keeping your powder dry—and even if you somehow could, the firelocks could not be protected. The flint would not strike a spark, and the powder would not ignite. Toward evening, fewer and fewer shots came from the English trenches—but by that time, few shots were coming from the French in the forest, either. Clearly, their usable ammunition was running low as well, and it must have been this that prompted the call across the field about eight in the evening: "Voulez-vous parler?"[29]

No, Washington replied. He would not parley.

His refusal was not empty gallantry. Washington may have been guilty of tactical blunders, but he knew men. A parley would give the French officers a close look at Fort Necessity, including the layout of the trenches. Suspecting "a Deceit"—why would the commander of so vastly superior a force be the first to call a parley?—Washington "refused to consent that they should come among us." In response to this refusal, the French commander asked for an officer to be sent to them, "and engaged their Parole for his Safety."[30]

Now this suggested to the colonel that the French sincerely wanted to offer terms. Yet, doubtless because of that very fact, he was still reluctant even to talk. Why were the French so willing to stop the fight?

It was quiet now, after a day of the continual roar of musketry. It was quiet, save for the moans of the wounded. Washington could see that more than a third of the men who had been fit for fighting were now either dead or hurt. His powder and cartridges were soaked, and the rain kept falling. Wet and fouled, the muskets needed to be cleaned, but among all of his men, there were only two screws—the long corkscrew-like instruments used to remove wet charges from firelocks. Most of the guns, therefore, were useless.

Washington looked around him. His cattle were dead. His horses, too. He had two bags of flour and a small amount of bacon. If he had any

more parched corn, his records at this time do not mention it.
At most, there were three days' short rations—starvation rations—
remaining.

What the men did have was rum. Of all things, the most recent convoy had brought up a supply of rum to be used as presents for the Indians
and to buck up soldiers on hard duty. The Indians were gone, and all of
Washington's soldiers were doing the hardest of hard duty. So, now that
the shooting had stopped, they helped themselves to the rum and heed-
lessly drank themselves into varying states of stupor. They would not be
fit to fight again any time soon.

George Washington summoned his two French-speaking officers,
Jacob van Braam and a scout named William La Péronie. He sent them
out to the woods, in the rain, to speak to the French.

10

ANATOMY OF SURRENDER

La Péronie and van Braam spent little time in conference with the French before returning to Fort Necessity. All the two men could convey was that the French were willing to allow the English to leave the fort and return to Virginia; they would not be made prisoners of war. Judging from the report Washington and Mackay prepared for Governor Dinwiddie, this was a lot better than they had expected: "From the Numbers of the Enemy, and our Situation, we could not hope for Victory; and from the Character of those we had to encounter, we expected no Mercy, but on Terms that we positively resolved not to submit to."[1] Yet Washington was not satisfied with the offer, most likely because the terms were so vague. He ordered La Péronie and van Braam to return to the French and talk some more.

Then something happened. Somehow, La Péronie sustained a serious wound, either during the parley or immediately after it. Was he shot? Was he injured in some other way? We do not know, but he collapsed and was unable to return to the French lines. This left van Braam—whose first language was Dutch, second language French, and third English—to han-

dle the parley on his own. The French commander, Coulon de Villiers,
recorded in his journal what he said to the Dutchman:

> *I sent M. le Mercier to receive [van Braam], and I went to*
> *the Meadow, where I told him, that as we were not at War,*
> *we were very willing to save them from the Cruelties to*
> *which they exposed themselves, on Account of the Indians;*
> *but if they were stubborn, we would take away from them*
> *all Hopes of escaping; that we consented to be favourable to*
> *them at present, as we were come only to revenge my*
> *Brother's Assassination, and to oblige them to quit the Lands*
> *of the King our Master; . . . We considered that . . .*
> *it was not proper to make Prisoners in a Time of Peace.*[2]

Around midnight, van Braam returned to Washington with the document of surrender—the *Capitulation*—Coulon de Villiers had prepared.
It was raining as usual, and the text, scratched out in a barely legible hand
to begin with, was runny and blurred on the damp paper. It now fell to
van Braam, using his knowledge of his second language, to translate the
terms into his third language; for La Péronie was disabled. Later, as we
shall see, another officer with a reading knowledge of French reviewed the
document, but only after it had been signed and the surrender made.
Why Washington did not call on this officer to review the French original
before signing it, we do not know. Nor do we know firsthand how van
Braam translated the document. His translation does not survive. The
original French document still exists in the Archives of the District of
Montreal, and a later English translation was republished in *The Papers of
George Washington,* edited by W.W. Abbott. The *Capitulation* begins:

> *As our Intentions have never been to trouble the Peace and*
> *good Harmony subsisting between the two Princes in Amity,*
> *but only to revenge the Assassination ["seulement de venger*
> *L'assasin"] committed on one of our Officers, bearer of a*
> *Summons, as also on his Escorte, and to hinder any*
> *Establishment on the Lands of the Dominions of the King*
> *my Master: Upon these Considerations, we are willing to*
> *shew Favour to all the English who are in the said Fort. . .* [3]

The document goes on to specify: "It shall be permitted him to go out,
and carry with him all that belongs to them, except the Artillery, which
we reserve." Moreover, Coulon de Villiers generously stipulated that "we
allow them the Honours of War; that they march out with Drums beat-
ing, and one Swivel Gun, being willing thereby to convince them, that we
treat them as Friends." Because the "*English* have but few Oxen or Horses
left, they are at Liberty to hide their Effects, and to come again, and
search for them, when they have a Number of Horses sufficient to carry
them off." Article VII stipulated that "as the *English* have in their Power,
one Officer, two Cadets, and most of the Prisoners made at the
Assassination of M. *de Jumonville* [l'assasinat du Sr. de Jumonville],"
Washington must promise to send them back. "For Surety of their per-
forming this Article as well as [the rest of] this Treaty, M. *Jacob Vambrane*
[van Braam] and *Robert Stobo,* both Captains, shall be delivered to us as
Hostages, till the Arrival of our *French* and *Canadians* above mentioned."[4]

The only point Washington negotiated further was a stipulation that
the English surrender their "munitions of war." Washington objected that
to do this would be tantamount to suicide. Without ammunition, his
men would be easy prey for Indians. Van Braam returned to Coulon de
Villiers, mentioned this point, and obtained from the French commander
a pen stroke through the phrase "*munitions de guerre.*"[5]

As the French quite reasonably saw it, they had extracted far more than the simple capitulation of George Washington and his command. "We made the *English* consent to sign, that they had assassinated my Brother in his own Camp," Coulon de Villiers wrote in his journal.[6]

For their part, neither Washington nor Mackay made any mention of the *Capitulation*—let alone of having admitted to assassination—in their July 19 report to Dinwiddie. Indeed, they ended the report on a note that made their defeat look suspiciously like a victory:

> *The Number killed and wounded of the Enemy is uncertain, but by the Information given by some Dutch in their Service to their Countrymen in ours, we learn that it amounted to above three hundred; and we are induced to believe it must be very considerable, by their being busy all Night in burying their Dead, and yet many remained the next Day; and their Wounded we know was considerable, by one of our Men, who had been made Prisoner by them after signing the Articles, and who, on his Return told us, that he saw great Numbers much wounded and carried off upon Litters.*

In addition, Indians told Washington "that the French had an Officer of distinguishable Rank killed." At any rate, Washington and Mackay reasoned, "Some considerable Blow they must have received, to induce them to call first for a Parley, knowing, as they perfectly did, the Circumstances we were in."[7]

Coulon de Villiers reported his casualties very differently: two killed, seventeen wounded seriously, and a "number so slightly wounded, as to have no Occasion for the Surgeon." Moreover, the Frenchman mentioned no loss of a high-ranking officer.[8]

What could account for the disparity? According to Parson Weems's celebrated cherry tree fable, Washington was incapable of telling a lie. And although Weems was writing fiction, his point was well taken. No one ever called Washington a liar. Almost certainly, the body count Washington and Mackay estimated was not a deliberate untruth, but the product of wishful thinking and as such, it was echoed in other British sources. There is, of course, no guarantee that Coulon de Villiers was any-more candid or accurate, but it is very likely that his figures are closer to the facts. As Washington's men were shooting from the cover of Fort Necessity and its trenches, outnumbered, all but starving, having to con-tend with rain and wet powder, it is a testament to the skill of his command that nineteen Frenchmen were killed or wounded. But *three hundred* slain? That, under the circumstances, seems simply impossible.

If Washington inflated—deliberately or unconsciously—what he had achieved at Great Meadows, it is difficult to imagine what he now thought of Fort Necessity as he prepared, under French eyes, to leave it. Perhaps it seemed much smaller now—deflated—as he and his men set about salvaging what equipment and supplies they could. The attack had left not a single horse alive, so everything would have to be borne on sol-diers' backs—including some of the wounded and sick. The precious rations amounted to three days' worth of short provisions. These were carefully apportioned among the troops. As for gunpowder, the soldiers took all they could, but some of it could not be carried and therefore had to be scattered to the four winds. A guard of eleven privates, a sergeant, and an ensign were, with French permission, left behind to tend to those

so badly wounded that they could not be moved and to watch over the
private baggage of the officers, which had to be left behind.

The French soldiers were remarkably quiet through the ordeal of their
enemies. There was no jeering, no interference of any kind—until the servant of Major Adam Stephen called out to his master: "Major, a
Frenchman has carried off your clothes!"[9]

Stephen spun about and recognized his portmanteau hoisted on the
shoulder of a French trooper, who now broke into a run as he made for a
knot of his fellow soldiers. Stephen gave chase, grabbed the portmanteau
from the soldier, and sent him off with a sharp kick, then started back for
his own men, who had been formed into marching order.

Not so fast. Two French officers confronted Stephen with a warning:
Assault a French soldier, and the terms of the Capitulation were void.

Adam Stephen was not accustomed to being threatened in such a
manner and responded to the French officers with what he later called
"pertness." Then he must have realized how he looked: covered in mud
and bereft of stockings, as well as any badge of rank. Clearly, the French
officers had not recognized him as an officer, but thought him a common,
ill-behaved English private—that is, until he rendered his "pertness."
Whatever he said, it was sufficient to prompt their startled question: *Are
you an officer?* Stephen answered wordlessly, directing his servant to open
the recovered portmanteau. From it, he had his man withdraw a "flaming
suit of laced regimentals"—his best dress uniform—which he instantly
donned over his mud-caked clothes. Yes, he was an officer.

With that, the incident was instantly defused. An officer, after all, has
every right to kick a soldier—regardless of nationality.

Why didn't you ask for hostages in exchange for the two you left? one
of the Frenchmen asked, laughing. Then he obligingly volunteered his
comrade and himself for hostage duty, explaining that they very much
wanted to go to Virginia, where (they had heard) there were so many
fine young ladies.

The matter of clothing occupied considerable time before the retreat from Fort Necessity finally got under way. Washington had some very fine clothes that he could not carry back with him, but was loath to leave in the care of the French. Since Jacob van Braam was remaining with them as a hostage, Washington offered him some of his finery—though at a price. A silver-fringed broadcloth coat went to van Braam for £6, and a fancy scarlet waistcoat for £7. Van Braam had a standing debt with Washington to the tune of £16, and agreed to assign two months' pay to the colonel.

As for whatever other belongings were left and could not be carried, Washington ordered their destruction. He did not want the French or the Indians to have them.

By ten o'clock in the morning, all had been loaded, sold, or destroyed. Granted the honors of war, Washington took them. He ordered the drums to beat and the colors raised high. At the head of his first major command, Washington marched out of Fort Necessity. The day was July 4, 1754.

*

At the end of that fourth day of July, Washington ordered a bivouac just three miles from Fort Necessity. In the morning, he called for a count. Virginia Regiment survivors numbered 293 officers and men. They trudged on to Wills Creek, reaching it by July 8 or 9. Here another count was ordered. The Virginia Regiment now numbered just 165. Some had died between the bivouac and Wills Creek, but most of the reduction was due to desertion. In addition, twenty-nine men had been left along the road, too tired, too hurt, or just too footsore to keep up with the others. As Washington tallied the actual combat casualties, he had lost thirty killed, seventy wounded, and nineteen missing.

It is painful for any commander to count his dead and wounded. We do not know if Washington felt any guilt or believed he deserved blame for his casualties, defenders of an ill-sited fort, victims of a battle he himself had provoked by his rash action at the bower. We can assume, however, that he considered the losses to have been incurred honorably. They were the price of battle.

But—probably as early as July 5—something far more disturbing than casualties came to George Washington's attention. An officer among the members of the regiment who possessed at least a rudimentary reading knowledge of French reviewed the signed *Capitulation*. In full daylight, not a rainy night, the rough handwriting was doubtless more legible. The officer stuck on two words, *l'assassin* and *l'assassinat*. He pointed these out to Washington. As mentioned, Jacob van Braam's translation is lost, but he had (according to Washington's later claims) translated these words as "loss," "death," or "killing"; that is, according to Washington, van Braam had never used the words *assassin* and *assassinate*, or *murderer* and *murder*—for the French terms do not necessarily carry the political implication of assassination, but they do carry the moral weight of murder. Washington began to understand that, in signing the *Capitulation*, he had effectively admitted to having ordered the assassination or murder of Jumonville or perhaps had even identified himself as the assassin or murderer.

Washington's biographers have traditionally taken the young commander at his word: that he relied solely on van Braam's translation, so that he was entirely unaware that he was signing what was in effect a confession. The early nineteenth-century antiquarian Jared Sparks issued a twelve-volume edition of *The Writings of George Washington* in 1837. In it, he reproduced a letter written about 1757 to an unspecified correspondent, who may have been the historian William Smith (1727–1803) of Philadelphia. The manuscript of the letter is lost, but there is little reason to doubt the authenticity of what Sparks reproduced. Washington angrily declared: "That we were willfully, or ignorently, deceived by our interpreter in regard to the word *assassination,* I do aver, and will to my dying moment; so will every officer that was present." Washington continued: "The interpreter was a Dutchman, little acquainted with the English tongue, therefore might not advert to the tone and meaning of the word in English."[10]

The blame, then, lay with van Braam. One theory Washington offered was that van Braam was ignorant. He went on, however, to intimate a second theory, one of willful deceit: "but, whatever [van Braam's] motives were for so doing, certain it is, he called it the *death,* or the *loss,* of the Sieur Jumonville. So we received and so we understood it, until to our great surprise and mortification, we found it otherwise in a literal translation."[11]

Landon Carter, the prominent planter who was a member of the Virginia Regiment, supported the deceit theory: "The only unpardonable blunder that Washington made," he wrote in his diary, was "making a confidant of [van Braam], for he was a poor juggling servant but by understanding French and having attended the Colonel on his embassy made in the Spring to the fort he became a favorite and was preferred."[12]

Writing in 1948, Washington's first great biographer, Douglas Southall Freeman, was inclined to give Jacob van Braam the benefit of the doubt. It was not that van Braam was either ignorant or treacherous, but, Freeman speculated, "in the flickering light," the word *l'assasin* scrawled on the rain-soaked, runny manuscript might easily have appeared to be *l'assaillir.* Seeing that this *verb* ("to assault") did not make sense where a *noun* was called for, van Braam used a non-specific and neutral English term for his translation: *death, loss,* or *killing.*[13]

Freeman pointed out that "at least one other translator" later "hesitated" over the word. Freeman did not, however, account for the mistranslation of *l'assasinat,* which occurs a few lines further on in the document.[14] Nevertheless, it is difficult to imagine what motive van Braam would have had for treachery. What could he have had to gain? Considering the combination of poor lighting, rain-drenched ink and paper, bad penmanship, the stress of a desperate battle just ended, and van Braam's imperfect knowledge of French and even worse command of English, it is more than likely that he simply made a poor translation—not once, but twice. Major Adam Stephen's recollection of the episode lends persuasive weight to what we might call the theory of the honest mistake. He recounted that when van Braam

> *returned with the French Proposals, we were obliged to take the Sense of them by Word of Mouth: It rained so heavily that he could not give us a written Translation of them; we could scarcely keep the Candle light to read them; they were wrote in a bad Hand, on wet and blotted Paper, so that no Person could read them but Van Braam, who had heard them from the Mouth of the French Officer. Every Officer, then present, is willing to declare, that there was no such Word as Assassination mentioned; the Terms expressed to us, were "the Death of Jumonville." If it had been mentioned, we could have got it altered, as the French seemed very condescending, and willing to bring Things to a Conclusion, during the whole Course of the Interview.*[15]

Over the next days and months, even after he returned to Williamsburg, the assault on his honor would stick in Washington's craw. However, the entire controversy seems to have disturbed Washington more than anyone else—which is not to say that there was a scarcity of critics of Washington's conduct of the failed mission to evict the French from the Ohio country.

William Johnson, provincial superintendent of Indian affairs and certainly the one English colonial official who enjoyed the most cordial and productive relations with the Indians, declared in a letter of July 29, 1754, that he wished "Washington had acted with prudence and circumspection requisite in an officer of rank, and the trust at the same time reposed in him, but I can't help saying he was very wrong in many respects and I doubt [suspect] his being too ambitious of acquiring all the honor or as much as he could before the rest joined him." Johnson believed that Washington's biggest mistake was "giving too much credit to the reports or accounts given him by the French deserters (which did not show him at all the soldier)." It would have been far better, Johnson believed, for Washington to "have avoided an engagement until all our troops were assembled."[16]

There were others who decried Washington's youth and lack of experience, and Governor Dinwiddie doubtless listened to them. After all, in a letter to Washington written on June 27, 1754, he had admonished the commander: "I wish You had suspended going to Red Stone Creek, 'till You was joined by other Forces, being much afraid of a Surprize." In a letter written to Maryland governor Horatio Sharpe on July 31, 1754, Dinwiddie, perhaps through faulty memory, transformed this after-the-fact admonition into a preemptive order not to attack until "the whole forces were joined in a body."[17] Actually, there is no record that Dinwiddie ever gave such an order, but, clearly, after the fact, he believed Washington had been reckless—yet he did not blame him greatly for this. He liked Washington and he continued to have confidence in him. The real blame, as far as the governor was concerned, lay with other colonies, which had failed to send sufficient numbers of troops in a timely manner. The soldiers promised by North Carolina and New York never materialized. Dinwiddie also had much to say against the Indian trader George Croghan, who had defaulted on the flour shipments he had been contracted to deliver.

Indeed, by the time Washington reached Williamsburg, on July 17, most of the carping had stopped, and he was generally greeted as a hero. Just two days after Washington arrived in the capital, the *Virginia Gazette* honored the "few brave men [who had] been exposed, to be butchered, by the negligence of those who . . . ought to have been with them many months before." Washington's name had even reached London, where the *Gentleman's Magazine* for July 1754 reproduced his letter to his brother, wherein he wrote of "something charming in the sound of bullets" as he fought the Battle of the Bower. George II himself read the article and reportedly remarked that Washington would not find the sound of bullets quite so charming "if he had been used to hear many."[18]

Official commendations would come, but they would have to await the convening of the General Assembly in its regular session. Governor Dinwiddie did take it upon himself to act immediately in granting a modest bounty to the men of the Virginia Regiment, using money that had been appropriated during the previous session. Washington was given 300 pistoles to distribute to his men "as a reward for their bravery."[19]

❧

Washington claimed to have destroyed whatever he and his men could not carry with them in their withdrawal from Fort Necessity. Certainly, he did not report any incident of French soldiers looting his baggage after the surrender. It is apparent, however, that they were not above rummaging—as Adam Stephen discovered when he chased down and kicked the soldier who had purloined his portmanteau—and it is apparent that French soldiers did examine some baggage either during the surrender or later, after Washington and his Virginians had left. They found some of Washington's clothing, books, surveying equipment, and—they claimed—a journal. Coulon de Villiers identified this document as Washington's diary and sent it on to his commanding officer, Contrecoeur, who, in turn, transmitted it to Governor Duquesne. After reading it, Duquesne wrote to Contrecoeur: "There is nothing more unworthy and lower, and even blacker, than the sentiments and the way of thinking of this Washington." Duquesne, in turn, sent the journal to Paris, where part of it was published in 1756 in a book called *Mémoire contenant le précis des faits, avec leurs pieces justificatives pour servir de response aux observations envoyées par les ministres d'Angleterre dans les cours de l'Europe.* This book was intended as a vindication of the French occupation of the Ohio country, and the portion of the Washington journal included in it was an account of the Battle of the Bower and the events leading up to it. The publication came to Washington's attention in 1757, when an English translation made from a copy of the *Mémoire* found in a captured French ship was published in New York. Washington responded to the document by pointing out that he "kept no regular [journal] during the expedition; rough minutes of occurrences I certainly took and find them [in the published journal] as certainly and strangely metamorphosed; some parts left out, which I remember were entered, and many things added that never were thought of." Indeed, comparing the translation of the French Washington "journal" with the material known indisputably to have been written by Washington reveals many instances of editorial license intended to make it look as if Washington had knowingly attacked at the Battle of the Bower a French "embassy," even as the French editor suppressed material suggesting that the so-called embassy was actually part of a larger force intended to drive the English out of the Ohio country by military means. Additionally, the French "journal" stressed passages that disparaged Britain's Indian allies, including the Half-King. Editorial footnotes ensured that the English were painted as the aggressors and that Washington was frankly depicted as the assassin (or murderer) of Jumonville.[20]

Thus George Washington was a victim of sufficient distortion to make him appear, at least to the French, as a villain—a murderer who got his comeuppance at Great Meadows. This, clearly, was propaganda, although by no means entirely unfounded in fact, and while Washington's officers

were, to a man, loyal, offering nothing but praise for their commander on
this mission, and while the governor and government of Virginia likewise
stood by the young colonel, modern historians have been harsher in their
assessment of George Washington's maiden command. Most see the
attack on Jumonville as reckless and the choice to defend Fort Necessity
as even worse—the product of a thoughtless excess of confidence and a
want of prudent judgment.

By any objective measure of military success, such modern assessments
are accurate. Washington picked a fight with a superior force, made grave
tactical mistakes defending against that force, and was defeated by that
force. In and of itself—again, objectively measured—the Battle of Great
Meadows was a small and shabby affair, a disproportionately bloody contest over a miserable pile of logs stacked between a pair of converging
rivulets in a Pennsylvania swamp.

But objective measurement is not always or necessarily an accurate historical tool. As the British letter writer and memoirist Horace Walpole
expressed it in his *Memoirs of the Reign of King George II (1822)*, "The volley fired by a young Virginian in the backwoods of America set the world
on fire." Few battles, no matter how great or small, have been of more
consequence than the one at Great Meadows. Here began the French and
Indian War, the commencement and North American theater of the cata-
clysmic Seven Years' War, truly the first "world" war, engulfing Europe,
India, the Caribbean, and vast portions of the Atlantic Ocean, killing
some 900,000 combatants, and savagely recarving the political contours
of the planet. It all started with Washington in a Pennsylvania swamp.

Great Meadows, the second battle of George Washington's military
career, was his first defeat. It would be one of many. In his highly percep-
tive *General George Washington* (2005), Edward G. Lengel wrote of the
colonel at Great Meadows, "His humiliation was complete."[21] True—
objectively considered—and yet Washington clearly experienced more
than humiliation in this battle and this defeat. He became in its harsh and
hasty process a soldier, a leader of soldiers—and more. He forged the

intellectual, visceral, and spiritual instruments that were indispensable to all that he would achieve militarily in the years that followed. Perhaps Great Meadows fathered the "Father of His Country." At any rate, in losing this youthful battle, Washington won what may be described with many words but that can be encompassed in a single word: *soul.* The battle that ended with Washington's surrender on the fourth of July 1754 was no mere humiliation, but a honing of character that would carry him to another July 4—in 1776—and beyond, from defeat to defeat punctuated by precious few victories yet culminating in the final triumph of independence.

Professor Lengel ends his chapter on Great Meadows not with the sentence about humiliation, but with words Washington himself wrote to William Fitzhugh (an old friend of his beloved half-brother, Lawrence) on November 15, 1754: "I have the consolation itself, of knowing, that I have opened the way when the smallness of our numbers exposed us to the attacks of a Superior Enemy; That I have hitherto stood the heat and brunt of the Day, and escaped untouched, in time of extreme danger; and that I have the Thanks of my Country, for the Services I have rendered it."[22]

EPILOGUE

OF A FIRE IN THE WILDERNESS AND THE SOUL OF A REVOLUTION

After Washington's return from the Ohio country, Governor Dinwiddie considered mounting a new expedition, presumably giving Washington another opportunity to command. By October 1754, however, Dinwiddie judged that the Virginia Regiment, even with assistance from other colonies—clearly an unlikely prospect—was insufficient to confront the French threat. He therefore decided to wait for help from the Crown in the form of some regiments of regulars, which were widely considered by the colonists to be invincible. While waiting, he did not disband the Virginia Regiment, but divided it into its constituent companies and sent the men to garrison what outposts the British still maintained. No soldier relishes garrison duty; moreover, Washington felt that each day the French were allowed to occupy the Ohio region—land of his king and of his country (by which he meant Virginia), and the land that represented the future of the Washington family fortune—was another surrender. He resigned his commission in disgust.

In truth, Dinwiddie responded to the crisis with calm intelligence and sound judgment. Washington's experience had proven that the French, in their current numbers and with the support of many Indians, were just too much for provincial forces. He reported the battles of the Bower and Great Meadows to the Lords of Trade in London, characterizing these exchanges collectively as a "small Engagement, conducted with Judgment by the Officers, and great Bravery by our few Forces," but went on to appeal for assistance in mounting a major offensive to evict the French once and for all.[1] The Crown agreed, and King George II's son, the Duke of Cumberland, as captain general of the army, laid out an ambitious four-pronged assault on all that France possessed—or claimed to possess—in North America.

The main prong was to consist of two regular British infantry regiments (plus provincials and whatever Indian allies could be recruited along the way) to follow Washington's route to the Forks of the Ohio. The mission of this group was to take and occupy Fort Duquesne. The other three forces would hit Nova Scotia, the Niagara forts on Lake Ontario, and the forts on Lake Champlain. Capture all of these forts, and the French would no longer be a presence in the Ohio Valley.

The commander of the Fort Duquesne expedition was Major General Edward Braddock. He was the typical professional British general officer; that is, he was old (sixty) and a lifelong military man (veteran of four decades), yet he was totally inexperienced in anything other than conventional European warfare. He had never fought a battle outside the continent and therefore knew nothing of wilderness combat. His ignorance did not prevent his assuming that Frenchmen, backwoods Canadians, and a horde of savage Indians could not possibly pose a serious challenge to British soldiers. For the "provincials" and Indian auxiliaries who were supposed to aid his expedition, he had, if anything, even less regard, dismissing both with utmost contempt. Such prejudicial attitudes were common in the British military of the time, but they may have been exaggerated in Braddock, who was considered a brave officer, but one wholly intolerant of opinions that differed from his and a bully to any who dared oppose him. As the Half-King had given Conrad Weiser his frank opinion of George Washington's shortcomings, so the Mingo chief Monacatoocha expressed himself freely to the Pennsylvania Council on Braddock. He was full of "pride and ignorance," the chief said, "a bad man when he was alive; he looked upon us as dogs, and would never hear anything what was said to him . . . he never appeared pleased with us and that was the reason that a great many of our Warriors left him and would not be under his Command."[2]

In sending Braddock in answer to Dinwiddie's plea, King George and his ministers were giving Virginia neither the best nor the worst officer in the British army. The governor, however, had reason to expect that the forces sent to him would be formidable, surely far larger, more impressive, and more capable than what he could muster in Virginia alone. In fact, the British army at this period was neither very large nor terribly impressive. Cumberland pulled two regiments, the 44th and the 48th Regiments of Foot, from garrison duty in Ireland. That they had been garrison soldiers is all that is needed to evaluate them. No army puts its best men—or even its reasonably good men—in garrison posts.

Perhaps realizing the relative weakness of the human material he had to work with, Braddock gathered together an unusually large panoply of artillery: four 12-pounder cannon, six 6-pounders, four 8-inch howitzers, and fifteen Coehorn mortars. The latter two weapons fired heavy projectiles in a high trajectory and were expressly intended to be used against fortifications in a siege. Braddock understood that his mission was to take a fort, so he brought along heavy siege artillery. What he did not understand was that the howitzers and Coehorns were massive overkill for taking a frontier stockade—they were intended to batter down stone walls or fly above such walls to the structures within—but, even worse, he did not appreciate the Herculean effort that would be required to transport a train consisting of such artillery through a nearly trackless wilderness over the rugged, thickly forested country between Alexandria, Virginia, and Fort Duquesne on the Ohio River.

Braddock, his regiments, and his hardware set sail in January 1755 and arrived in Virginia on February 20. Six weeks of stormy sea passage could not have improved the irascible commander's humor, and when he set foot ashore to find the Virginians going about their business as usual, lives apparently unperturbed, he was livid. Where was the stockpiling of arms? The recruiting of regiments? The drilling of companies? What was the plan? He demanded and secured an audience with Governor Dinwiddie, who in the end could offer him only two things.

The first was a map of Braddock's objective. Captain Robert Stobo, whom Washington had left with Coulon de Villiers as a hostage, was still being held, because Governor Dinwiddie refused to give up the prisoners Washington had taken at the Bower. Stobo had occupied his time most productively by drawing a detailed plan of Fort Duquesene, which he managed to smuggle out in a packet of letters. The biggest news in Stobo's account was that the fort was garrisoned by just four hundred men. Braddock must have brightened at this—for his two regiments mustered about two thousand regulars, plus some nine hundred provincials—but somebody in the governor's quarters warned the general that the biggest problem was not *taking* the fort, but *getting to* the fort. He would need help, someone who had both firsthand knowledge of the Alleghenies and military experience.

That's when Dinwiddie offered his second item: George Washington. Indeed, Washington had already made overtures of his own, having wasted no time in dispatching a letter congratulating General Braddock on his safe arrival in Virginia. Clearly, he wanted the general to know his name. Yet when the prospect of service in the expedition was actually raised, Washington balked. His experience with Captain Mackay and the independent company had left a distinctly bitter taste. As a provincial colonel, he was certainly inferior to one of the king's majors and, at best, the equivalent of a regular captain—although most regular captains would regard him as an inferior. Braddock was persuaded that a man like

Washington would be invaluable to him, but he did not have it in his power to secure for him a royal commission as a captain of regulars. He therefore proposed an alternative, suggesting to Dinwiddie that this provincial colonel might serve him as an aide-de-camp. That would circumvent the established chain of command, because Washington would report directly to Braddock, bypassing all other officers.

Braddock agreed, and Washington was thrilled. Not only would this put him in action again—among the charming sound of bullets—it would afford him what he himself realized he so desperately needed: an apprenticeship with an experienced officer of a regular European army.

*

The very first lesson Washington learned was one of which he already had more than an inkling. The bigger the army, the harder it was to move. What must have dismayed Washington, however, was that Braddock seemed to be learning this very lesson right along with his apprentice.

Early in April 1755, Braddock sent his army on ahead of him, from Alexandria to the British outpost at Wills Creek, while he held a council of war with Dinwiddie and the governors of Maryland, Pennsylvania, New York, and Massachusetts. When he caught up with his troops later in the month, he was confounded with rage to find his forces idling, awaiting supplies promised by various colonial purveyors. Local pledges, it seems, were freely made, but little or nothing was actually delivered. It was a situation that would have tried the patience of a saint, and Edward Braddock was anything but that. He railed against the damned provincials, even as his quartermaster, Sir John St. Clair, loudly threatened to ride, "Sword drawn . . . through the Province and treat the Inhabitants as a parcel of Traitors."[3]

As Washington looked on, this is what he saw and learned: the more the British commanders blustered and threatened, the less willing were his fellow Americans to help. It would be presumptuous to conclude that Braddock's young aide saw in this situation the seeds of revolution, but he did learn that the logistics of even the mightiest of armies depended heavily on the cooperation and goodwill of local civilians.

Even well supplied, an army encumbered with the baggage and artillery Braddock lugged was grotesquely out of place in the American backwoods. On April 23, Washington wrote to William Fairfax: "Our march must be regulated by the slow movements of the [artillery] Train." This was not so much a lesson to Washington as confirmation of what his brief experience already told him; the difficulty, he wrote, was "answerable to the expectation I have long conceived, tho' few believ'd."[4]

It was April 21 before Braddock reached Frederick, Maryland, and May 10 when he reached Fort Cumberland, the British forward outpost at Wills Creek. En route, anticipated Indian allies failed to materialize at Winchester, Virginia. Now, with potential Indian allies gathered all around Fort Cumberland, Washington saw how Braddock managed to alienate them by haughtily refusing to concede to them certain rights within the territory of the Ohio Valley. ("He looked upon us as dogs," Monacatoocha would later say.)

Then Washington saw how the great army—2,900 men and all that artillery—struggled piteously to move out of Fort Cumberland from May 30 to June 10. Unable to move heavily laden wagons over the rugged trails, even after these had been "improved" by the time-consuming labor of his men, Braddock ordered some supplies to be left behind at Fort Cumberland. This helped a bit, but even Braddock despaired of reaching Fort Duquesne in anything under a matter of months. Washington, the apprentice, at last chimed in. He suggested detaching a "flying column" to make the initial assault. Braddock agreed. Stobo had said that only four hundred men were garrisoned; therefore, Braddock handpicked eight hundred of his regulars, plus about six hundred provincials, chose eight artillery pieces, and hauled thirty wagons. The rest of the force would catch up when it could.

George Washington must now have felt the satisfaction of having offered an idea that proved a success. The rate of march instantly quickened. But then the conventional soldier in Braddock reemerged, and Washington experienced renewed frustration as the general slowed the pace so that his men could clear and level a better road—one that the streamlined flying column did not require (as Washington saw it). Worse, Washington soon fell ill and, on June 23, asked Braddock to leave him behind near the Youghioheny River until he recovered. He would then catch up with his commander and the flying column. Although it is unclear at this point what Washington thought of Braddock, the general's genuine regard for his aide-de-camp is apparent. He left him with a packet of Dr. James's fever powder—which Washington found most efficacious—and promised that he would not fight without sending for him first.

On June 24, the flying column encountered the first signs of the French and Indian presence—abandoned campfires, canoes, and taunting messages painted on the trees. On the 25TH, when the soldiers stirred from their night's bivouac, they woke to another, far more ominous sign: three of their number had been killed and scalped. No one had heard their cries in the night—if the stealthy attackers had even allowed them to make a sound.

By July 8, when Washington, barely recovered from his bout of fever, rejoined Braddock, the flying column was quite near Fort Duquesne. Weak, apparently afflicted with hemorrhoids so painful that he ordered his servant to affix cushions to his saddle, Washington rode out on the next day with Braddock and five hundred regulars. Ahead of them was an advance party of three hundred led by an officer Washington quite admired, Lieutenant Colonel Thomas Gage of the 44TH Regiment of Foot. In May 1774, Gage would take up the post of royal governor and military commander-in-chief of Massachusetts, sent by George III to crush the incipient rebellion there. Behind Gage's three hundred regulars were the one hundred men of an independent company from New York, led by co-captains Robert Cholmley and Horatio Gates, the latter of whom, in the American Revolution, would be credited with victory at Saratoga in 1777. Always jealous of General Washington, Gates would be implicated in the so-called "Conway Cabal," which sought to remove Washington as commander of the Continental Army and replace him with none other than Horatio Gates. The Independent Company served as guard to a working party of two hundred fifty under St. Clair. Braddock, Washington, and the five hundred regulars were behind the working party. Behind them, acting as the flying column's rear guard, were one hundred Virginia provincials under the redoubtable Adam Stephen.

Braddock's main body finished crossing the Monongahela at about two in the afternoon. Aside from the three killings discovered on May 25, the approach to the outskirts of Fort Duquesne had been remarkably unremarkable. The absence of opposition suggested to some that the French, hearing of or even seeing the approach of the British with their lordly train of artillery, had abandoned the fort.

Then, as the main body settled into an encampment some ten miles from the fort, the distant rattle of musketry dispelled such pleasant thoughts. Gage and his three hundred were under attack.

For armies in conflict, nothing ages more quickly than intelligence. Stobo's report of a weak garrison of four hundred was accurate—when he made it—but by July 6, Fort Duquesne had been reinforced. Despite the increase in numbers, Commandant Claude-Pierre Pécaudy de Contrecoeur quite reasonably feared a siege by superior British forces. He contemplated surrender, but his young second in command, Captain Daniel Liénard de Beaujeu, persuaded him neither to give up nor to wait for a siege, but to make a preemptive attack.

Assigned to lead the assault, Beaujeu knew he would be going up against a force that outnumbered him two to one. However, French scouts had watched the way Braddock marched. They knew his forces were slow and clumsy, and although he had sent a substantial body of men in advance of the main column, Braddock had failed to send a smaller scouting force ahead of them. Surprise, therefore, would be easy. Nevertheless, Beaujeu exercised the precaution of taking communion before dawn on July 9. Then, having assembled seventy-two regulars of the Marine and 146 Canadian militiamen—637 Indians would rendezvous with them outside of the fort—he set out on a ten-mile march southeast to meet Edward Braddock.

Braddock sent half his regulars to reinforce Gage, holding the rest behind to guard the wagons and baggage. He ordered an aide to ride ahead to see what was happening, but even before the aide returned with a report, the rising volume of fire persuaded Braddock himself to gallop to the front. Washington and the general's other staff officers were close behind. They soon collided with retreating—routed—regulars. Breathless officers reported that St. Clair's work party and Gage's advance party had been set upon by French, Canadians, and Indians. In the initial exchange, the leader—Beaujeu—was killed, and that nearly brought the attack to a halt—but then the Indians fell upon them, and the French (rallied by Beaujeu's lieutenant, Jean-Daniel Dumas) started firing again. It was chaos—a massacre. Some redcoats fired wildly, and others just threw down their weapons, huddled like sheep, and, like sheep, were slaughtered.

Even before the telling of this terror was finished, the retreating advance party and work party collided with the advancing reinforcements. Maneuver became impossible, and the French and Indians, always pressing in, opened fire on a jumble of soldiers, horses, baggage, and artillery.

Braddock did precisely what George Washington would do on more than one occasion during the American Revolution. He waded into the disaster, defying the gunfire to ride among his troops in an attempt to rally small groups into some semblance of effective order for a defense or a counterattack. But in an era long before the invention of "smokeless" gunpowder, the scene was soon shrouded in smoke and dust. Redcoat fired on redcoat, and what had been an army was now a mob. These were not, after all, crack frontline troops, but, until recently, denizens of the Irish garrisons. In an American wilderness, they were, quite literally, bewildered.

In the thick of it with the rest of Braddock's staff officers, Washington was unhurt—even though (as he wrote to his mother on July 18) "I had four Bullets through my Coat, and two Horses shot under me."[5] Everyone else attending the general was soon either dead or wounded. Whether or not Washington knew it at the time, the Virginians under Adam Stephen did much better than the regulars—dissolving at last not from the bullets of the French or the hatchets of the Indians, but under confused friendly fire from those regulars.

Braddock, for all his stubborn, uncomprehending bluster, acquitted himself as a hero. Four horses were shot from beneath his sturdy frame. Each time he seized a new mount and continued to pit his sheer bulldog will against the surrounding chaos. But then he himself fell, a ball having penetrated (according to Washington) his shoulder and lodged in his "Breast."[6]

There are conflicting accounts of what happened next with the commander. Some say he asked nothing more than to be left behind. Others that he asked for a pistol with which to take his own life. Some accounts record his last words (pronounced when he died three days after having been wounded) as oddly hopeful: "We shall do better next time." Others report he simply uttered a dazed "Who would have thought it?" All that is known for certain is that his faithful aide-de-camp Washington put him on a wagon and sent him toward the rear. Some time after this, those who were still fighting—or still going through the motions—made for the rear as well, abandoning to forest, French, and Indians the richly laden baggage train that they had hauled so far and with such infinite agony. It was a good thing that they did. Instead of pursuing the survivors, the attackers fell upon the baggage and looted it.

Retreating with the last survivors from the front, Washington found Braddock, lying alone and near death in the wagon he had commandeered for him. The general was conscious and ordered his aide-de-camp to ride back to Colonel Thomas Dunbar, who was at the head of the rest of the army, the portion from which the flying column had been detached, and to tell him to send food and medicine forward as quickly as possible.

Almost harder than living through the battle was riding through that night, back through what remained of the flying column. Washington wrote of "shocking scenes" and of the "dead—the dying—the groans—lamentations—and crys along the Road of the wounded."[7] He reached Dunbar on July 10, having ridden all night.

Dunbar's troops joined the shattered flying column at the place of its retreat, Great Meadows, on July 13. There Braddock succumbed to his wounds, and Washington directed that he be shrouded in a pair of blankets and buried in an unmarked grave. The site was no more than a mile from the ruins of Fort Necessity. It was familiar ground to George Washington, who there had lost 119 men, killed, wounded, or missing. Braddock, more experienced than Washington by four decades, lost 456 killed, 520 wounded, and perhaps a dozen given up as prisoners. A total of 1,373 men had been engaged.

The slaughter Washington survived—historians would call it the Battle of the Wilderness—was a lesson for which Great Meadows had prepared him as much as one could be prepared. Despite the disparity in numbers engaged and lives lost, the two battles were of a piece. Both taught the great law of war, that its essence and object was bloody death. And now Washington understood from firsthand experience that death could be dealt in an orderly, disciplined fashion, or it could come as an overwhelming chaos. The successful commander sought order in death, but he had to learn to accept the chaos as well and, if possible, survive it to fight another day.

Washington had survived.

Part of the reason, to be sure, was luck. As many hardships and defeats as Washington would endure—most of them years off, in the American Revolution—he was an incredibly lucky soldier. A tall target who always led from the front, deliberately making himself conspicuous in combat, he was never wounded.

Part of his ability to survive—and his capacity to lead others in survival—also derived from his commitment to discipline. There is a popular belief, reinforced by generations of history writers, that Braddock's defeat at Great Meadows was for the colonists a sudden and dramatic epiphany, revealing that the touted invincibility of the British regulars was a myth and that the shattering of this myth broadcast the seeds of the revolution, which took root two decades later. There is some truth in this. Washington himself wrote to his mother from Fort Cumberland on July 18 that the "Regular Soldiers . . . were struck with such panick, that they behavd with more cowardice than it is possible to conceive"; in contrast, "The Virginia Troops shewd a good deal of Bravery, & were near all killd." He went on to call the conduct of the British regulars "dastardly." They broke and ran "as Sheep pursued by dogs; and it was impossible to rally them." To Governor Dinwiddie on the same day, he wrote essentially the same thing, of regulars "immediately struck with such an inconceivable Panick, that nothing but confusion and disobedience of order's prevailed amongst them," in contrast to "The Virginian Companies," in

which the troops "behavd like Men, and died like Soldier's." He also
repeated what he had written to his mother: how the "dastardly"
regulars "broke & run as Sheep before Hounds." Trying to rally them
met with "as little success as if we had attempted to have stopd the wild
Bears of the Mountains."[8]

Washington was appalled by the behavior of the regulars and proud of
the conduct of the Virginians, yet there is no evidence that he thenceforth
decided that American soldiers were invariably better than those of the
king. It was others who drew this conclusion. Virginians circulated
rumors that, with his dying breath, Braddock had cried out for his "dear
Blues" (the Virginia Regiment wore blue uniforms) because they, at least,
had fought like men. Others even claimed that Washington had begged
General Braddock to allow him to take charge of all the provincials and
lead them into the woods, where they could fight the French and Indians
on their own terms.

But Braddock did not cry out for his "dear Blues" any more than
Washington had asked to fight like an Indian. It is true that Washington
discovered that the British regular soldier was vulnerable—but not
because he failed to fight like a Virginian or like an Indian. At the Battle
of the Wilderness, Washington saw, British regulars had failed to fight like
soldiers. Braddock was known as a stern disciplinarian, but in these two
garrison-bred regiments, it was precisely discipline that was lacking.
When it came to fighting the American Revolution, Washington was glad
that his men (some of them) had a frontiersman's skill with a rifle and
could, when necessary, fight in the manner of an Indian. Yet it was to the
European military model he consistently looked for the order and discipline he wanted for his Continental Army, and he was grateful to
European officers like DeKalb and Steuben, who helped his officers train
American troops in the ways of European soldiery.

Washington benefited personally from the rumors and myths that circulated throughout Virginia and the other colonies following the Battle of
the Wilderness. In letters, newspapers, and the talk of the tavern, he was

widely hailed a hero. None of that would be forgotten when in 1775 the Second Continental Congress voted on John Adams's nomination of George Washington as commander-in-chief of the newly authorized Continental Army.

Lessons in survival, leadership, the inevitability of death in war, and the even greater danger of the chaos that may accompany death; lessons, too, on the importance of logistics, on adapting forces to prevailing conditions, and on discipline—all of these Washington learned at Great Meadows then learned on an even larger, more horrific scale in the service of Edward Braddock. But these do not constitute the full measure of what the young leader learned in his first encounters with the enemy.

From both Great Meadows and the Wilderness, Washington returned neither shocked, nor cowed, nor chastened. He returned blooded, a mature soldier, prepared to fight, prepared to lead, prepared to prevail. The example of his courage, amply demonstrated in these first battles, never deserted him, but continued to make him an extraordinarily effective military leader. He did not learn—not at Great Meadows, not at the Wilderness, not even later, during the American Revolution—all that a general should learn of the military art. Many of his technical and tactical shortcomings would never be fully overcome, and in the fight for independence he lost more battles than he won.

Yet win or lose, he always prevailed. In 1776, after relinquishing both Long Island and Manhattan to the British, Washington wrote: "I trust the experience of error will enable us to act better in the future." It would be easy to dismiss this as easy wisdom, even something of a throwaway line. But to do so would be to ignore the profound personal transformation that had already come two decades earlier, during 1754 and 1755. While others died or panicked or despaired in contests for the Ohio wilderness—the ground that marked the very future of America—George Washington fought, led, watched, and learned. Washington survived. More than that, he prevailed.

Military triumph in the American Revolution was wrested from more defeats than victories because Washington truly believed in the last word of that remark he made in 1776. His faith was in the *future*. It was a uniquely American faith, a belief that it is not only possible to rise from the ashes of loss, but that those ashes are, in fact, indispensable to the rise. They are the foundation of a character capable of enduring without despair all manner of disappointment and defeat, no matter how bloody. For Washington, they were the foundation of command and the heart of leadership—the soul of a revolution.

NOTES

1: The Flesh Beneath the Marble
1. Freeman, Douglas Southall, *George Washington: A Biography* (New York: Scribner's, 1949), vol. 1, 69; Abbot, W.W, ed., *Papers of George Washington: Colonial Series* (Charlottesville: University Press of Virginia, 1983), vol. 1, 118.
2. Freeman, *George Washington*, 71.
3. Moore, Charles, *George Washington's Rules of Civility and Decent Behaviour in Company and Conversation* (Boston and New York: Houghton Mifflin Company, 1926), passim.
4. Ibid.
5. Washington, George, *Writings* (New York: The Library of America, 1997), 11.
6. Conrad, Joseph, *Lord Jim* (1900; reprint ed., Boston: Houghton Mifflin, 1958), 11; Washington, *Writings*, 12–13.
7. Washington, *Writings*, 13–14.
8. Freeman, *George Washington*, 250–251.
9. Ibid., 257.
10. Abbot, *Papers of George Washington*, 41, 42, 43.
11. Ibid., 46.
12. Ibid., 49.
13. Freeman, *George Washington*, 263.

2: Of Empires and Self-Interest
1. Quoted in Heat-Moon, William Least, *Columbus in the Americas* (New York: Wiley, 2002), 146, 63.
2. Ibid., 65.
3. Quoted in Axelrod, Alan, *Chronicle of the Indian Wars* (New York: Macmillan General Reference, 1993), 11.
4. Ibid.

3: Errand into the Wilderness
1. Abbot, *Papers of George Washington*, 50.
2. Axelrod, Alan, *The International Encyclopedia of Secret Societies and Fraternal Orders* (New York: Facts on File,

1997), 94; Wood, Gordon S., *The Radicalism of the American Revolution* (New York: Vintage: 1993), 223; Cook, Ezra A., *Eminent Men on Secret Societies (Washington Opposed to Secret Societies)* (Chicago: Ezra A. Cook, 1880), 12–27.
3. Freeman, *George Washington*, 272–273.
4. Twohig, Dorothy, ed., *George Washington's Diaries: An Abridgment* (Charlottesville: University Press of Virginia, 1999), 17.
5. Ibid., 17; Abbot, *Papers of George Washington*, 58, 60.
6. Abbot, *Papers of George Washington*, 61.
7. Ibid.
8. Freeman, *George Washington*, 277.
9. Ibid., 284.
10. Twohig, *George Washington's Diaries*, 19–20.
11. Ibid., 20.
12. Ibid.
13. Freeman, *George Washington*, 291.
14. Washington, Writings, 19.
15. Twohig, *George Washington's Diaries*, 20.
16. Ibid., 20-21.
17. Washington, *Writings*, 20–21.
18. Ibid., 21.
19. Ibid., 22.
20. Ibid., 21.
21. Ibid.
22. Ibid., 22–23.
23. Ibid., 23.
24. Ibid., 23.
25. Ibid., 23.
26. Ibid., 23–24.
27. Ibid., 24.
28. Ibid., 24.
29. Ibid., 24.
30. Ibid., 25.
31. Ibid., 25
32. Ibid., 25–26.
33. Ibid., 26.

4: LE BOEUF

1. Twohig, *George Washington's Diaries*, 23.
2. Ibid.
3. Ibid.
4. Ibid.
5. Ibid., 23.
6. Ibid., 23–24.
7.. Ibid., 23–24.
8. Freeman, *George Washington*, 305.
10. Ibid
11. Twohig, *George Washington's Diaries*, 24.
12. Ibid., 24–25.
13. Ibid., 25.
14. Ibid.
15. Freeman, *George Washington*, 307.
16. Twohig, *George Washington's Diaries*, 25.
17. Ibid., 25–26.
18. Ibid., 25.
19. Ibid., 26.
20. Freeman, *George Washington*, 309–310.
21. Twohig, *George Washington's Diaries*, 26.
22. Ibid.
23. Ibid., 26–27.
24. Ibid.
25. Ibid.
26. Ibid., 27.
27. Ibid., 27–28, n.
28. Ibid., 28.

5: MURTHERING TOWN

1. Twohig, *George Washington's Diaries*, 29.
2. Ibid.
3. Ibid.
4. Ibid., 29, n.
5. Ibid., 29.
6. Ibid.
7. Ibid.
8. Freeman, *George Washington*, 318, 319.
9. Twohig, *George Washington's Diaries*, 29–30.
10. Freeman, *George Washington*, 319–320.
11. Twohig, *George Washington's Diaries*, 30.
12. Freeman, *George Washington*, 320–321.
13. Twohig, *George Washington's Diaries*, 30.
14. Ibid.
15. Ibid.
16. Ibid.
17. Ibid.
18. Ibid., 30, n.
19. Ibid., 30.

20. Ibid., 31.
21. Ibid.
22. Freeman, *George Washington*, 326.
23. Twohig, *George Washington's Diaries*, 32, n.
24. Ibid., 33, n.

6: A NEW MISSION

1. Freeman, *George Washington*, 328.
2. Ibid., 330.
3. Ibid., 333.
4. Abbot, *Papers of George Washington*, 70.
5. Ibid., 73, 72.
6. Ibid., 74.
7. Freeman, *George Washington*, 337.
8. Ibid., 339, 340.
9. Abbot, *Papers of George Washington*, 76.
10. Freeman, *George Washington*, 341.
11. Abbot, *Papers of George Washington*, 78.
12. Ibid., 78 and 65, n. 5.
13. Freeman, *George Washington*, 348.

7: BATTLE IN A BOWER

1. Twohig, *George Washington's Diaries*, 40.
2. Ibid.
3. Ibid., 40–41.
4. Abbot, *Papers of George Washington*, 85–86.
5. Freeman, *George Washington*, 294.
6. Quoted in Jennings, Francis, *Empire of Fortune: Crowns, Colonies, and Tribes in the Seven Years War in America* (New York: Norton, 1988), 66.
7. Ibid.
8. Abbot, *Papers of George Washington*, 87–88.
9. Twohig, *George Washington's Diaries*, 43.
10. Abbot, *Papers of George Washington*, 92.
11. Ibid., 96–97.
12. Freeman, *George Washington*, 365.
13. Ibid., 366.
14. Abbot, *Papers of George Washington*, 105.
15. Freeman, *George Washington*, 368.
16. Abbot, *Papers of George Washington*, 105–106.
17. Ibid., 118.
18. The *Sommation* is discussed in Abbot, *Papers of George Washington*, 113–114, n. 12 and 13, and in Twohig, *George Washington's Diaries*, 50–51, n.
19. Abbot, *Papers of George Washington*, 116–117.

8: "A CHARMING FIELD FOR AN ENCOUNTER"

1. Abbot, *Papers of George Washington*, 111.

2. Twohig, *George Washington's Diaries*, 52; Abbot, *Papers of George Washington*, 112–113.

3. Abbot, *The Papers of George Washington*, 116.

4. Ibid., 116–117.

5. Ibid., 112.

6. Ibid.

7. Ibid.

8. Ibid., 117.

9. Ibid., 118.

10. Quoted in Jennings, *Empire of Fortune*, 67.

11. The following discussion of the Fort Necessity site is based on Frederick Tilberg, *Fort Necessity National Battlefield Site* (National Park Service Historical Handbook Series No. 19) (Washington, D.C.: National Park Service, 1954). The handbook is available online at http://www.cr.nps.gov/history/online_books/hh/19/index.htm.

12. The material from shaw and Burd is quoted in Tilberg, *Fort Necessity National Battlefield Site*, in the unpaginated section titled "Discovery of the Original Fort." Online, see http://www.cr.nps.gov/history/online_books/hh/19/hh19e.html.

13. Ibid.

14. Abbot, ed., *Papers of George Washington*, 98–99.

15. Ibid., 102.

16. Ibid., 103.

17. Ibid., 107.

18. Ibid., 109.

19. Ibid., 123.

20. Ibid.

21. Ibid., 123–124.

22. Ibid., 124.

24. Ibid., 131.

22. Freeman, *George Washington*, 383.

25. Abbot, *Papers of George Washington*, 126–127, 129–130.

9: The Battle on the Meadow

1. Twohig, *George Washington's Diaries*, 54.

2. Ibid., 54–55.

3. Ibid., 55.

4. Ibid.

5. Abbot, *Papers of George Washington*, 136–137.

6. Ibid., 138.

7. Ibid., 137.

8. Twohig, *George Washington's Diaries*, 55; Freeman, *George Washington*, 391.

9. Twohig, *George Washington's Diaries*, 55.

10. Ibid.

11. Ibid., 56.

12. Ibid., 56–57.

13. Ibid., 57.

14. Freeman, *George Washington*, 394.

15. Abbot, *Papers of George Washington*, 155.

16. Freeman, *George Washington*, 400.

17. Ibid.

18. Abbot, *Papers of George Washington*, 155.

19. Quoted in Jennings, *Empire of Fortune*, 66–67.

20. Ibid., 66.

21. Abbot, *Papers of George Washington*, 159.

22. Ibid.

23. Ibid., 160.

24. Ibid.

25. Abbot, *Papers of George Washington*, 161, n. 2.

26. Freeman, *George Washington*, 404.

27. Abbot, *Papers of George Washington*, 160.

28. Ibid.

29. Freeman, *George Washington*, 405.

30. Ibid.

10: Anatomy of Surrender

1. Abbot, *Papers of George Washington*, 161.

2. Ibid., 163, n. 4.

3. Ibid., 166.

4. Ibid., 167.

5. Ibid., 163, n. 4.

6. Ibid.

7. Ibid., 161.

8. Ibid., 164, n. 8.

9. The anecdote of Major Stephen's purloined clothes is related in Freeman, *George Washington*, 409–410.

10. Abbot, *Papers of George Washington*, 169–170.

11. Ibid.

12. Freeman, *George Washington*, 423.

13. Ibid., 407.

14. Ibid.

15. Abbot, *Papers of George Washington*, 167–168, n. 1.

16. Freeman, George Washington, 415.

17. Abbot, *Papers of George Washington*, 150; Freeman, *George Washington*, 416.

18. Freeman, *George Washington*, 423.

19. Ibid., 424.

20. Lengel, Edward G., *General George Washington: A Military Life* (New York: Random House, 2005), 46; Freeman, *George Washington*, 540.

21. Lengel, *General George Washington*, 46.

22. Ibid., 48.

Epilogue: Of a Fire in the Wilderness and the Soul
of a Revolution

1. Brock, R. A., ed., *The Official Records of Robert
Dinwiddie, Lieutenant-Governor of the Colony of
Virginia, 1751–1758* (Richmond: Virginia Historical
Society, 1883–1884), vol. 1, 242.

2. Hazard, Samuel, ed., *Minutes of the Provincial Council
of Pennsylvania* (Harrisburg and Philadelphia, n. pub.,
1838–1853), vol. 6, 589.

3. Sargent, Winthrop, *The History of an Expedition
Against Fort Du Quesne, in 1755* (Philadelphia:
Lippincott, Grambo & Co., 1855), 159.

4. Abbot, *Papers of George Washington*, 258.

5. Ibid., 336.

6. Ibid., 340.

7. Humphreys, David, *Life of General Washington*
(Athens: University of Georgia Press, 1991), 18.

8. Abbot, *Papers of George Washington*, 336, 339–340.

INDEX